A CENTURY IN THE WEST: LIFE OF A PIONEER WOMAN – MARY POPP'S STORY

Written by
Mary Popp

Edited by
Donald H. Layh

Illustrated by
Janet A. Layh

Printed by Hignell Printing Limited, 488 Burnell Street, Winnipeg, Manitoba, R3G 2B4 Phone (204)784-1030, Fax (204)774-4053

Published by Twin Valley Consulting Ltd., Box 250, Langenburg, Saskatchewan, SOA 2AO Phone (306)743-5520 Fax (306)743-5568

ISBN:

0-9684093-0-X

Cover:

Pencil sketch of Mary Popp drawn by Jan Layh from a photograph taken about 1912.

TABLE OF CONTENTS

FOREWORD

The history of Mary Popp's family reflects the history of many German Lutheran families which settled in the Beresina, Hoffenthal and Landestreu districts extending in an arc north of Langenburg, Saskatchewan. These families have frequently referred to themselves as *Schwabs* and to their language as *Schwabisch*. More accurately, however, Mary Popp's ancestors and other families in the Langenburg area[1] originate from a triangular sweep of land bordered by the Rhein and Moselle Rivers and the French border, an area commonly called the Rheinland - Pfalz. Their language, is more correctly called *Pfalzisch* rather than *Schwabisch*.

Mary Popp's ancestors left their homeland in the Rheinland - Pfalz over 200 years ago, carrying with them only a few earthly belongings, their Lutheran faith and *Pfalzisch* language. Among this group were all of Mary Popp's great great great grandparents, coming from towns like Harxheim, Kaiserlautern, Bechtolsheim, Reichenbach, Staudernheim, Rockenhausen and Nussbaum.

To understand why Mary Popp's ancestors left the Rheinland - Pfalz one must appreciate that Germany in the closing decades of the 1700s did not present ideal living conditions. The Seven Years War between Austria and Prussia had embroiled most of Europe. Young men were conscripted into armies for which they had little allegiance. Religious persecution and intolerance was rife. Land was scarce and often available only through a serf relationship with landowners who exacted a heavy toll of taxes and rent.

Austria was a dominant European power in the 1700s. In 1772 Austria gained the new territory of Galicia lying to the north of the Carpathian Mountains, land that had formerly belonged to Poland. Today this land lies within the Ukraine and eastern Poland.

---

[1]These famililes included the following families: Adam, Baumung, Bieber, Bessler, Burkhardt, Busch, Dietrich, Dressler, Geres, Haas, Haberstock, Kandel, Kendel, Kentel, Kitsch, Koch, Layh, Lowenberger, Mack, Mattheis, Nerbas, Schappert, Werschler, Wirth and Zorn.

Joseph II, the Austrian Emperor, wanted to attract German farmers to Galicia and Bukovina (additional territory to the east of Galicia taken in 1775) to act as model farmers to the indigenous Polish and Ukrainian farmers.

In 1782 Joseph II issued a proclamation promising free land, religious freedom, military exemption for the oldest son of the family, free transportation from Vienna (the capital of Austria) and a ten year exemption from taxes. To many people of the Rheinland - Pfalz the proclamation was alluring and they took up the invitation. Included in this group were Mary Popp's ancestors.

The most likely route followed by these *Pfalzisch* farmers from the Rheinland to Galicia started with an overland trek to Ulm, a German city on the Danube River, a distance of approximately 200 kilometres. Upon arriving at Ulm the emigrants would have boarded flat bottomed barges for a journey of approximately ten days down the Danube to Vienna. Conditions on the barges would have been crowded and families would have eaten and slept without shelter. Imagine the reaction of these hardy German farmers as they passed through some of Europe's most renowned scenery and glided through cities like Regensburg and Linz to Vienna.

In Vienna petitions were filed with the Austrian government requesting permission to settle in Galicia. From Vienna the third and most arduous leg of the migration began. The trek from Vienna to the Galician capital of Lemberg (now L'vov) was approximately 720 kilometres. Traveling probably 35 kilometres a day, six days a week, the wearisome journey would have taken five to six weeks. Along the way children would have been born and family members buried in roadside graves.

One group of settlers to Galicia, including Mary Popp's ancestors, formed a German village in 1784 called Landestreu, meaning "true to the land". Landestreu formed a common parish with the neighbouring German Lutheran village of Ugartsthal. As often happens with neighbouring communities, these two villages were often greater rivals than co-operative neighbours. Aside from other German villages in the area, Galicia was predominantly populated by Poles, Jews and Ukrainians. The German settlers considered themselves more industrious than their Slavic neighbours. Each group maintained its own identity and intermarriage between the groups was uncommon and generally frowned upon.

Landestreu was renowned for its beauty, nestled in the hills of the northern flank of the Carpathian mountains. The village was called the "Pearl of Galicia" and was especially renown for its spectacular beauty during spring blossom time. The climate was mild enough to allow the extensive cultivation of many fruit trees.

Landestreu was well known throughout Galicia for the Geib family's skill in bell casting. The Geibs brought this tradition from Germany to Landestreu where it flourished until the early 1900s. Landestreu was also famous for its salt springs from which salt for table and livestock use was produced. The women of the village soaked flax in the stream that separated the village into upper and lower streets. They spun the flax and wove it for bed and table linens.

In 1811 a Lutheran Church was built. A steeple was added in 1821. Until that year the law of Austria, a Catholic state, did not permit steeples on Lutheran churches to ensure they would remain as inconspicuous as possible. A brick school house was built in 1847 and, at times, had over 100 children enrolled.

During World War I Austrian troops and officers were stationed in Landestreu. The village was equipped with electric lights. A theatre and bath house were built for the soldiers and officers. The village did not then realize that its favoured position was a short lived benefit. Landestreu eventually fell to the Russian advance in 1917. The village was heavily bombarded. Forty-six dwellings were destroyed. The church was hit by two grenades but it was not destroyed. The school and bell tower were burned to the ground.

Mrs. Mary Becker (Schaan) was born in Landestreu, Austria in 1902. She reported her experience as a young girl in Landestreu during World War I in Those Were the Days: The History of MacNutt, Calder, Dropmore and the Surrounding Districts:

> Landestreu was a pretty village and all went well until the war began in 1914. Father, and other men of the village left to take part in the war. Mother remained behind to look after the family and plow the fields with oxen. Life in the Village

suddenly came to an end. We awoke to hear the firing of guns, the Russian soldiers coming in one side of Landestreu and the German troops approaching from the other...

As we took refuge under the bridge, we saw the village go up in flames. All but one building was burned. When we returned to our yard sometime later, all we could find were the corners of a shed that remained unburnt. Looting and burning took rampage. The soldiers took everything that was useful... Fortunately for us, the German soldiers rescued us from beneath the bridge, because only moments after we left, the bridge exploded in flames as a bomb shell passed through. Bombardment was terrible. Shots fired often traveled two hundred miles and the force of explosions were so great that many people were knocked off their feet.

Life during the war years was unforgettable. The young men and women were immediately drafted into service by either German or Russian troops. I and a number of other friends were involved in many varied tasks. One of the tasks was to dig trenches for soldiers, which required fourteen days for that particular occasion, all digging was done by spades. Grain from the fields were used to line the trenches until after the war. We were also assigned the task of clearing the snow away so that troops could pass by. Our reward was a bit of food or cloth which we used to make clothes or shoes. One day's reward was a small dish of potatoes (left over after digging). These potatoes were so small that only soup could be made from them.

We not only suffered from the pangs of war but also from the plague of cholera, typhoid and fleas. Death was everywhere. Rivers used for water supply were contaminated with bodies of horses and people. Very little was known about cholera and typhoid other than the fact that they were contagious diseases. People died by the hundreds and burial occurred without ceremony. Officials dressed in rubber garments removed bodies with large poles fitted with hooks on the end which were used to pull the corpses into their graves. Caskets were not used. The body was simply covered with lime and buried.

...

Although our life was filled with tragedy and sadness, it seemed that we accepted war as part of our everyday life. We were happy to live with our friends and were happy when members of our family were still alive. The sound of the roar of battle made our nights sleepless, but we tried to muffle the sound by burrowing our ears into our pillows in order to get

> some sleep. It seemed that the sounds only became louder. Exhaustion took its course and sleep eventually came.
> When the war was over, food was very scarce. We had to salvage as much as possible. The grain was removed from the trenches, dried, and flour was ground from the wheat by gristing it between two stones especially used for this purpose. We had gone a whole year without eating a slice of bread. Our village was destroyed and we, the family, had to seek a new life, new hardships and new friends.

By World War I many families had left Landestreu, immigrating to Canada. Beginning with Mary Popp's parents and three other young married couples, villagers started to immigrate to Canada as early as 1889. From 1902 to 1908 a wave of emigration led to a change in the purely German make-up of Landestreu. Landestreu became an ethnic mixture of Germans, Poles and Jews. The last German *Ortsschultze* (village overseer) was Christian Haberstock from 1912 - 1919. After World War I, Galicia fell to Polish rule. From 1919 all decisions were made by the Polish majority.

In 1939 Hitler invaded Poland. Poland was divided between Germany and the Soviet Union with the proviso that the German minorities would be permitted to leave the Soviet-held portion of Poland which included the village of Landestreu. Germans in Galicia knew nothing of these secret arrangements. The people of Landestreu were loathed by the Polish majority - understandably so since the German army had overrun Poland in a few short weeks. The villagers worried when the German army did not advance to Landestreu. It was the greatly feared Russian army that first reached Landestreu.

Rudy Schaan, a 12 year old boy in 1939 has recounted the events of the autumn of 1939 as experienced by the people of Landestreu:

> So, instead of Germans in our village, we had the Russian army as saviors. We seemed to be safe from the Poles. The Polish army was no where to be seen. The Russian army did not seem to have any animosity towards the German population. Between the Russians and the Poles, there was always tension and they never liked each other. This was September, 1939. The village survived this fast turn of events, no shots fired, no fires, no major damage, no lives lost. This

> was not what this tiny German village expected. After coming so close and being part of a safe environment with German protection, we how had another problem. The Poles hated us and now we had the Russians. For how long? Would there be other "solutions"? Surely this was not what was expected nor hoped for - the Russians? But all was peaceful, at least for now. Germany and Russia were not at war but were actually allies.
>
> What transpired in those next three months only the powers that be know that. The deal was made for the Germans to leave the Russian occupied part of Poland with apparently no strings attached. Where to, we did not know, nor did we care, as long as we could get away from the Russians.
>
> Finally, in December, 1939, the deal was made. We, the Germans, would leave everything behind and be moved to German-occupied Poland to the west of us. No compensation to anyone regardless of wealth, status or size of family. The date was set, January 4, 1940.

On the evening of January 3, 1940, the villagers said a sad farewell to their beloved Landestreu. Arm in arm they walked through the village, singing their farewell. They visited the cemetery to sing hymns to commemorate family members who had died before and who would forever stay in Landestreu. On January 4th, 1940, the women and children gathered at the train station in Kalush and boarded cattle cars heated with iron stoves to travel westward. The men started their trek by horse and wagon. Many of these men eventually became part of the German army. The women and children became part of an occupation army, living on farms taken from Polish farmers in German-annexed Poland.

Herman Schick, the Lutheran Pastor from Ugartsthal, a neighbouring German village, wrote about the departure from the two villages in "*Erinnerungen an das Pfarramt Ugartsthal - Landestreu*" in *Zeitweiser der Galiziendeutschen, 1976*:

> The men started their "Grossen Treck" [their great trek] on January 20, 1940, with the tearful farewell handshakes and "buwajte zdorowy" of the Ukrainians who kissed the hands and coat sleeves of the German commissioners sending along greetings to Germany. In total darkness, under the ringing of church bells, the column of wagons of Ugartsthalers and their pastor departed for the "Kaiserstrasse" [Imperial Highway] at Holyn where they were to meet the Landestreuers. It was a

> blessing that it was still dark. The history of a Pfaelzerdorf [village of the people from the Pfalz] in the Carpathian country came to an end forever.

The German government gave eastern European Germans farmland in western Poland. Polish farmers were dispossessed of their homes and German farmers were instructed to farm this newly annexed German territory. Polish farmers quickly became servants of German owners. Understandably, the arrangement was not readily accepted by the Polish resistance which killed many of these new German settlers during the war.

In the winter of 1945, the Landestreuers living in Poland scrambled westward ahead of the advancing Russian army anxious to seek revenge against anyone of German origin. Many lives were lost in this human exodus, including Mary Popp's maternal uncle, Johann Friedrich Baumung who briefly stopped in a bread line and lost contact with the rest of the group. Many of these families escaped Soviet-occupied Germany; others were left behind the Iron Curtain to eke out a new life under a communist regime.

After World War II, some of the families that had left Landestreu in 1940 eventually joined other family members in Canada. As late as 1948 Mary Popp's cousin, John Baumung and his wife Marie arrived in Langenburg, almost 60 years after Mary Popp's parents had first settled in the Hoffenthal District.

The fate of Landestreu after World War II was never certain since travel to the Ukraine was restricted. Since the fall of Communism, several people born in Landestreu have returned to the village to find approximately 40 barrack style houses formerly used to house Russian officers on holiday leave. A few of the old German built houses can still be identified.

Mary Popp's story chronicles a long life shaped largely by the values and customs of the people from the "Pearl of Galicia". Little could her parents have predicted that in spite of burying many of their infant children in the prairie soil, one daughter's life would span over 100 years and that her keen sense of observation would record and immortalize their efforts to start a new life on the Canadian prairie.

EDITOR'S NOTE

Mary Popp began writing her memoirs in 1967 at the age of 70. She quit writing in 1996 at the age of 99. During 30 years of writing, she chronicled the extraordinary life of a Saskatchewan woman -- a pioneer, a mother of three children, a wife, and a person involved in her community.

Mary Popp was born on January 18, 1897 in the Hoffenthal District northeast of Langenburg. Her parents, Jakob and Augustina Lowenberger, German immigrants from Austria, arrived in Canada eight years before her birth. In her writings Mary Popp recalls stories told by her parents -- their life in Landestreu, Austria and their arrival in the Hoffenthal District of Saskatchewan with three other young German couples. She describes the Lowenberger family's heroic and successful efforts to establish a farm on the Canadian prairie. Mary never expressly states the respect she held for her parents, but her admiration of their work ethic and ability to create a home for their children is implicit in the vivid descriptions of the farm life of the Lowenberger family.

Mary's marriage to Henry Popp on October 20, 1914 at the age of 17 begins a 58 year relationship. In the first years of marriage she struggles with her inability to have an equal say in matters of family finance. Henry's spendthrift ways are at odds with Mary's dreams of saving money to build a new house with the "modern" conveniences of electric lights and central heat. In characteristic understatement, Mary reveals that Henry's occasional fondness of alcohol is the source of considerable concern for her. Throughout her marriage, however, her unquestioning loyalty to Henry requires no direct confirmation; theirs is a relationship that anticipates and endures any and all manner of hardship. Mary's unwavering care for Henry is evident as she watches his mental health disintegrate and he slowly dies of prostate cancer.

Mary's memoirs chronicle the birth of her three children on the farm in the Landestreu District south of the village of MacNutt.

She records with motherly care the children's buggy accidents, their illnesses, confirmations, their leaving home and enlisting in the armed services. She follows their marriages and the birth of grandchildren and great grandchildren. Tragically she also chronicles the death of all her children.

Mary continued to regularly write her memoirs until 1992, with sporadic writings until 1996 when she was 99 years old. She attempted to type a postscript to her memoirs at the age of 101 years, but her failing eyesight prevented her from continuing.

Mary wrote her memoirs in a language and style as though she were sitting across the kitchen table chatting to her neighbour. Her prose has a conversational feel. You can hear her speak, often in abbreviated partial sentences as one uses when speaking to a good friend.

In preparing Mary Popp's memoirs for printing, changes were made to clarify the meaning of passages and add conventional punctuation. Because she wrote her memoirs over a long period of time, she often partially or completely repeated stories she had earlier recounted. Her memoirs have been reorganized to avoid duplication and to present her stories in chronological order. The essence of her writing has been preserved to the greatest possible extent.

All of Mary Popp's memoirs were handwritten until she learned to use a typewriter at the age of 83. At that time, her handwriting was still legible and clear. Even though English was Mary Popp's second language, her writing evokes strong sentiments, often humorous, but just as often profoundly sad.

Footnotes have been added to give the background to many persons, places or circumstances described by Mary Popp.

Genealogical Charts

MARY (LOWENBERGER) POPP'S ANCESTORS

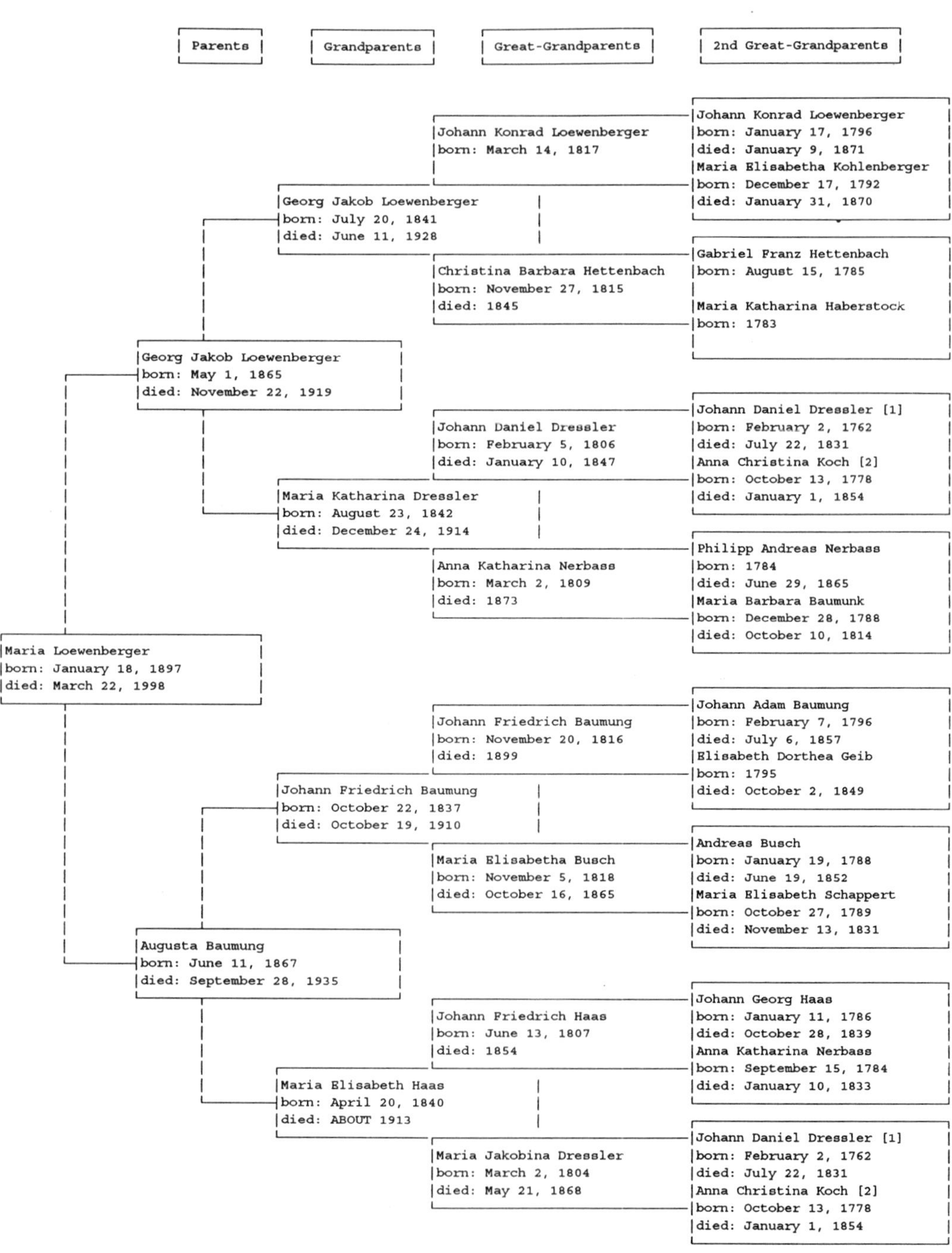

AUGUSTA (BAUMUNG) LOWENBERGER'S ANCESTORS

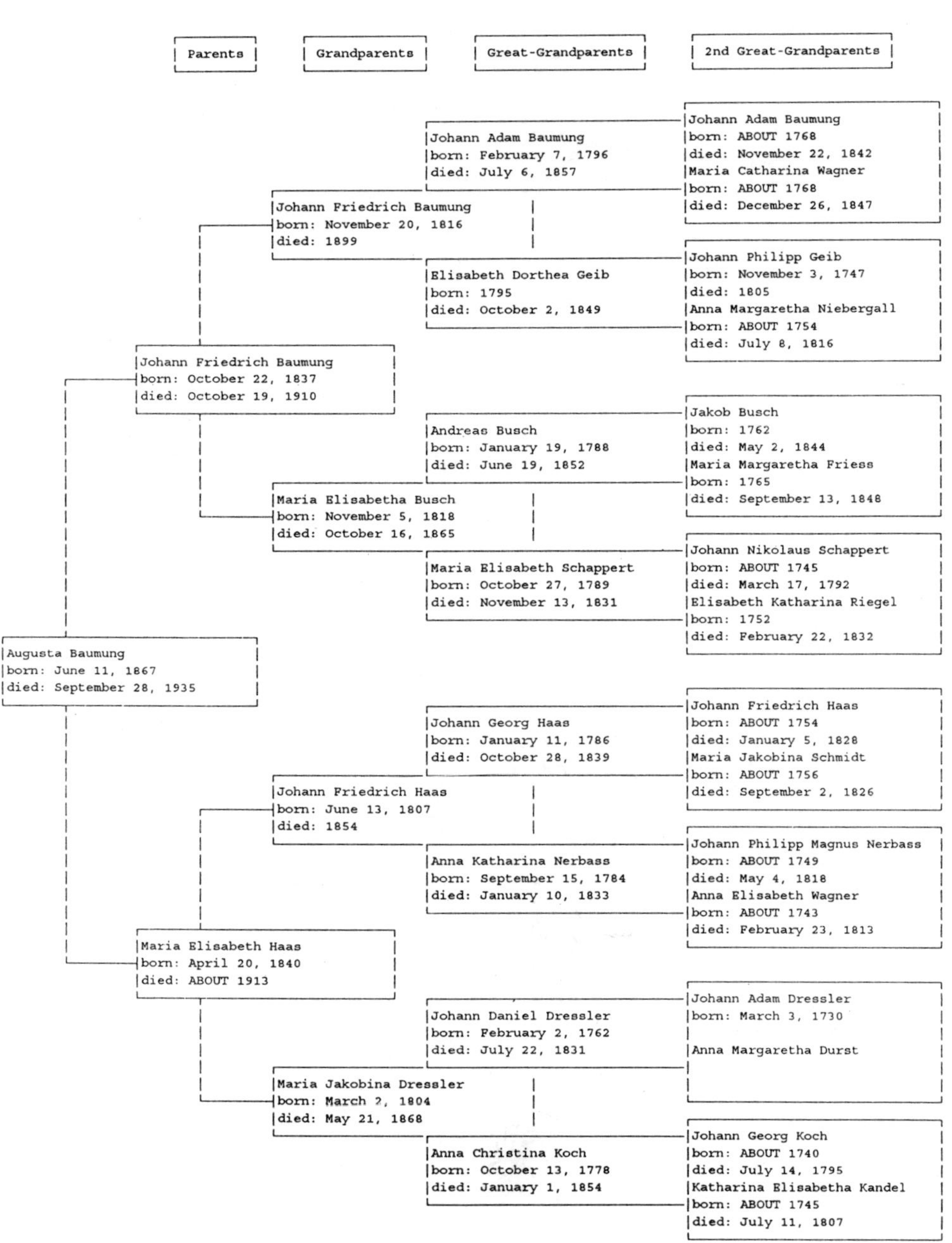

GEORG JAKOB LOWENBERGER'S ANCESTORS

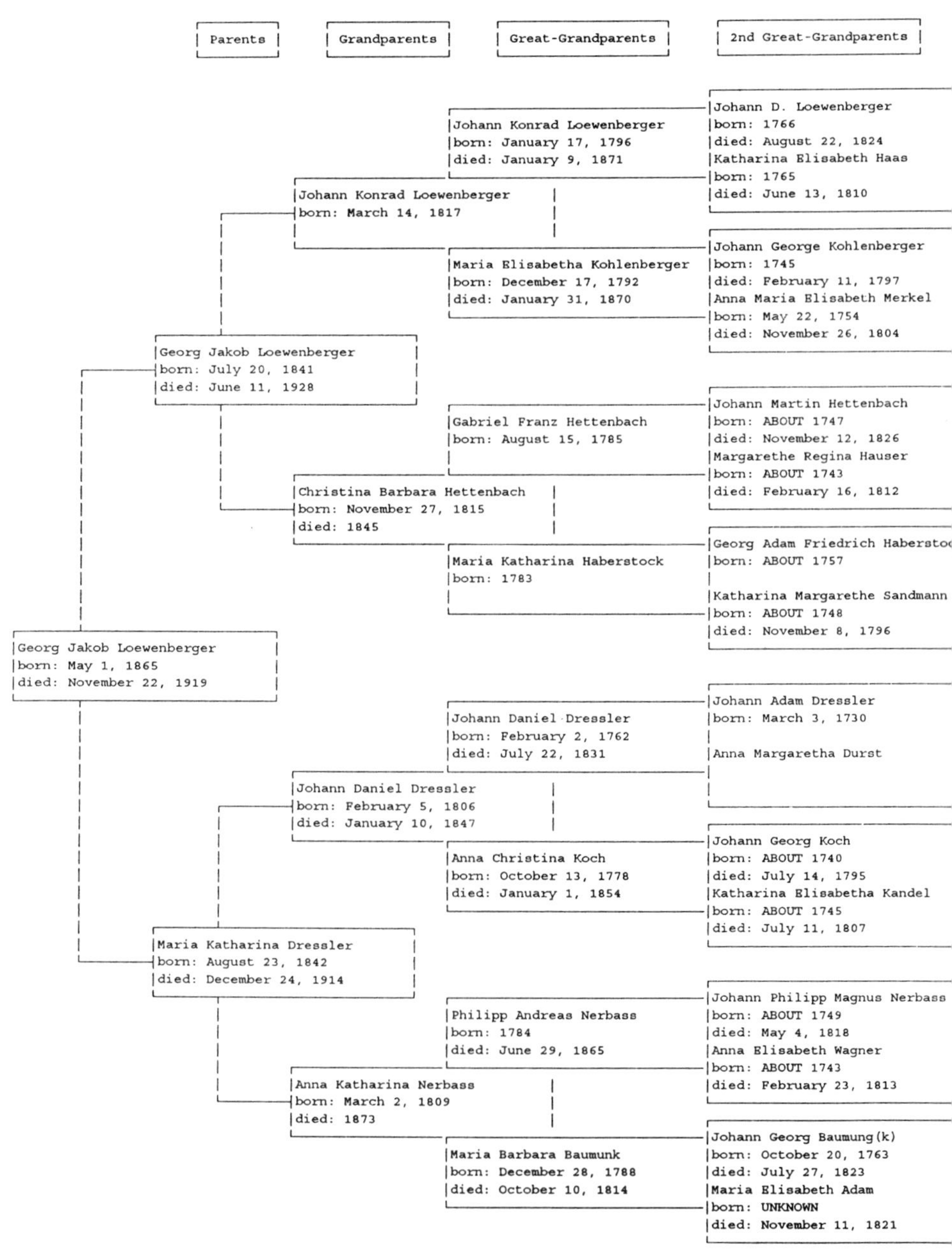

DESCENDANTS OF HENRY AND MARY POPP

HEINRICH POPP
Jan. 16, 1891 - July 17, 1973

MARIA LOWENBERGER
Jan. 18, 1897 – Mar. 22,1998

ARNOLD POPP (Dec. 14, 1915 - Nov. 1, 1965)
m. May 28, 1935
META KENDEL (Oct. 22, 1914 -
Children: **Jeanette Popp** (May 13, 1934)
m. Sept. 15, 1951
William Langila (Oct. 6, 1931)
Children: **William Langila** (Feb. 29, 1952)
m. Donna Methot
Douglas Langila (Sept. 14, 1959)
David Langila (Feb. 23, 1960)
m. Elaine Roulston
Children: **Michael Langila** (Jan. 2, 1987)
Melissa Langila (Sept. 30, 1988)

RICHARD POPP (Jan. 20, 1919 - July 5, 1997)
m. Jan. 1, 1943
IRENE MITSCHKE (Aug. 18, 1921 -
Children: **Brian Popp** (Oct. 24, 1945)
m. Jan. 1, 1972
Louise Krefting
Children: **Melanie Popp** (Dec. 7, 1974)
Michelle Popp (Oct. 20, 1976)

Barbara Popp (Aug. 27, 1947)
m. Aug. 30, 1968
Daryl Lentz (June 22, 1946 - Feb. 14, 1973)
Children: **Darren Lentz** (Feb.19, 1971)
m. Sept. 6, 1975
Frank Schmidt
m. Sept. 5, 1992
Frank Daley

Paula Popp (Feb. 24, 1952)
m. Aug. 7, 1971
Daryl Orth (Nov. 15, 1951)
Children: **Warren Orth** (Nov. 15, 1972)
m.
Paula Urzada
Children: **Carter Orth** (April 14, 1996)
Makail Orth (Nov. 29, 1997)
Trevor Orth (July 28, 1976)
Darla Orth (Jan. 14, 1978)

Brant Popp (Sept. 29, 1954)
m. Aug. 22, 1975
Joan Zuk
Children: **Grier Popp** (Mar. 25, 1988)

m. MARY JACOB

ELLA POPP (Jan. 15, 1924 - Mar.19, 1990)
m. June 16, 1946
ERNEST PARKINSON (Mar. 11, 1992)
Children: **Fredricka Parkinson** (Nov. 2, 1948)
m. August 17, 1968
Carlyle Murray
m. August 9, 1975
Thomas Jackson

Beverly Parkinson (Dec. 13, 1952)
m. January, 1970
Roy Feguson
m. August 13, 1983
Steve Kesslering (January 5, 1957)

CHILDREN OF PHILIPP AND MARGARET POPP (HENRY POPP'S PARENTS)

PHILIPP POPP (June 11, 1854 - July 6, 1926) — **MARGARET WAGNER** (August 13, 1854 - May 11, 1917)

KATHERINE POPP (Dec. 20, 1876 - Dec. 23, 1918)
m. November 26, 1896
FERDINAND BECKER (Nov. 8, 1873 - Jan. 16, 1965)
Margaret (Adolph Kendel), Adolf (Mary Mack), Minnie (Rueben McRae), William Friedrich (Ethel Lelond), Helena (Russell Wark), Joseph Frank (Lillian Lelond) Philip George (Eleonora Lohmeyer) Wanda Katherina (John Werschler) Adela Elisabeth (Stuart MacDonald) Frank Ferdinand (Emilie Bechtloff) Edwin Martin (Ella Miller)

ROSINA POPP (May 15, 1879 - Nov. 17, 1964)
m. October 20, 1896
WILLIAM CHITTICK (Jan. 10, 1864 - Dec. 3, 1938)
Mary Anne (John Moore), William (Hughena May MacDonald), Clara Elizabeth (Robert Irwin), Evelyn Jessie (Howard Avery), Philip Walter (Ruth Nicholson), Violet (George Schaan), Arta Eileen (Ernest Turley), Shirley Rosilyn (Robert Taverner)

JACOB POPP (June 20, 1881 - July 18, 1957)
m. July 7, 1903
ELISABETH SCHOEPP (Mar. 28, 1883 - July 18, 1917)
Ferdinand (Dora Hoar), Mary Rosa, Joseph (Wilhelmina Andrews), Katherine Pauline (Anthony Senger), Margaret Wilhclmina, Elisabeth Helena, Elsie Elenora
m. December 3, 1919
KAROLINA AICHELE (June 15, 1886 - May 15, 1966)
Fredrick Frank (Agnes Hanoski), Thelma Mae (Bernhardt Peppler)

JOSEPH POPP (March 11, 1883 - Oct. 17, 1904)

MARY POPP (Jan. 30, 1885 - Feb. 17, 1981)
m, November 20, 1902
ALAN BARKER (April 20, 1871 - May 24, 1950)
Gertrude Elisabeth (Albert Rettinger), Florence Edna (Barrie Taylor), Ella Marguerite (Thomas Mann), Minnie Mary (Francis Creighton), Leonard John (Lillian Scott), Lila Pearl (Leslie Wright), Arthur Herbert (Wynne Cheeseman), Doris Helen (Leslie Yerya)

ELISABETH POPP (Jan. 6, 1887 - Feb. 14, 1973)
m. January 1, 1906
HALVOR HANDE (Nov. 25, 1820 - Jan. 25, 1936)
Henry William (Lillian Nelson), Frank Bernhard, Ernest Alfred (Vera Isabel Bennett), Philip Halvor (Frances Pringle)

PHILIP POPP (Dec. 3, 1888 - Oct. 24, 1994)
m. October 29, 1922
ELEANOR WAGNER (Feb. 15, 1892 -
Lenard Ewald (Helen Ohlinger), Frank Albert (Martha Schepp), Alvin Philip (Louise Baumung), Edgar Benjamin (Eilene Peppler), Morley Gordon

HEINRICH POPP (Jan. 16, 1891 - July 17, 1973)
m. October 20, 1914
MARIA LOWENBERGER (Jan. 18, 1897 - Mar. 22, 1998
Arnold William (Meta Eleanor Kendel), Richard Arthur (Irene Mitschke), Ella Cecilia (Ernest Parkinson)

ADAM POPP and CHRISTINE POPP (twins)

FRANK POPP (Oct. 5, 1895 - Sept. 15, 1971)
m. August 6, 1917
ELISABETH MENSCH (Jan. 18, 1897 - April 15, 1956)
Frances Katherine (Norman McKinnon), Florence Valinda (David Cross), Leslie Duane (Eileen Rathgeber), Bernice Verdna Elisabeth (Donald Webster)

CAROLINA POPP (Feb. 20, 1899 – Feb. 23, 1989)
m. August 8, 1917
ARTHUR MCRAE (August 3, 1893 - January 22, 1956)
Margery Grace (John Harold Stewart), Norma Faith, Doris Beth (Douglas James Bailey)

DESCENDANTS OF JAKOB AND AUGUSTA LOWENBERGER (MARY'S POPP'S PARENTS)

GEORG JAKOB LOWENBERGER	**AUGUSTA BAUMUNG**
May 1, 1865 - November 27, 1919	June 11, 1867 - September 28, 1935

ELISABETH LOWENBERGER (Dec. 7, 1885 - Jan. 13, 1932)
m. April 16, 1914
JULIUS METZ (December 8, 1891 - July 15, 1967)
Gertrude Metz (Oct. 17, 1914), Elsie Metz (Nov. 12, 1916), Arthur Metz (Sept. 25, 1920), Frieda Metz (July 4, 1922)

KATHERINE LOWENBERGER (July 9, 1892 - Sept. 29, 1953)
m. November 10, 1914
PETER RATHGEBER (September 12, 1894 - November 5, 1963)
George Rathgeber (Dec. 10, 1915), Helma Rathgeber (April 14, 1918), Freda Rathgeber (Nov. 19, 1920), Lillian Rathgeber (June 11, 1923), Alice Rathgeber (Sept. 26, 1925), Rudolph Rathgeber (June 18, 1927)

MARIA LOWENBERGER (Jan. 18, 1897 - Mar. 22, 1998)
m. October 14, 1914
HEINRICH POPP (January 16, 1891 - July 17, 1973)
Arnold Popp (Dec. 14, 1915), Richard Popp (Jan. 20, 1919), Ella Popp (Jan. 15, 1924)

RUDOLPH LOWENBERGER (Mar. 26, 1899 - Feb. 16, 1986)
m. December 21, 1928
BEATRICE KAEY (May 21, 1908 -
Doreen Lowenberger (Aug. 14, 1930), Marilyn Lowenberger (Aug. 1, 1932), Bernice Lowenberger (Nov. 7, 1933), Wayne Lowenberger (Jan. 24, 1941), Linda Lowenberger (May 11, 1944)

JACOB LOWENBERGER (May 12, 1901 - July 18, 1975)
m. December 16, 1925
STEPHANA BELL (September 26, 1902 - April 8, 1988)
Sybil Lowenberger (Oct. 17, 1928), Melva Lowenberger (July 19, 1931), Robert Lowenberger (Jan. 11, 1939)

GEORGE LOWENBERGER (May 23, 1902 - August 23, 1987)
m. October 16, 1922
ADELHEID MACK (October 4, 1902 - April 15, 1997
Norma Lowenberger (May 11, 1923), Luella Lowenberger (July 19, 1924), Jean Lowenberger (May 7, 1927), Ruth Lowenberger (July 25, 1929), Esther Lowenberger (July 25, 1929), Kenneth Lowenberger (Aug. 7, 1932), Richard Lowenberger (Oct. 2, 1934), Joan Lowenberger (May 28, 1937)

ADOLPH LOWENBERGER (Jan. 12, 1905 - Aug. 29, 1989)
m. Dec. 17, 1927
ANNE ELIZABETH DAWSON (Aug. 17, 1905 - Aug. 29, 1939)
Patricia Lowenberger (July 24, 1932)

HELEN LOWENBERGER (Sept. 17, 1912 - July 14, 1947)
m. May 15, 1932
WILLIAM HAUSER (Oct. 21, 1912 - Jan. 2, 1975)
Elaine Hauser (April 30, 1936), Brian Hauser (Jan. 21, 1943)

MARY POPP'S MATERNAL COUSINS

MARIA KATHARINA BAUMUNG (Mar. 11, 1861- 1898)
m. JACOB KENDEL (July 2, 1856 - ?)
Children: Jacob (Wilhelmenia Geres), Dorothea (? Klayh), Friedrich (Anne ?), Elisabeth (Wilhelm Fingas/ Wagner/Kendel), Maria (John Aasen), Rudolf (Lorna Greensides), Wilhelm (Amelia Baumung), George, Amelia (Jacob Mack/Joseph Rosner)

AUGUSTA BAUMUNG (June 11, 1867 - Sept. 28, 1935)
m. GEORG JAKOB LOWENBERGER (May 1, 1865 - Nov. 22, 1919
Children: Elisabeth (Julius Metz), Katherine (Peter Rathgeber), Maria (Heinrich Popp), Rudolf (Beatrice Kaey), Jacob (Stephana Bell), George (Adelheid Mack) Adolf (Anne Dawson), Helen (William Hauser)

ANNA MARIA BAUMUNG (Oct. 3, 1868 - Sept. 15, 1954)
m. JOHANN GEORG BAUMUNG (Nov. 22, ? - May 8, 1948)
Children: Elisabeth (Jacob Kandel), Katharina (Wilhelm Harth), Friedrich (Katharina Bahsler), Freda (? Lange)

DOROTHEA CAROLINE BAUMUNG (Mar. 19, 1870 - ?
m. ? BARON

RUDOLF BAUMUNG (June 11, 1871- Nov. 7, 1941
m. DOROTHEA DRESSLER (Mar. 21, 1881 - Nov. 7, 1952
Children: Friedrich, Katharina (Filip Nerbas), Elisabeth (George Busch), Johanette (Paul Geith), Amelia, Eleonora (Markus Geith), George (Annie Rosin)

JOHANN FRIEDRICH BAUMUNG (Dec. 13, 1876 - Sept. 29, 1945)
m. ELISABETH HABERSTOCK (Feb. 15, 1884 - May 29, 1956)
Children: Elisabeth (Rudolf Kandel), Friedrich (Marie Kandel), Rudolf (Emma Kandel), Johann (Marie Haas), Jacob, Hildagaard (Adolf Kendel)

JACOB BAUMUNG (May 6, 1882 - Aug. 13, 1964)
m. ELISABETH NERBAS (Dec. 8, 1887 - June 12, 1977)
Children: Friedrick (Amelia Segate), Amelia (Wilhelm Kendel), Jacob (Elna Mitschke), Rudolf (Elisabeth Tollman), Anna Marie (Rudolf Zorn), Lydia Katharina (Jacob Andre), Helen Auguste (Eitel Zorn), Sylvia Margaretha (Lloyd Lundgren)

CHRONOLOGY

August 23, 1853	Margaret Wagner (Mary Popp's mother-in-law) born in Austria.
June 11, 1855	Phillip Popp (Mary Popp's father-in-law) born in Kolomea, Galicia, Austria.
May 1, 1865	Georg Jakob (Jakob) Lowenberger (Mary Popp's father) born in Landestreu, Austria.
June 11, 1867	Augustina (Augusta) Baumung (Mary Popp's mother) born in Landestreu, Austria.
December 7, 1888	Elisabeth Lowenberger born in Landestreu, Austria.
1889	Jakob and Augusta Lowenberger and daughter Elisabeth immigrate to Canada.
1889	Twins, Fredrick and Jacob, are born to Jakob and Augusta Lowenberger. Both die.
January 16, 1891	Henry Popp (Mary Popp-Lowenberger's husband) born.
March 1892	Phillip and Margaret (Wagner) Popp, (Henry Popp's parents) immigrate to Canada.
July 8, 1892	Katharina Lowenberger born in Hoffenthal District, Saskatchewan.
January 18, 1897	Mary Lowenberger born in Hoffenthal District, Saskatchewan.
March 26, 1899	Rudolph Lowenberger born in Hoffenthal District, Saskatchewan.
May 12, 1901	Jacob Lowenberger born in Hoffenthal District, Saskatchewan.
May 23, 1902	George Lowenberger born in Hoffenthal District, Saskatchewan.
1902	Lowenberger family moved to new farm on Section 1-23-30 WPM.
September 2, 1903	Twin daughters, Emma and Margaretha, are born to Jakob and Augusta Lowenberger. Both die.
January 24, 1905	Adolph Lowenberger born in Hoffenthal District, Saskatchewan.

May 29, 1909	Friedrich Lowenberger born in Hoffenthal District, Saskatchewan.
July 9, 1910	Friedrich Lowenberger dies, 14 months old.
1910	Mary Lowenberger confirmed by Pastor Wiegner at Hoffenthal Lutheran Chruch.
September 7, 1912	Helen Lowenberger born in Hoffenthal District, Saskatchewan, last child of Jakob and Augusta Lowenberger.
April 16, 1914	Elisabeth Lowenberger marries Julius Metz.
October 20, 1914	Mary Lowenberger marries Henry Popp.
November 10, 1914	Katie Lowenberger marries Peter Rathgeber.
December 14, 1915	Arnold Popp, first child of Henry and Mary Popp, born in Landestreu District.
May 11, 1917	Margaret Popp (Mary Popp's mother-in-law) dies, age 64 years.
January 20, 1919	Richard Arthur Popp, second child of Henry and Mary Popp, born in Landestreu District.
November 22, 1919	Georg Jakob Lowenberger dies at 54 years of age.
January 15, 1924	Ella Popp, third child of Henry and Mary Popp, born in Landestreu District.
December 23, 1925	Jacob Lowenberger marries Stephana (Fantie) Belle in Presbyterian Church in Shellmouth.
July 6, 1926	Phillip Popp (Mary Popp's father-in-law) dies in MacNutt, age 71 years.
December 17, 1927	Adolph Lowenberger marries Anne Drawson.
October 1928	Henry and Mary Popp leave the farm and move to MacNutt.
December 21, 1928	Rudolph Lowenberger marries Beatrice Keay.
January 13, 1932	Elisabeth Metz dies in MacNutt.
May 15, 1932	Helen Lowenberger marries William Hauser.
1932	Henry and Mary Popp move from MacNutt to Calder.
September 28, 1935	Augusta Lowenberger dies in Winnipeg at 65 years of age.

August 1938	Henry and Mary Popp move to Langenburg and live in Burkhardt house until 1951.
1942	Ella Popp begins nurse's training in St. Boniface Hospital.
January 1, 1943	Dick Popp marries Irene Mitschke.
1943	Henry Popp breaks his leg in elevator accident in Langenburg.
June 16, 1946	Ella Popp marries Ernie Parkinson.
July 14, 1947	Helen Hauser (Mary Popp's sister) dies in Winnipeg, Manitoba, 34 years old.
1950	Mary Popp goes on trip to Port Arthur Ontario to visit Arnold and Meta Popp.
1951	Henry and Mary build new house in Langenburg.
April 1951	Dick Popp becomes Hospital Administrator.
September 29, 1953	Katie Rathgeber dies in Winnipeg, Manitoba.
1956	Henry Popp retires from the Pool Elevator.
1957	Mary Popp travels to Ontario with Schendels and to California with Brenners.
November 1, 1965	Arnold Popp dies, 49 years old in Port Arthur, Ontario
July 17, 1973	Henry Popp dies, age 82 years old.
July 18, 1975	Jacob Lowenberger dies, age 74 years.
August 23, 1984	George Lowenberger dies, 82 years old.
February 16, 1986	Rudolph Lowenberger dies, 86 years old.
August 29, 1989	Adolph Lowe dies, 83 years old.
March 19, 1990	Ella Parkinson dies, 66 years old.
1993	Mary Popp takes residence in Langenburg Centennial Care Home.
January 18, 1997	Mary Popp celebrates her 100th birthday.
July 5, 1997	Richard Popp dies, 78 years old.
March 22, 1998	Mary Popp dies, 101 years old.

MAP OF LANGENBURG AND SURROUNDING AREA

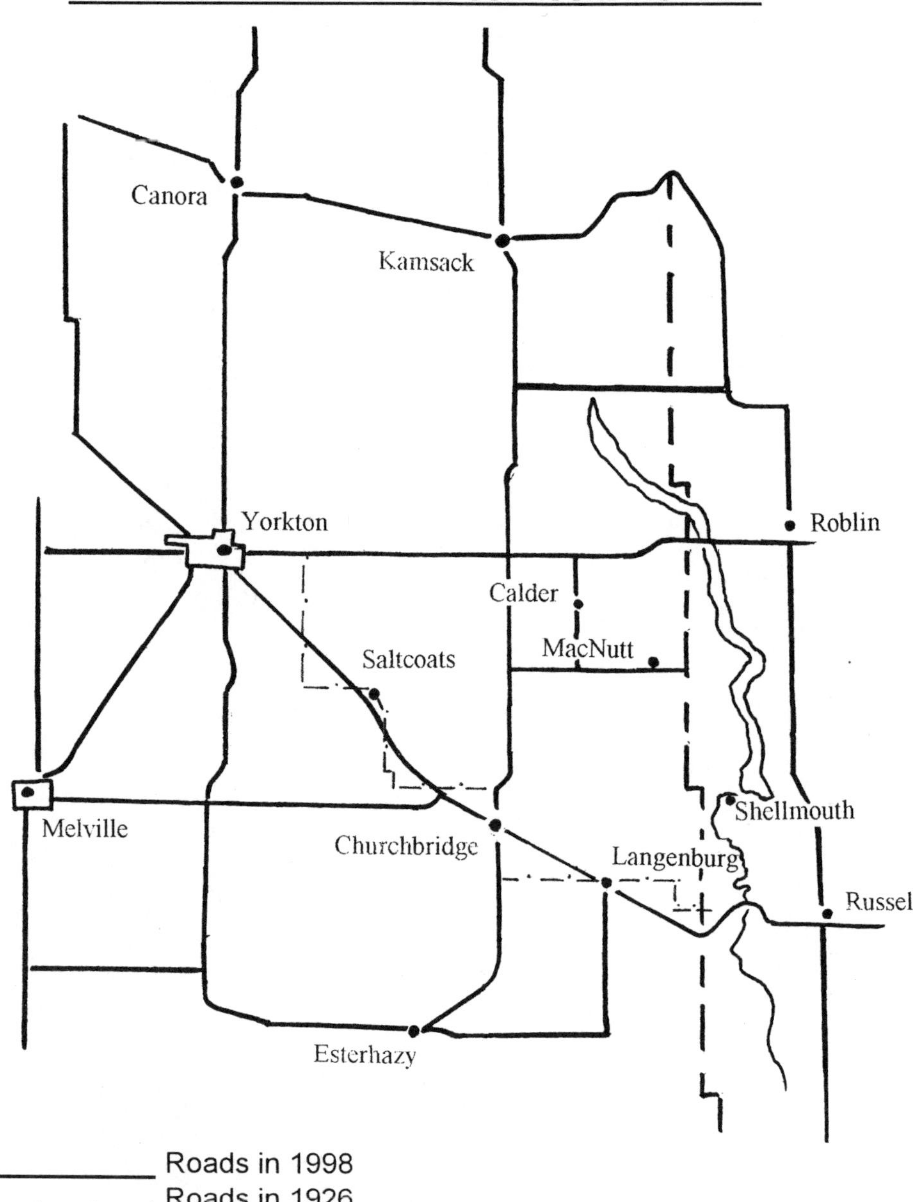

THE AUSTRIAN PROVINCE OF GALICIA
Lemberg (L'vov)
Dnjestr River
Stryj
Ugartsthal
Landestreu
Horocholina
Kolomea
Katharinendorf
Poland
Ukraine

From Austria to Hoffenthal

I am now 70 years old[1], and my thinking is not of the future, or not much --- but of the past. This is a time when people have no time for story telling, or if some have time to tell, nobody has time to listen. What with TV and radio, so much reading and so many, many other activities there just is no time.

When I was young and we lived on the farm,[2] there were many times that our mother would tell us of their early lives. She would tell us while we were working, while we were cooking or washing dishes, or picking and carding wool which would take hours or days, or desprouting and sorting potatoes in the cellar, or knitting.

There were so many things we would work at together, my sisters, my mother and I. She would often tell us the same thing over and we wouldn't want to listen, but it made the time go faster and the work easier. I remember a lot of what she told us, but now

---

[1] Mary Popp began writing her memoirs in 1967.

[2] Mary Popp's parents first homesteaded on the NW 1/4 16-22-30 WPM, eight miles northeast of Langenburg, Saskatchewan.

I am beginning to forget. When I start thinking about some of the things she told us, I would give anything to be able to ask her now.

Both Mother and Dad[3] were born in Austria. Their parents had small holdings of land on which they made their living. They lived in a village they called a *Dorf*.[4]

On this land they planted grain for their own use and all their vegetables. Their cattle were taken to pasture in the morning. My mother's father[5] kept bees. I had seen a picture of all the bee

---

[3] Mary Popp's parents were Georg Jakob Lowenberger, commonly called Jakob, (May 1, 1865 - November 22, 1919) and Augusta Baumung (June 11, 1867 - September 28, 1935). As was common with many marriages in Landestreu, Jakob and Augusta shared several common ancestors. In their case, they shared Dressler, Nerbas and Baumung ancestors - families who had settled in Landestreu in the 1780s. Mary's surname was originally spelled Löwenberger. The two dots above the "o" (called an umlaut) change the pronunciation of the "o" to a sound unfamiliar in English. It is a common practice when dropping the umlaut from a vowel to add an "e". Thence "Löwenberger" was commonly spelled "Loewenberger", with the "w" pronounced as an English "v". Today, most families spell the name as "Lowenberger" and the original pronunciation has correspondingly changed using a long "o" and the English "w" sound.

[4] *Dorf* is a German word for village. The *Dorf* was called Landestreu meaning "true to the land".

[5] Mary's grandfather, Johann Friedrich Baumung (October 22, 1837 - October 19, 1910) was known as an industrious and enterprising man in Landestreu. In Heimat Galizien, Ein Gedenkenbuch, 1965, edited by Julius Kramer, Elinore Volker (nee Kandel) wrote about Johann Friedrich Baumung, also her grandfather:

> Alone of all the German villages in Galicia, Landestreu had an aqueduct, even if it was just for watering cattle. It was laid by the parish alone. In our highlands (Carpathian Mountains) there was an exceptionally strong spring which was discovered by Friedrich Baumung. He planned how to get the water into the village. Nice straight trees were hollowed out and skillfully joined together for a pipeline through which the water ran down into hollowed-out oak tubs spaced through the village. Water ran from one tub into the other. Summer and winter the cattle had water. ...
>
> Whoever came to Landestreu looked with wonder at the apiary that belonged to [Friedrich Baumung]. In his fruit garden, fenced with a high woven willow fence, stood many beehives. Friedrich Baumung had steady customers outside the village. In the village a glass of honey was got whenever somebody had a bad cough, a sore throat or other ailment for which honey was considered an ailment. [Friedrich]

hives. Mother told how she helped look after the bees. They also grew some flax and made linen. She had done a lot of spinning and weaving and made all their bed linens and also their underclothes. She had bedspreads finely woven with four inch crocheted inserts and lace. She also did some netting and fine work. I have a bonnet which was supposed to have been her wedding bonnet --it would be over 100 years old.[6]

Their food was plain without much waste. They had ways of using everything. They also grew fruit trees, so they made plum jam[7] and apple cider.[8] They cooked noodles, potato pancakes,

---

> also had a fruit press. On his press the whole village made their cider. When it was cider-making time, a big holiday for us children, a big wagon box was loaded with apples. When the sweet juice started flowing everybody would generously taste it. This often lead to many bellyaches. [Friedrich Baumung was also the "Oilmiller".] Every litre of oil used in the village was made on Oilmiller's mill. Most of the oil was made from flax and rape seed with smaller quantities being made from poppy seed and pumpkin seed. The latter two made a very tasty oil used just for special purposes.

Friedrich Baumung died in Landestreu at 75 years of age. Of his ten children, three eventually came to Canada: Augusta (Mary's mother), Jakob Baumung and Rudolf Baumung.

It is thought that the name Baumung (sometimes spelled Baumunk) came from France when Balthasar de Baumong left France after the Thirty Years' War and settled in Reichenbach, Germany. In 1788 two Baumung brothers left Reichenbach for Galicia where they settled in Landestreu: Johann Adam Baumung (1768 - 1842) who married Maria Wagner and Johann Georg Baumung (1763 - 1823) who married Maria Elisabeth Adam. The Baumung family became a large family in Landestreu and many villagers could trace an ancestor to either Johann Adam or Johann Georg Baumung. Johann Adam Baumung was Mary Popp's ancestor on her mother's side; Johann Georg Baumung was an ancestor on her father's side.

[6] The date of marriage of Mary Popp's parents is unknown. The wedding bonnet is owned by Mary Popp's granddaughter, Ricki Jackson.

[7] Making plum jam in Landestreu was an annual community event. Rudy Schaan described making plum jam in Landestreu in his unpublished memoirs, *Landestreu: A Village No More*:

> Bushels of ripe plums were made ready - washed, pitted and put in a giant copper kettle over an open outdoor fire. It was cooked until it was fairly stiff and would be considered good enough for keeping without further preservatives. You could not spread it once it cooled so it had to be sliced into thin pieces and used that way in baking as

cabbage rolls,[9] dumplings, *borscht,*[10] *berhae*[11] made with cheese and plums, *kuchen*[12] of all kinds, strudel, and fancy pastries. They did not eat as much meat as people do now.

When Mother and Dad married, Dad being the oldest son was to inherit the home and take over, but his parents were quite young yet and there were four younger children.[13] They lived with his family but that did not last long. Then they got work, working

---

> well as spread on bread. It was a very tricky process and required constant mixing with a large ladle to prevent the mass of fruit from burning. The fire had to be just right and it took an entire day to get it done.

[8] Apple cider was called *Moscht.* Rudy Schaan described making *Moscht* as follows:

> *Moscht* was their hospitality drink. It was quite an art to produce good cider other than vinegar. The Baumungs had a facility which was a piece of art in itself. The crusher was a huge curved log. This was hollowed out and looked like a very deep bent canoe. The apples to be crushed were dumped into this canoe and a huge stone wheel the width of the cut out was rolled over these apples in a back and forth motion. The stone had a centre hole in which a long pole was fitted and secured on both sides of the stone with dowels. The other end of the pole was secured to a post. Two or more people used this pole to roll the stone back and forth over the apples until the desired mash was achieved. It was then put into a huge wooden press. The juice was collected in wooden barrels and with a lot of patience a potent cider produced many a glow in the dreary cold winters. The animals got the pulp. Nothing got wasted.

[9] The Germans living in Galicia borrowed many dishes from their Slavic neighbours. *Holopchi* or cabbage rolls are leaves of soured cabbage wrapped around a mixture of rice and meat and then boiled. They continue to be a popular dish in the Langenburg area.

[10] *Borscht* or *Borsh* is beet soup. Typically it is a Russian dish. Again, it was adopted by the German settlers from their Slavic neighbours.

[11] *Berhae* or perogies is a Ukrainian dish. Various fillings - potatoes, cheese, plums, rhubarb, even sauerkraut - are wrapped in a dough covering and boiled. *Berhae* are often served with sweet or sour cream.

[12] *Kuchen* is a German word for "cake". Its more specific meaning, however, refers to a special cake made with a base of sweetened raised dough upon which fruit or poppy seeds are placed. A crumb mixture of brown sugar, flour and butter is sprinkled over the fruit. The cake is then baked.

[13] Jakob Lowenberger had one brother, Friedrich, and three sisters, Elinora, Dorothea and Maria. Only Jakob came to Canada.

for a big land owner who had many servants. Mother and Dad were overseers, but they were to eat with the servants. They got chopped barley bread, very dark. Mother cried. She could not eat that bread, so they were allowed to eat separate and could have white bread. All the food was locked up and each one was doled out his portion. Mother had the key to the store room and was overseer of the maids and Dad was overseer of the man servants.

I don't know how long they worked there, but not more than a year or so. Then they heard about people immigrating to Canada. So they, with three other young couples, the Friedrich Nerbases[14], the Jacob Busches[15] and John Burkharts[16] immigrated to Canada with their worldly possessions packed into a big home-made trunk. They said good-bye to their parents, never to see them again. Mother's two brothers[17] came to Canada later but Dad never saw any of his family again. Later nephews and nieces from both sides came.

My oldest sister[18] was a year old when they came to Canada and the other couples each had one child about the same age. They landed in Winnipeg in the fall. It must have been in the year 1889. The four families lived in a four room house in Winnipeg, each having a room. They had come to a new land and a new language which they did not understand. There was no work for them. They watched when a load of wood would go by and they would take their saws and follow it, but others would do the same - Winnipeg was small then.

---

[14] Friedrich Nerbas (November 18, 1867 - September 6, 1940) and Dorothea Mack (October 8, 1867 - January 6, 1946) and their daughter Elisabeth, born December 8, 1888.

[15] Jacob Wilhelm Busch (1863 - 1932) and Eleanora Schappert (1870 - 1954) and their infant daughter, Anna. The Busch family settled in the Beresina District northeast of Langenburg. Jacob and Eleanora had 15 children.

[16] Johann Burkhart (March 15, 1861 - May, 1949) and Eleanore Bieber (February 1871 - March 15, 1910). Mr. Burkhart outlived four wives and was married to his fifth before his death.

[17] The two brothers who later came to Canada were Jacob Baumung (1882 - 1964) and Rudolf Baumung (1871 - 1941).

[18] Elisabeth (Lizzie) was the oldest daughter, born December 7, 1888 in Austria.

Now here is where I would like to ask my mother questions, but I think there was an immigration agent who helped them. In the spring, they got a 400 dollar loan each, with which they bought a wagon with double box, a breaking plow, some seed grain, a pair of oxen or horses and one or two cows and drove out from Winnipeg.[19] That's where I got stuck in my story. There were no highways. How would they know where to go? My brother's wife has told me that Mother told her that in Winnipeg homesteads were assigned to them. With this loan they bought what they needed most and an immigration agent led them out to Langenburg[20] to

---

[19] By late fall of 1886 the railway had reached Langenburg. Earlier that year the Kieper and Welke families arrived in Langenburg. William Welke Sr. recounted that in September 1886 the railway ended in Binscarth. There they loaded their implements on wagons and made the last leg of the trip with wagon and oxen. It seems unusual that Mary Popp's parents would have trekked from Winnipeg by horse and wagon when the railway would have brought them to Langenburg. Could they not afford the fare? Mary Popp's brother, George Lowenberger, born in 1902, suggests in his writings that his parents travelled to Langenburg by train and lived under the wagon box until a cave was dug in the south side of a hill.

[20] The origins of the name "Langenburg" has been recorded by Bill Barry in *People Places: Saskatchewan and Its Names* as follows:

> The German influence in Saskatchewan has been very strong, and German Canadians have been the second largest ethnic group in the province since it was created.
>
> ...
>
> With such widespread influence, it is no surprise that a number of Saskatchewan names honoured famous Germans. One of the more interesting was Feurst (prince) Hermann of Hohenlohe - Langenburg. He was one of many wealthy young Europeans who came to central North America in the mid to late nineteenth century on hunting trips. Unlike numerous other adventurers, the *feurst* does not seem to have left a chronicle of his experiences. In 1884 a group of Germans trekked north from Moosomin to begin a new life on the prairies. They named the northern part of their settlement HOHENLOHE and the southern part LANGENBURG to houour their compatriot, even though it is not likely that the prince got any closer to the area than Moosomin. The Langenburg post office opened in 1888, and its future was secured when the railway began operating through the settlement a few years later. [In fact the railway reached Langenburg late 1886.] Hohenlohe was not so lucky. No school was organized until 1910, and when it closed in 1965 the name disappeared. Had the railway passed

their homesteads. They were days driving. At night they would unload the wagon and turn the box upside down and sleep under it.

I've been told that my parents had twins born in Winnipeg. The boys' names were Friedrich and Jacob. Both of them died on the way from Winnipeg and were buried on the prairie somewhere along the way. One died a few days before the other.

Their homestead was eight miles north east of Langenburg. I do not know if the other families came out at the same time,[21] but they all lived just a few miles apart on new unbroken land, not much bush, tall grass, rich soil.

They dug a cave[22] in the side of a hill for their first home. Later Mother said they dug a cellar in the cave. Dad dug and she

---

half a dozen miles to the north, however, we might have a Hohenlohe today instead of a Langenburg.

[21] It would seem all four couples must have travelled together. Mary (Nerbas) Becker wrote of her parents' history in *Shellmouth Our Century*: "My parents Friedrich and Dorthea Nerbas came to Winnipeg, Canada from Austria in 1889 with Elisabeth who was one year old. They stayed the first year in Winnipeg, arriving in the Hoffenthal district in 1890. They homesteaded NE-20-22-30, with their neighbours, Mr. and Mrs. Jake Lowenberger, John Burkhardt, and Jake Busch.

[22] In 1889 Pastor Schmieder was in Langenburg organizing a Lutheran congregation when he travelled to the Beresina district to visit Esslingers who had arrived a year earlier. In a written report he described the cave-like dwelling used by the Esslingers, undoubtedly the same type of shelter used by the Lowenbergers:

> At the edge of a bit of bush two rooftops became visible; the remainder of the houses were completely underground and buried in the earth. One had to bend down and descend a few steps in order to reach the one and only room in the dwelling. At first I was inclined to consider these houses well suited to the purpose and practical, because I felt they would be cool in summer and comfortably warm in winter. But now I am convinced that they are just as difficult to heat as log houses since the frost penetrates so deep into the ground. The only advantage that such a house has is that these people can construct them with an outlay of a mere $3.00 for nails, hinges and two small windows. And that is indeed very important, since these people are still deeply in debt and will need one or two years before they can pay for their farm implements and provide something better. The beds, table, chairs and benches in these dugouts are put together with inadequate carpenter tools by the people themselves.

carried the dirt up and out. If they did the same for a barn, I do not know.

In the winter they would get bad blizzards with high drifts. One time a missionary drove out to visit the new settlers and he drove over the roof of my parents' dwelling. They heard this noise on the roof. When they went out to look, he had driven over the roof and didn't know it.

They broke some land. Seeding and harvesting was done by hand. The cows on that good grass gave so much milk Mother made cheese but they couldn't eat it all. She would churn butter but couldn't use or sell it so they greased the wagon wheels with it. She made a small wooden tubful of about ten pounds and carried it on her head to Langenburg but she could not sell or trade it. The store[23] would not take it. As small children we were not taken along to town. But we were very happy when our parents came home and brought five cents worth of candy. Candy then was in round blocks about an inch thick with either "Patrick" or "Miller" printed through it. The candy was chopped in pieces with a big knife or small axe and we would each get a piece. That was Langenburg to us.

They bought a pair of young pigs and made a woven willow fence for them, but the pigs got out and into the tall grass. Mother and Dad chased them. They could see where they were, where the grass moved. They chased them until both they and the pigs wore out, but they got them.

Then Mother wanted some chickens. A few miles away there lived people by the name of Burton, who must have homesteaded there before. They had chickens. So Mother walked there, but she could not speak English and they could not speak German. They asked her if she wanted hens or roosters. Since the word for *hens* in English sounds like the German word for *roosters*, she asked thought she was asking for *hens.*[24] She got two in a box and carried them home on her head. (Mother could carry everything on her head; perhaps that's why she used to get such

---

[23] By the time the railway reached Langenburg two stores were in operation, one owned by Helgi Johnson and the other by Christian Hinck and Paul Ulrich.
[24] Rooster in German is *Hahn*.

severe headaches in later years.) Anyway she set her box in the kitchen. Next morning what she thought were hens crowed. She took her box on her head and carried them back and exchanged them for hens.

Mother told us that in the first or second year they were here, Dad and some men walked to Oregon to look for work.[25] They were gone for months and she was alone with the children. She said how she got so homesick. Tommy the dog would go and sit on the hill at twilight and howl and Mother would cry. The men were looking for a warmer climate and better land. But they came back and stayed -- I don't know if they found work.

Other settlers kept on coming, relatives, friend and others, all settling in the neighbourhood.[26] Most came from my folks' village of Landestreu, Austria, people that had known each other in the old country.[27]

---

[25] It seems likely that they walked to North Dakota. Mary (Nerbas) Becker, the daughter of Frederick and Dorthea Nerbas, the couple who accompanied the Lowenbergers to Canada, wrote in *Shellmouth Our Century* that "The men walked to North Dakota to find work. The women worked alone and kept the home."

[26] Other families that arrived in the Hoffenthal District included Georg and Carolina (Kullmann) Phillips (1890), Valentin and Dorothea (Lowenberger) Schappert (1889), Johann and Maria (Phillips) Schappert (1891), Wilhelm and Katharina (Haas) Mensch (1892), Philipp and Margaretha (Kitsch) Nerbas, Georg and Margaret (Klei) Haas, George and Catharina Werschler, Ludwig and Elisabeth Goehring, Alfred and Jakobina (Mack) Kendel (1901), Friedrich and Maria (Wirt) Werschler, Heinrich and Catharina (Neuerschmidt) Haberstock, Friedrich and Sophia (Schramm) Mayer, Peter and Katharina (Urscahl) Gretzinger, Philipp and Katharina (Wehrle) Dietrich, Jakob and Magdalena (Kullmann) Metz, Andrew and Caroline (Prinz) Koch (1904), Philip and Caroline (Schappert) Kendell (1903), Anton and Maria Elizabeth (Lowenberger) Hofer (1891), Rudolf and Dorothea (Dressler) Baumung (1904), Valentine and Katharine (Nerbas) Mack.

[27] Many of the families in Landestreu had nicknames. These nicknames were also used in Canada for a number of years and are still known among the older citizens of Langenburg. The Geres family was called *Buttermilch* (Buttermilk); the Mack family, *Pankucha* (Pancakes); the Baumung family, *Schumacher* (Shoemaker); the Kendel family, *Futschjer* ("Playboy"); one group of the Koch family, *Schumichel* (Shoe Michael); another group of the Koch family, *Schwabisko Koch* (Schwabisch Koch); the Lowenberger family, *Kloo Loberjer*

On July 9, 1892 another daughter was born to my parents, Katherina. She was baptized by Pastor Buegel who had held his first service in the Hoffenthal[28] District on May 1, 1892. Since there was over five years between the birth of my two older sisters, there probably were children born in that span who died in infancy.

How long my folks lived in the cave, I don't know. I don't think I was born in it, but I do remember the house they built after. It was a log house plastered inside and out with clay and white washed both inside and out. The roof was covered with sods, with grass growing on it. There was a big room and a kitchen which must have been built after, as there was about a six inch space between them. The kitchen had some corner logs sticking out. You could climb onto the roof to look for the cows. Even our dog Tommy could climb up and when he was shown where the cows were he would go and get them.

The inside of the house, the big room, as I remember it, had a board floor scrubbed white. The kitchen had a mud floor plastered with clay. The big room had beds in three corners. Between two of them was a cradle and in the fourth corner stood a big trunk, painted brown, where most of the clothes were kept.

I remember just one thing in the kitchen - the cook stove. It was big, with a lot of embossing and oven doors on both sides that swung open like a door. On the front it had drafts and a shelf with an ash pan and a swinging lid. Little doors in front would open and you could bring the ashes out into the ash pan. It was a friendly looking stove and it would crackle and spark when there was a good fire on.

When it rained a lot or for long, Mother would have to put all the pans and pails on the beds and all over where the water would drip through. Father would light the lantern and go up to the attic by an outside ladder to look if the roof wasn't caving in when the sods were soaked with rain.

My parents also told us of blizzards in the early years. They were so bad that Dad would tie a rope to the house and then to the

---

(the Little Lowenbergers); the Schaan family, *Kuhhirt Schaan* (Cowherder Schaan).

[28] Hoffenthal means "Valley of Hope".

barn to find his way back and forth. One time he got lost when he was getting a bag of oats from the granary to the barn. It was very difficult for him to walk in the deep snow because of his asthma. In those years there wasn't much shelter to break the wind. Prairie fires used to burn down any bush.

After my oldest brother Rudolph was born on March 26, 1899 my Mother wasn't well, so they hired a Ukrainian couple who had two boys. The older one went to work out; the younger one stayed with us. His name was Donella. He stuttered so badly he could hardly talk. His parents stayed for some time, until Mother was well. I was learning to talk then, so I learned Ukrainian.[29] Both Mother and Dad could speak it well and my two older sisters also learned it. But since I was so young, I forgot how to speak it. Donella stayed on at our place when his parents left --- must have been for a couple of years, because I can remember him, perhaps because he stuttered so badly. Then many years later, when I was married for some time, he lived at Wroxton. He took annual trips, walking to Langenburg and he found out who I was. We lived by the road. He came in to see us and stayed for a couple of days. After that he made our place a stopping place on his trips, until we left the farm. His stuttering had become worse. He was such a little man.

My Aunt Lizzie Baumung[30] has told me that the first grave in the Hoffenthal cemetery was that of Henry Kriewaldt.[31] He and

---

[29] Most of the German settlers from Galicia could speak Ukrainian and Polish because most of the neighbouring villages were Slavic.

[30] Elisabeth Baumung (nee Nerbas) was the oldest daughter of Friedrich Nerbas and Dorthea (Mack), one of the four couples who emigrated to Canada with Mary Popp's parents. She married Jacob Baumung, Mary Popp's mother's brother.

[31] Heinrich Kriewaldt (June 6, 1864 - 1901) married an Irish school teacher by the last name of Quinn. They lived in the United States. They had one boy, Wilhelm (1886 - 1954) who married Louise Haas in 1914 and two girls who died of diptheria. Heinrich remarried and moved to Canada. The Hoffenthal Church records show an entry for Heinrich Kriewaldt married to Lisetta ?, who was born June 7, 1872. Heinrich and Lisetta had five children: Rosa, Rita, Lili, Lisette and Magdalena. Heinrich's brother, Ferdinand Kriewaldt, came to the Hoffenthal area on May 1, 1896. Ferdinand and Heinrich's sister, Ida, was married to Reverend Carl Geith. On November 18, 1897 Ferdinand married

his wife were good friends of my parents. In 1901 on Pentecost my parents were having my brother Jake baptized. He was born May 12, 1901. Mr. and Mrs. Kriewaldt were to be the sponsors, but they didn't arrive at church. It seems Mr. Kriewaldt had gotten up and went to get the horses to go to church. When he didn't come back everybody looked for him. He wasn't found for a couple of days. When they found him, the crows and flies had been at him. They had men then that would do certain things: Mr. Burkhart made coffins and Mr. Valentine Mack[32] would get the dead ready for burial. Apparently he got quite sick after that case.

Thc barn was part log and part layered sods. One Saturday night just before Pentecost in 1902, my oldest sister was polishing the stove which was close to a window. We were having a thunder storm. There was a heavy crash, and my sister's arm got numb. Our parents were in bed already. Mother got up and looked out the window and the barn was on fire. Lightning had struck the barn and killed the horses. I don't know how many horses we had. One pair belonged to my cousin. A bull and six calves were killed. They were in the log barn. The cows and one mare, Nellie, with a new colt, were in the sod part of the barn which had not burned. They were not harmed. I was very young then but remember it clearly.

The next day was a beautiful day and Dad got somebody else's team of horses and pulled all the dead animals away. Many people were there to see what had happened, and the neighbours came running, some in their underclothes, helping to put the fire out.

Beatha Lowenberger (1880-1919), daughter of George and Eleanor Lowenberger. Ferdinand and Beatha had six children: Athalia (Phillips /Nerbas), Edwin, Minna (Campbell), Herbert, Clara and Harold.

[32] Valentine Mack (August 26, 1855 - May 9, 1940) and his wife Katharina (Nerbas) (November 19, 1864 - July 1, 1930) also emigrated from Landestreu, Austria. (Valentine's first wife, Elisabeth Farber, had died in Europe.) Valentine and Katharina's daughter, Adelheid, married Mary Popp's brother, George Lowenberger in 1922.

My cousin Mary Kendel[33] has told me that she was at our place when lightning struck the barn. She and my older sister were in the kitchen, and later helped carry water to put the fire out. My brother Jake said one team of horses that was burned had been bought from Mr. Beaton and had not been paid for when they were killed. Mr. Beaton gave Dad another pair.

Our house was on a hill. We had to go down hill to the barn, the well and the garden. The garden was fenced with woven willows; other fences were made with poles and posts. The well had three poles standing in a tripod shape. A pulley and rope with an attached pail were used to draw up water.

In one of the severe winters my dad got sick. They said he had the grippe. He had to be in bed and couldn't sleep for days and nights. When he thought he couldn't stand it any longer, he asked Mother for his pipe. He scraped some of the nicotine out of it and ate it. Then he fell asleep and Mother couldn't wake him. Nor could she go for help. She left the children while she went to feed the stock and do all the other chores but could not walk a couple of miles for help while Dad was so very ill. There was no doctor to get anyway. After days, my dad woke up. He did not know what had happened to him. Some time later his uncle came. When he learned what had happened he said that Dad could have poisoned himself. He was surprised he hadn't died. After that our dad always had asthma, which kept getting worse as he grew older.

Mother would help with all the outside work. One day she was helping to haul and stack hay. A small baby was in the cradle. My two older sisters, Lizzie and Katie, were playing outside. Lizzie, maybe seven years old, was to listen at the door if the baby cried, then call Mother. It didn't cry. When it was time to nurse the baby, Mother went in. They had a cat that could open the door by stepping on the latch. The cat had gone in and lain on the baby's face. When Mother came in the cat got up and the baby was dead.

Another time Mother and Dad were milking in the corral. My second oldest sister, Katie, was picking flowers and there was a big stray tom cat around. When my sister was making funny noises

---

[33] Mary Kendel was the daughter of Jacob Kendel and Maria Katharina Baumung. She came to Canada as a young woman and married John Aasen.

they thought she was trying to make noises like the cat. When the noise got worse, they went to look. The cat had put its paws on Katie's shoulders, pulled her down and eaten a hole in her head. She always had a place the size of half a finger without hair on her head. You would think after that they would never have kept cats, but that was the only way to keep the mice down.

My parents' house was a stopping place or home for many people coming from the old country. My uncle Jake Baumung,[34] my mother's brother, and my cousins, Fred Kendel,[35] came, young men about twenty years old. Our place was their home. They would get jobs, but when they weren't working or had time off they would come home. Later, Fred's sister came, Mary Kendel, a young girl 13 years old, my mother's sister's daughter. Their mother had died[36] so they came to Canada and got jobs, young as they were. To us children, they were our children, our family, and we hated to see them leave when they went to work out.

We just had two rooms and three beds so when somebody came we had to double up. The bigger ones slept at the head end of the bed and the little ones slept at the foot end of the bed. If there were too many, beds had to be made on the floor.

---

[34] Jacob Baumung was born in Landestreu, Austria on May 6, 1882. At 17 years of age he came to the Hoffenthal district and stayed with the Lowenbergers. Jacob married Elisabeth Nerbas on November 17, 1903. They raised eight children. Fred, Emelia (Schaan), Jake, Rudolf, Mary (Zorn), Lydia (Andres), Gustie (Zorn) and Sylvia (Lundgren). Jacob died August 13, 1964; Elisabeth died June 12, 1977.

[35] It was commonly known that Jake Baumung and his nephew, Fred Kendel, were sent to Canada by their parents. Apparently they had gotten into an altercation with a Mr. Geib, the *Glockengeisser* (bell caster), at a dance in Landestreu. Mr. Geib apparently had told them they were too young to be at the party. The young men in retaliation smashed his bell moulds. Apparently, to avoid the consequences of their action, they either chose to come or were sent to Canada. (Related by Mary Baumung and Gustie Zorn).

[36] Friedrich and Mary Kendel were Mary's cousins, the son and daughter of Maria Katharina Baumung and Jacob Kendel. Maria Katharina died in Austria in 1898 at 37 years of age. Later more Kendel siblings would emigrate from Landestreu, Austria: Elisabeth (Fingas/ Wagner/ Kendel), Wilhelm, who married his cousin Amelia Baumung, Amelia (Mack/ Rosner) and Rudolph who married Lorna Greenside.

I remember one summer night we could hear somebody coming walking on the road talking very loudly. They were two Ukrainian men who had landed in this country. The mosquitoes were very bad. They had green netting fixed onto their hats. It was very hot so they were perspiring and rubbing their faces. It was dark when they got to our place. When they came in their faces and hats were all green from the netting. Mother and Dad could speak Ukrainian to them, but I remember being very scared of those green men that talked differently. It wouldn't wash off either. They stayed over night and maybe a few days. Mother had bought a pair of white wool blankets with rainbow coloured borders. They were new and on the bed they slept in. When Mother made the bed there were body lice crawling in the bed. She could boil the rest of the bedding but not those blankets so the men bought the blankets. I felt very bad about those green men carrying away our new blankets. I couldn't understand why.

There were no highways or graded roads, no road allowance, just trails. The roads were very crooked as they went around sloughs and hills. The ruts were worn deep from the wagon wheels. There was one endless one, called the Pelly Trail.[37] It ran over the land we moved to later. I never knew why it was called the Pelly Trail until reading in later years about some early settlers in the Pelly area. That road was deeply worn.

Prairie fires were common in those years. I guess that was why there was not much bush growing. But the grass was so tall and in the fall when it was dry, if a fire started there was no stopping it. Dad would plow a fire guard about eight furrows around all the buildings, and if a fire came and it was windy they had to watch so the fire wouldn't jump the guard or sparks fly into the yard. They would have pails of water and wet bags to put out any sparks that would get across the guard.

---

[37] It seems more than one trail may have been called the Pelly Trail. They all led to Fort Pelly. It is thought that the Pelly Trail branched off a major trail from Fort Gary to Fort Ellice, at a point south of present day Shoal Lake, Manitoba. Another "Pelly" Trail went on the west side of the Assiniboine Valley from Fort Ellice to Fort Pelly. It would seem that Mary Popp was referring to this trail. From the Lowenberger land the trail continued south and passed by Wolverine House now marked by a cairn northeast of Marchwell.

My dad's uncle[38] came later and lived a half mile east of us. There was a grain field between the two places. I was sent to take a message to their place. There was a path through the wheat field, but coming back I got off the path and got lost in the tall wheat field. The wheat was a lot taller than I was. I remember how frantic I was until I got out of that field. I was crying.

In the winter Mother would melt snow for soft water, but in the summer, she could not catch rain water off the sod roof so she would fill a barrel with well water and dump the wood ashes in, let it stand a few days until it was clear, and use it for washing. As far back as I can remember, Mother made all our laundry soap.

Wood for the stoves was hauled from the river,[39] which was about eight or ten miles away. I guess that's where they got the logs for our first buildings. Later when there were fewer prairie fires, a lot of bush grew that could be used for fuel. The fires would go out during the night and it would get quite cold, but there was always kindling made the evening before to get a quick fire started in the morning.[40]

One of the times when Dad was getting ready to leave for the sawmill,[41] brother Rudy who was quite small, said when he

---

[38] Johann Georg Lowenberger (July 2, 1854 - March 28, 1924) was married to Elinora Koch in Austria. After she died, he and several children immigrated to Canada where he married Margarethe Trapp (1877 - February 19, 1953). Georg and Margarethe had twelve children.

[39] Assiniboine River.

[40] This is as much as Mary Popp wrote in 1967. On February 1, 1968 Mary began writing again, noting that 1967 was "not an easy year for us". Henry Popp had been diagnosed with prostate cancer. She also wrote that she would continue her history, noting "Am now a year older, 71 years old and a little more forgetful, but will try."

[41] The sawmill was at Asessippi, now a ghost town just west of the 83 Highway where it crosses the Shell River. In *My Dear Maggie* edited by Kenneth S. Coates and William R. Morrison, Canadian Plains Research Center, University of Regina, 1991 William Wallace described Asessippi as it stood in 1883:

> Last Monday Papa and I drove up to the Assissippi Saw Mill for lumber boards for the granary. I have been near but never at the place before. It is a pretty but perilous looking hole. The Shell River flows down from the north to this point, after which it turns a right angle and flows west, and the town is situated at the point. You see it almost directly underneath when driving along the banks - the descent is very

grew up he was going to have a beard, a long fur coat with a sausage in the pocket and go to the bush just like his dad. Rudy also reminded me of another time, after we had moved to our new place. There were taller buildings and there were a lot of long dry sticks in the bush. He got one and climbed onto one of the buildings, pushing that stick up. When Mother asked what he was doing he said he was going to push a hole in the sky. He wanted to see the Father in Heaven.

One time we saw a gopher go into a hole. So we carried water from the slough and poured it in the hole until the gopher came out. We caught him, put a string around him and took him in the house and tied him on the stove leg to dry. We had plans - we were going to make a harness and hitch it up for a horse. We told the younger boys not to tell, but they didn't know how not to tell. When Mother and Katie came in, Jake said "We haven't got a gopher under the stove." Well there went our gopher. Katie threw him in the bush.

I don't remember the first church that was built,[42] but I remember the mission festivals. Everybody took their noon meal

---

steep. The town itself is not much, but promises well. It boasts a store, a gristmill, nearly finished, a sawmill working, a smithy, and a "Hotel".

[42] Mary Popp refers to the Hoffenthal Church. The first church building was a log building, consecrated July 15, 1896. In 1900 a new frame structure measuring 24 feet x 36 feet was built on the SE 1/4 28-22-29 WPM, on a two-acre piece of land in the southwest corner, donated by Anton Hofer. The settlers in the Hoffenthal area were first served by Reverend Berthold who began a ministry in 1891 from Langenburg. By 1892 a dispute had arisen between the Pastor and the congregation over the celebration of the Lord's Supper. Reverend Berthold believed in the *Apfelschnitzel Theorie*, that apple slices could replace unleavened bread and apple juice could replace wine in the celebration of the Eucharist. Seventeen members from Hoffenthal sent a letter on March 12, 1892 to Reverend Buegel in Winnipeg. He came to investigate. Pastor Buegel must have been in Langenburg in July 1892 because the Church records show that he baptized Katherina Lowenberger born July 9, 1892. On September 4, 1892 Reverend T. Hahn was installed as pastor of the Hoffenthal congregation. He was followed by Reverend Starck for one year. Reverend Geith then served Hoffenthal from 1895 to 1902. Reverend Dommann, a colourful and controversial minister, served from 1905 to 1908. Sources: *One Hundred Years in the Fellowship of the Holy Spirit, St. Paul's Evangelical*

and sat on the ground. Maybe two or three families would go together to eat and visit. There were no telephones and no cars. People were very happy to see each other. They visited back and forth, mostly by walking. If it was summer, the horses had to rest.

The Hoffenthal records show that a log house was bought and moved to Hoffenthal in 1895 and used as a small church until the other one was built in 1900. The graveyard was on the southwest corner of my parents' quarter section of land until the new church was built. Now the graveyard is plowed over as a field.

Why was the graveyard on our land? Perhaps our parents were the first to bury a child. I found the names of those buried in this cemetery in a church book: Jacob Lowenberger (July 11, 1895 - September 13, 1895); Katherine Nerbas (February 12, 1895 - September 1895 [drowned]); Elenore Lowenberger (1860 - January 25, 1898); Friedrich Lowenberger (January 2, 1897 - October 10, 1898); Emma Schappert (July 15, 1899 - November 2, 1899); Anna Marie Burkhart (January 31, 1898 - November 21, 1898); Valentine Nerbas (1899 - 1899); Heinrich Haberstock (December 23, 1899 - July 9, 1900); Gustie Burkhart, burned; and Ferdinand Lowenberger (January 22, 1898 - October 10, 1898).

Lutheran Church, Langenburg, Saskatchewan edited by Irene Adams, 1989; *Evangelisch Lutherische Gemeinde Hoffenthal, 1892 - 1992* printed by Jasper Printing Group Ltd, Edmonton, Alberta; Memoirs of George Lowenberger.

New Farm at Flower Valley

In 1901 or 1902 Dad bought the south half of section 1-23-30, four miles north of where we lived. I was six years old when we left our first home and moved to this new house. My parents must have lived on the first place about 15 years and paid the loan when they moved to the new place.

When we moved Mother rode on a wagon loaded with chickens, pigs, furniture and the smaller children, one a tiny baby, George, who had been born at the old place on May 23, 1902. She drove the team. Dad was on horseback and my sisters and I drove the stock. And of course Tommy the dog helped. I was just to help until they got started, but had to help all the way. I was very tired, but also proud I had walked all the way.

Dad would go to Asessippi to bring logs to the new farm and to the sawmill to have lumber cut into boards and rough lumber. He took food and perhaps would be gone for a week. When he had a lot ready, the neighbours would go and help bring it home. Then there was all the work to get those logs ready and build the house.

It was a big house, four rooms, big living room and kitchen downstairs, two big rooms upstairs, plastered with clay with a shingle roof. Later siding was put on the outside; later still a big lean-to kitchen was built on the length of the house which was divided into a big pantry at the end and a little porch to hold the cream separator and the milk pails. It was a nice big roomy kitchen, but had a drawback - it was too cold to use in the winter, it froze so we had to move into the other kitchen for the winter.

The house was surrounded by a big bush with cherry, chokecherry and saskatoon trees which all of us loved. But there was no well. The closest place Dad could find water was about one half mile away which made it very hard. In the summer we would just have to get the water for drinking and cooking. We would have rain water for dishes and washing. There was a big slough by the yard for the stock but in the winter it would freeze over. We would have to take the horses and cattle to the well then bring water home in barrels for the rest of the stock. We carried water into a big barrel in the kitchen, otherwise it would freeze. We also carried in and melted snow for washing as the homemade soap would curdle in the well water.

The dog Tommy was old by the time we moved. After lightning struck our barn, he was very scared. When there was a thunder storm he would go frantic so he had to be shot. We children couldn't have felt worse if it had been one of the children.

The first years on the new place we had to herd the cattle in the summer so they wouldn't stray and also not get into our or other people's grain until fences were built. My sister and I would take our lunch. The days were very long. We had no watch to know the time - we would have to go by the sun. Sometimes we would eat our lunch too early and then get very hungry by the time the sun was low enough to go home. Sometimes we would dig senega roots,[1] but it took a lot of roots to get one pound of washed dried senega roots which sold at thirty cents a pound.

Even though we were surrounded by bush, it was too young so the fuel still had to be brought from miles away. Dad would be

---

[1] Senega is the dried root of a native plant used medicinally as an expectorant (used to assist in the discharge of phlegm).

away many days getting firewood. It all had to be cut and hauled inside into big wood boxes. We put a log on a long saw horse. My two sisters would cut with a cross cut saw. I would be bundled up to sit on the log to hold it, but if the log rolled I would go with it. I suspect they sometimes rolled the log on purpose. Wood had to be cut everyday. On Friday nights we would try to cut and split enough to last over the weekend.

Sometimes we had a hired man. If we didn't have a man, we would have to help feed and water the stock and clean the barns. When the work was done we would be on the frozen slough sliding (no skates) and playing on the ice until we got tired. Then we would howl like dogs. The dogs would bark and the coyotes would start howling. Then we would go inside in a hurry.

My oldest sister, Lizzie, was ten years older than I. My other sister, Katie, was five years older than I and I was small and skinny so I would just help. Since our brothers were all younger, the girls had to work outside and also help do the house and garden work. We had to work very hard. When Lizzie went to work in the Langenburg Hotel, I had to take the other end of the saw to cut wood.

In the early 1900s more relatives came, Mother's brother, the Rudolf Baumung family,[2] came with three or four children. They bought land about one mile from us and built a house and other buildings. Then more of the Kendel cousins came, Lizzie, Willie, Mollie and Rudolf. They all got work and got married and settled not too far away. Later more cousins came from both sides of the family.

Also there were more babies born, and some died. Alive when we moved to the new place, were Lizzie, my oldest sister ten years older than me, Katie, five years older then me, Jake, four

---

[2] Rudolf and Dorothea (Dressler) Baumung left Landestreu, Austria on April 27, 1904. They arrived in Langenburg by train from Winnipeg on May 21, 1904. They homesteaded about four and one-half miles west of Shellmouth on the SW 1/4 2-23-30 WPM, the section neighbouring Jakob and Augusta Lowenberger's farm. Three children were born in Landestreu, Austria: Katherina (Philip Nerbas), Elisabeth (George Busch) and Johannette (Paul Geith). Amalia (Louis Kotny), Elenora (Markus Geith) and George (Anna Rosin) were born on the homestead.

years younger, and George a baby. Then Adolph and Helen were born in the new home, Adolph in 1905 and Helen in 1912.[3]

The big room was often used for dances - "*Fastnacht*".[4] The stove and table would be moved out, sometimes even the bed. All the neighbours would come and have a good old-time dance. I remember the big kitchen table would be moved to one corner for the musicians to sit on and my cousin Katie Baumung[5] and I would dance together every dance, no matter what they played.

Dad would do the bindering.[6] Sometimes we would have to stook the grain. Then later we stacked the grain, as often it wasn't threshed until after it had snowed. Dad bought the first threshing machine in partnership with others. I only remember they

---

[3] The Lowenberger children (surviving infancy) were: Elisabeth born in Landestreu, Austria December 7, 1888; Katherina born July 8, 1892; Mary born January 18, 1897; Rudolph born March 26, 1899; Jacob born March 12, 1901, George born May 23, 1902, Adolph born January 24, 1905; and Helen born September 7, 1912.

[4] *Fastnacht*, the night of Shrove Tuesday, was a time of merriment in anticipation of the somber season of Lent. House parties and dances that lasted the entire night were common. Plenty of food was served. At every *Fastnacht* a donut made of raised dough, called *Fettkuchelja* was served.

[5] Katharina Baumung, born in Landestreu, Austria January 16, 1899, was the daughter of Rudolph and Dorothea Baumung who had immigrated to Canada in 1904. She married Philip Nerbas (1893 - 1978). They had one daughter, Lydia.

[6] A binder was a piece of farm equipment that revolutionized the harvesting of grain. Invented in the United States, it was originally drawn by horses. It cut the grain which then fell onto a moving canvas. Another canvas moved the cut grain to a binding mechanism that pushed a large metal needle threaded with twine through the grain and tied a knot around a certain amount of grain. The resulting tied grain was called a sheaf. The sheaf fell to a carriage attached to the side of the binder. A person sat upon the binder and adjusted the height of the cutting blade and the reels. The operator would also trip the carriage at certain intervals so that when the field was completely "bindered" the sheaves would lie in rows across the field. The sheaves would then be placed into groups of approximately eight with the cut end sitting on the ground and the heads braced together to form a pyramid shape called a stook. "Stooking" was an arduous task done by hand or sometimes with a pitch fork. The stooks shed rain or snow until the threshing crew arrived at the farm. The sheaves would then be hauled to the threshing machine which separated the grain from the straw.

called it the coffee mill. Twin cutters cut the twine on the sheaves. The grain was let into bags from the spout, taken to the granary and emptied. It was an exciting time for us children when the threshers came. We would stay home from school in case we were needed.

Later the wheat was again filled in bags, loaded on sleighs or wagons and sold at Langenburg.[7] We had to clean it first by putting it through a fanning mill. One person would turn the wheel by hand to run the mill and another would put wheat on the mill. I found it hard to do either job. My sister Katie was stronger so we would change off. I would turn the wheel, then I would feed the mill. We had to clean a load a day for Dad to take to town the next day. It would take him all day. He would leave really early in the morning to drive 12 miles with horses. Then there would be a line up. Others from closer were ahead of him so he had to wait. He would get home late but we would still have to fill up the bags to be loaded early next morning to go again. It was hard work for us all.

In the summer the grain fields had to be weeded, pulling out ball mustard, black mustard, sunflowers, later French weed, Canadian and sow thistle.[8]

We milked about 12 or more cows. A cream man came with big cans on a wagon. He tested our cream, then poured it with the rest in a big can. Sometimes he brought our mail, or a plug of tobacco for Dad. We had to watch for him and go to the road to get it. Once I was sent and it was the wrong wagon so I started looking for gooseberries and missed the cream man. I got a licking. The cream was taken to Shellmouth[9] where they had built a creamery.

---

[7] Although Shellmouth was much closer than Langenburg, the railroad did not come to Shellmouth until 1909. British American Grain Co. built the first elevator in Shellmouth in 1910. Agents were D. McFadyen and G. Jackson. N. M. Patterson Co. built an elevator in 1918. In 1940 the National Grain Co. bought both elevators which were operated by Jacob Haas. Jacob was born in 1904, the son of J. G. and Elisabeth (Adam) Haas. He married Emilie Bezo. They had two children: Melvin and Marjorie. Jacob was killed in an accident on March 11, 1950. Source: *Shellmouth Our Century*

[8] Herbicides to control weeds did not become common until after World War II. Before then weeds had to be picked by hand and carried off the field.

[9] In 1881 Major Charles Boulton acquired a site for a town on the east banks of the Assiniboine River and had it surveyed. By 1885 the hamlet boasted a saw

Going to Shellmouth wasn't easy. There were very steep hills on the old road going down the Assiniboine valley so the wheels of the wagon or buggy were tied together to brake them from going too fast. When the new road was built, it was a lot easier. But when the first cars started going, the horses got scared.[10]

We would go picking cranberries, chokecherries, pincherries and nuts in the Shellmouth hills. Sometimes we walked the three miles just to go picking berries. Then we carried them home. Although Lizzie was away a lot, and the brothers were all younger, we did have a nice family life, what with teasing, fighting, playing and later on dancing, practicing the newer dances, two-step, three-step, four-step, Jersey, French Minuet and new square dances. We could all play the mouth organ[11] and even though our brothers were too small and not enough to make a set for square dancing, we would still practice. Sometimes the hired man, if we had one, or cousins would fill in. Even if we worked very hard during the day we still played at night, sometimes we played cards or just told stories.

There didn't seem to be as much school homework as there is now. When we grew older, there were choir practices, dances, concerts and parties. Our house was a gathering place with the older people in the living room and the younger people in the kitchen, playing full show. Sometimes we would dare to go and get some of the parents in our games. Then we played the mouth organ or somebody would have an accordion and we would have a few dances. There wasn't always lunch since people would eat supper late. Sometimes we made coffee and *kuchen* or we would get a dishpan full of apples from the cellar and pass them out.

---

mill, a four story hotel, a large stone livery barn, three stores, two blacksmith shops, a large number of dwellings and stopping houses and a population of 118. Source: *Shellmouth Our Century*

[10] The hill approaching Shellmouth from the German settlement to the west is still called "German Hill".

[11] On Mary Popp's 100th birthday celebration the Langenburg Centennial Care Home presented Mary with a gold plated mouth organ. When asked if she would play a tune she asked for requests. She played *Ach! Du Lieber Augustine* and other German songs.

Apples were bought in barrels. We would get three or four barrels of different kinds of apples. We always had apples before we went to bed, while they lasted. They were also used for pie, *kuchen* and strudel.

In later years we got an organ, ordered from the States, and would have singsongs if somebody could play. None of us learned to play as we didn't like the teacher who stayed at our place and was supposed to teach us.[12]

There was no school close to our new farm. My sisters had gone to Echo School[13] but that was too far so Dad started working to start a school. Flower Valley School[14] was built, a one room school with a back porch. There were windows on the east and west walls and a blackboard on the south wall. There was also a five-foot pointer, a teacher's desk and chair, a globe, waste basket and a shelf with a pail of water with a dipper in it. Three rows of double desks could seat about thirty students.

The new school was opened in 1905. I was eight years old and my brother Rudy was six. We were very scared the first day we went to school. We sat together in one desk. Our feet didn't even touch the floor. There were just two other boys in school that day - English boys, a Scott and a McFadyen. They couldn't speak German and we couldn't speak English. But the teacher could talk a very little German which helped a little. The next day more children came until the desks were occupied. Most of the children had not been to school before. We didn't learn much that first year.

---

[12] Mary later records the following note: "This organ stayed with my brother George Lowenberger. When they left the farm it was sold. After changing owners a couple of times it was sold to the Lutheran Ladies Aid and used in the church basement. Ella Parkinson, my daughter, bought it from the Ladies Aid and spent hours picking out tunes on it."

[13] The Echo School District Number 455 was established September 8, 1897. School opened July 4, 1898 with Miss M. E. Sibald as teacher. Among the first students appear the names Elisabeth and Katie Lowenberger.

[14] Flower Valley School District No. 1098 was organized in 1904. George Haas had suggested the German name "*Blumenthal*". The English translation, "Flower Valley", was eventually agreed upon. Jakob Lowenberger was elected as one of the three trustees at the first public meeting on August 20, 1904. The schoolhouse was built on the N.E. 1/4 2-23-30 WPM. In 1905, 33 children were enrolled.

It was hard for that young teacher - a young girl so far away from home. On the last day of school we said good-bye and cried a little. She cried, too. We never saw her again.

I have nice memories of the schoolhouse. Most of our social life was at the schoolhouse where we would have Sunday School concerts and dances. It was just one and a half miles from our place if we cut across fields and prairie, and over sloughs when they were frozen. Once when I was on the middle of a slough, I broke through with our lunch which was tied in a bundle. I got out and went on as it was over halfway. My brother and the Koch children[15] were further back and did not fall in. Our lunch was partly soaked but we had to eat it anyway. I dried myself at the heater at school.

The first years there was no school in the winter, just summer school without summer holidays. But later when there was school in the winter, we would drive. They had built a barn for the horses.[16] The school was over two miles away by the road and there were often horse races on the way home.

The first teacher we had in Flower Valley was Miss Amy Spencer from Ontario. She was very young, pretty and nice; she played horsey with the kids. If they would fall, she would kiss their sores and wipe their tears. She had a little party the last day. She made us all write our names on a card for her and she gave little gifts - Bible pictures.

The second teacher was also from Ontario, Miss McKay. She boarded at our place. She had a temper, strapped the kids and slapped their faces. We were not to speak German during school hours, but we didn't know how to speak English. She had us all scared stiff. I got a strapping for not being able to spell "children",

---

[15] These were the children of Andrew Koch Sr. and his wife Carolina (Prinz) who emigrated from Landestreu, Austria with Rudolph and Dorthea Baumung. The Koch children were John, George, Elisabeth (Haberstock), Andrew, Fred, Christian and Katherine (Haberstock).

[16] At an October 8, 1908 meeting a tender was put out to erect a stable 24 feet by 22 feet. George F. Haas' tender of $305.00 was accepted.

but I still helped her sweep the school after four o'clock and walked home with her.[17]

Then we had a Mr. Peiepus, Mr. Onhauser, Mrs. Stringlund, then Mr. Dorsett[18] who studied German while he was at Flower Valley. He was old and had white hair and beard. He taught Sunday School Sunday afternoons, in both English and German. If we knew our lessons we would get a ticket. If we had ten tickets we would get either an English or German New Testament. We had small English songbooks and *Die Frohe Botschaft*[19] in German. We all loved to go to that Sunday School. The young people would come and sometimes the parents too.

In 1909 Reverend Wiegner[20] came to Hoffenthal. I was in his first confirmation class, a big class,[21] all raw material, as he said.

---

[17] In a conversation in July, 1997 Mrs. Popp, then 100 years old, easily recalled the names of her teachers and described how the children had enjoyed Miss Spencer. But for Miss McKay she had less kind words. She said that Miss McKay was mean to the children and at one time had struck Johnny Koch across the face. Then she paused and asked, "Is Johnny still with us?" "I guess not", she rhetorically replied.

[18] The following teachers taught at Flower Valley between 1905 and 1920: Miss Spencer (1905 - 06), Miss McKay (1907), Mr. Dorsett (1908 - 1912), Mr. V. F. Onhauser (1912 -13), Mr. J. Stringlund (1913), Mr. Paul Peters (1914 - 1918), Miss Blanche Gorman (1918), Miss Margaret Paton (1919) and Miss Ada M. Comber (1920).

[19] *Die Frohe Botschaft*, in English, is "The Joyful Message".

[20] Reverend Wiegner served Hoffenthal from 1909 to 1927. In 1910 the church was enlarged when the bell tower was added. A parsonage was built in 1912. Reverend Wiegner served Hoffenthal until 1927 when he accepted a call to serve in Winnipeg. Reverend J. Dreyer served from 1927 to 1932. Reverend A. Fuhr served from 1932 to 1951. In 1947 the third and present church was built. In 1951 Reverend A. O. Borchardt began to serve Hoffenthal.

[21] Mary was confirmed at Hoffenthal by Reverend Wiegner on April 10, 1910. There were twenty young people confirmed that day, the second largest confirmation class in Hoffenthal's history: Ida Philipps (October 8, 1895), Philipp Mueller (July 10, 1895), Eva Geith (May 21, 1896), Jakob Schmidt (December 3, 1896), Maria Mack (March 6, 1896), Mary Lowenberger (January 18, 1897), Heinrich Schappert (September 23, 1895), Valentin Mack (November 24, 1894), Louise Haas (July 23, 1896), Heinrich Haas (June 26, 1894), Johann Schappert (January 30, 1895), Gustav Werschler (September 8, 1895), Emilie Burkart (June 23, 1895), Wilhelm Lowenberger (September 13, 1895), Elisabeth Mensch (January 18, 1897), Rosa Eckert (May 10, 1895),

Reverend Wiegner was very strict. We had to do much memory work to get ready for confirmation in six weeks. When Reverend Wiegner came we had our first Christmas program in church. He started a choir, some more raw material. He worked very hard.[22]

After I was confirmed in 1910, I had to stay home to help with the summer work, so I just went to school sometimes. I lost interest and none of the other children my age went anymore. But I did go along to choir practice on Sunday nights. If we had young folks visit us they would come along in the big sleigh. We would sing on the way there and home if we wasn't too cold. When there wasn't choir practice young people would gather at our place, 15 to 20 or more. No one was invited, everybody just came. We would play games after supper. We usually ended up with somebody playing the mouth organ and people dancing.

Sometimes in the evening Katie and I would go to visit at Jack Haas' farm.[23] He was very good at story telling and would end up by telling ghost stories. Then we would be so scared going home on the prairie trail about three quarters of a mile with bushes on the side with caterpillar webs that looked like heads and fire flies here and there. We would walk close together, too scared to talk until we got in the yard. Then we would run into the house, but we would go again.

One thing we always, always looked forward to and waited for was the Langenburg Sports Day. We hoped it wouldn't rain. We would all pile into the democrat with our best clothes on. We would have to have new dresses made for the Sports Day and get new hats, real fancy ones and a couple of yards of sheerest chiffon

---

Elisabeth Backes (December 13, 1895), Katharina Nerbas (August 22, 1896), Eleanora Burkart (February 21, 1897) and Johann Haberstock (August 7, 1895).

[22] The Lowenberger family developed a close relationship with Reverend Wiegner. In 1935 he returned from Winnipeg to conduct Mrs. Lowenberger's funeral service. In 1964 he attended Henry and Mary Popp's 50th Wedding Anniversary in Langenburg.

[23] Jacob Haas (July 2, 1882 - January 16, 1942) was the fourth child of Georg Haas (January 24, 1844 - August 28, 1924) and Margarethe Klei (February 3, 1846 - September 17, 1909). Jacob married Eleonoria Schappert on February 13, 1906.

veils to tie on the hats if it was windy. Those Sports Days started out with a parade in the morning with clowns and the band. Then at the sportsgrounds there was a merry-go-round with music, wire walkers, all kinds of races - running, three legged, egg, nail driving, fat mens, fat womens, catching a greased pig, climbing a greased pole and many others. We enjoyed buying ice cream and other things we hadn't had before and just being at the Sports Day. Then there were horse races. Mr. Berger had a car, and for 25 cents you would get a ride in that car, once around the race track. It was all so exciting.

Then we had the long ride home, with mosquitoes swarming around and biting you. When we got home we had to do the chores, milk the cows, feed the calves and pigs. The chickens would have gone to sleep before that. Sometimes we would get caught in a rain storm and our new clothes would get wet.

There would be the odd concert or show that would come to Shellmouth or MacNutt. But it was still a long way to go by horses, though we did get to see the Swiss Bell Ringers and sometimes magicians or concerts. But we had to make most of our entertainment ourselves. There were no phones, no T.V. or radios, not even too much reading material. But there wasn't too much time either, as each one had their work to do during the day. In the evening we would play cards, casino, black pedro or checkers. But the evenings were short as we went to bed early.

One time our bachelor neighbour, Chris Paulson, came over and brought a talking machine with a big horn and round records. Well that was just the most wonderful machine we had ever seen. It could talk and sing. He would come often to entertain us.

Another bachelor neighbour was Mr. Drake.[24] I don't think we ever heard his first name. He was “Mr. Drake” to us. Since he was alone, Dad would help him and he would help us. So he would be at our place for meals at times. His buildings looked very dilapidated. And when we saw the inside of his shack, it was so dirty. We just couldn’t see how a person could live like that, especially an educated man. I disliked him because he teased me.

---

[24] Mr. Drake may have returned to England.

But on our wedding day he sent his hired man over with a wedding present - three pieces of cut glass which we still have.

Most of the dances were on Sunday nights. They would start early, maybe at eight o'clock and last until three. Then we had to drive home by horse and buggy. We would get home when the rest of the family was getting up. So there was no going to bed; just change your clothes, go milk the cows, stack hay or grain, or dig potatoes. There was no resting. Maybe we could get a little sleep on a load of hay, driving from the field to the barn where all the hay was stacked for the winter. It wasn't easy after having a few minutes sleep to build hay stacks and tramp them down.

Dad was forever trying to find water close to the yard by using the divining rod.[25] A well was dug right beside the kitchen; but there was no water, so it was closed up again. Then a boring outfit came and bored holes about two feet across, one just west of the house. They went as deep as they could go. No water. Then a hole up on the hill got some water. But we couldn't water all the stock at once, so we would have to wait for it to refill. And it was still too far to carry all the water for the house, the pigs and poultry. So we would fill cream cans with water and pull them on a little sled. Then a well drilling outfit came around and they drilled a well between the house and barn. It was over 100 feet deep. We had to have a gas engine to pump the water that height. Then we had enough water. I think it is still in use.

We never had a washing machine. We washed on the wash boards. Katie had one tub and I another. There were always five or six beds in use. It would take us all day to do the washing. The white clothes had to be boiled. There would be lines and lines full of washing. In the winter we had clotheslines upstairs and in the kitchen, since even if we hung the clothes out to freeze, they still had to be dried. Ironing was the same. We would both iron all day while Mother mended, sewed on buttons and repaired and darned socks.

---

[25] A divining rod was commonly a forked willow stick. A person walked with the stick, one fork in each hand, with the forks spread open. When the stick started to twist downward, it was thought that an underground stream of water was directly below.

A highlight was when peddlers came and opened up their wares. It was so exciting to see those cases with trays of jewelry, threads, thimbles, needles and sometimes even little knickknacks for us kids. They also carried yard goods. If Mother had saved money from the cream cheques she would buy material for dresses for the family or maybe just flannelette for underclothes. But we would just be happy to sit on the floor and watch him open those boxes. Sometimes he would have lovely dress material.

After sister Lizzie had worked in the Langenburg Hotel for a while and earned some money, she went to Winnipeg and took a dressmaking course. She was able to sew us nice dresses. As far as we were concerned, they were the latest style. She would make her own patterns then make ours first. But she would often use the same pattern to make dresses for other people. Sometimes we wouldn't like that.

One time she had made both Katie and me two dresses each. They were hanging on one coat hanger and a mouse got at them and ate holes in one sleeve of all four dresses. We were heartbroken and mad that all the cats we had would let a mouse get into the house. But Lizzie fixed the dresses by either putting new sleeves in if there was enough material, or fixing them so the inserts looked like trimming. I had to help Lizzie a lot when she was sewing. If she made a mistake, I had to rip the seams for her. Or I would cover buttons and sew them on. She did not trust me to make button holes. Both Katie and I had to try dresses on and stand while she fitted them. Sometimes we would just hold the lamp for her. One time while I was holding the lamp on a Monday night after I had been to a dance on Sunday night, I dozed off and the lamp chimney fell off and broke. I was sent to bed but couldn't go to sleep after that crash.

When we first moved to that new place our closest neighbours to the east were Dan McFadyens.[26] They had children. We saw them a lot and I learned a little English and was so proud

[26] Dan McFadyen married Janet Gourlay in Minnedosa, Manitoba on April 12, 1899. They homesteaded the NW 6-23-29 where they lived for a few years before selling the farm and moving to Langenburg to open a butcher shop. Mr. McFadyen died of pneumonia on August 27, 1907, leaving his wife and five children: Sandy, John, Isabel, Dan and Archie.

of it. When I started school, one of the German children was crying and didn't know how to tell the teacher in English what the problem was. I was pleased to be able to tell the teacher that the student had a headache.

Christmas was always a happy time. When we were smaller we believed the Christ child came during the night and brought the tree and the gifts. It was a disappointment when I found out different, but then I could help make tree trimmings, paper flowers and chains, string popcorn, stick nuts on the tree with sealing wax, and put candy canes on the tree. Mother bought red and green sugared cookies and chocolate-covered marshmallow figures for the tree. I loved those Christmas trees with all those edibles on.

Our tree was always hung from the ceiling. Candles were placed on the trees but were just lit at certain times. The toys weren't wrapped, they were hung on the tree - dolls, bugles, and toys which you would wind up so they would run.

One Christmas I had a very bad cold, headache and sore throat. The day before Christmas was Sunday. I stayed in bed, but that night was the concert at church and nobody wanted to stay home with me. So Katie tried to doctor me. She fixed me a hot drink. I remember talking to myself. Then I fell asleep. When I woke up, I vomited all over the floor and poor Katie had to clean it up. But I felt better, and they bundled me up and took me along the four miles to church. I don't think I got cold, but I felt sick.

The next day I stayed in bed until noon. Then I got up because there was a dance in our kitchen that night. Dad, Mom and Katie went to church. Then the folks were asked someplace for dinner after church. Katie got a ride home with Henry Popp[27] and Fred Werschler[28] who came to our place for dinner. Lizzie had cooked dinner, and I had just come downstairs when they came in.

---

[27] Mary's future husband.

[28] Friedrich Werschler was the son of Friedrich and Maria (Wirth) Werschler who emigrated to Canada from Landestreu, Austria. On June 21, 1917, at the age of 29 he married Karoline Haberstock who was then 20 years old. They moved to Portland Oregon in the 1920s where Fred died in 1931 or 1932. Fred and Lena had at least four children: Friedrich Henry, Philip William, Margarethe Emily and Maria Elfriede. Fred Werschler was known in the area as an excellent butcher, a skill he shared with other Werschler family members.

Henry said, "Did you just get up? Are you that lazy?" I was too shy to say I'd been sick. That was the first time Henry had spoken to me. I was just 14 years old, nearly 15 since my birthday was in January. He was 20 years old, nearly 21. No wonder I was shy.

A large number of people came to that dance, but it wasn't too crowded as there were other rooms to go into. I danced a lot and my cold got better. From then on Henry came quite often, usually with Fred Werschler. There were always others there too, so we didn't know who he came to see. He did try to kiss me once, but I ran away. Later he would come every two weeks because his brother Frank[29] would get the horse and buggy the next Sunday to see Lizzie Mensch.[30] And so Henry's visits went on.

As we grew older, the brothers got bigger and could do a lot of outside chores. With a well in the yard we didn't have to haul all that water. Then Dad bought a coal stove. We didn't have to cut and carry in as much wood so it was easier, even though there were more ashes to carry out.

Our walls were still whitewashed about twice a year and the floors scrubbed with a brush. Then the folks heard of some plaster called wood fiber. You would mix it with water and put it on the clay walls. It dried like plaster. They got some and put it on. Mother bought paint and Katie and I painted the ceiling (which was 'V' joint boards). Then we painted the walls. The floors were very worn, what with dances and general wear and tear. But we tried it. It took a lot of paint; it was a big floor. After we painted it we didn't have to use the brush anymore to clean it. But there was no more dancing on it either. By then the kitchen had been added and Katie and I painted it, inside and outside. By then we thought we were good painters. If there was any paint around we would paint anything that needed painting.

---

[29] Frank Popp was Henry's younger brother, born October 5, 1895. He married Elisabeth Mensch on August 6, 1917. Frank Popp died September 5, 1975. Elisabeth died April 15, 1956. They had four children: Katie, Florence, Leslie and Bernice.

[30] Elisabeth Mensch (1897 - 1956) was the daughter of Wilhelm Mensch and Katherine Haas, who arrived in Canada in 1894 from Austria and homesteaded on the NE 1/4 12-23-30 WPM.

Then we decided we wanted a flower garden by the house. We chopped down some trees and made posts and peeled them. We found some boards and made a picket fence. I remember it wasn't a very good looking fence, but we planted nice flowers in our new garden. Our vegetable garden was away from the house, a very big garden. We would plow it then help plant and hoe it. In the fall we put all the vegetables in the cellar. There was no canning. We would make a barrel full of sauerkraut, with cabbage heads in for *holopchi*, and put down a barrel full of dill pickles. The peas and beans were let ripen and threshed out with a stick. We let the wind blow all the chaff away and they were stored for cooking. Mother would also dry some green beans to be soaked and cooked. We had gooseberries, black currents and rhubarb in the garden and wild cranberries, chokecherries and pincherries to make jams and jellies.

We butchered about five pigs during the winter and made all kinds of sausage - breakfast, blood and liver sausage as well as *Schwarte mah.*[31] Butchering was a community affair. At the end of a day of butchering and sausage making *metzelsuppe*[32] was a must.

In the fall Dad would take enough wheat to the mill[33] to have flour made to last all year. With hams and bacons, and milk and cream, there always was enough to eat. Liquor was never bought in bottles, but in gallon jugs. I remember Dad once bought a five gallon keg of liquor. It was put in gallon jugs and the keg was used for making pickles.

---

[31] *Schwarte* means rinds; *mah* means stomach. *Schwarte mah* was made by boiling pig rinds (skin) in a boiler. Once boiled, the rind was ground up with other meat cut off the pig's head. Then this preparation was put into the cleaned pig's stomach and boiled again. Once it was cooled, the stomach and its contents were sliced and served with vinegar and bread. Today this dish is commonly called head cheese.

[32] *Metzelsuppe* was made by putting in a large container all the drippings left over from boiling sausage. This was heated on the wood stove. A thin mixture of flour and eggs was dribbled into the drippings. The soup was thickened with a paste of browned butter and flour and served with potatoes, *sauerkraut* and sausage.

[33] The mill was the gristmill at Asessippi.

Mother had many heartaches throughout her life. I remember she had twins who died[34] and a little boy, Freddie,[35] who died. Then on September 17, 1912 we had a little sister. We all tried to pick a name for her. She was called Helen, after a story we all had read. We all spoiled her. The youngest brother, Adolph, was about five years old then.

Mother could not nurse the younger children. In those years, before fridges, how could we keep milk sweet without even a well close to hang the milk in?[36] In the first years there weren't even screens to keep out the flies and mosquitoes. There were no sprays, just poison pads to put on plates and sticky pads and coils to catch the flies. We would put a piece of net over the cradle to keep the flies away from the babies. Smudge piles were made for the cattle and horses to make smoke to keep the mosquitoes away. Sometimes we made a smudge in a pail if we wanted to sit outside. With all the cattle in the yard and all the bush around, the mosquitoes and flies were very bad. Driving at night was torture at times.

---

[34] The Hoffenthal Church Registry shows twin daughters born to Jakob and Augusta Lowenberger on September 2, 1903. They were baptized Emma Löwenberger and Margaretha Löwenberger on September 8, 1903. Margaretha's death is recorded October 27, 1903. The cause was described as "General Weakness". Emma's death is not recorded. George Lowenberger, Mary Popp's brother, recounted in his memoirs the death of an infant sister:

> I well remember one of my sisters died. I was not going to school yet and was at home. Mother had the baby on her lap. I was in the room when the baby had no diaper on and all of a sudden a stream of fluid came from her rectum and flew a few feet. Mother screamed and told me to run and call Dad. It was fortunate Dad was bindering on a field just west of the house, so it did not take me long to locate him. He called the hired man but I had to stay and watch the horses until the hired man came. From then on I can't remember whether Dad got there in time, but the baby passed away.

[35] On May 29, 1909 a son Friedrich was born. His death is recorded in the Hoffenthal Church Registry as July 9, 1910.

[36] Without refrigeration dairy products were often kept cool in summer by placing them in a container and hanging the container in the well. Some families had ice houses which sat over a hole into which large blocks of ice were placed during the winter months. The ice was covered with saw dust. The ice would last through most of the summer and keep food cool.

At school we played ante over[37] and pom pom pull away. Then we got a football and played football. Baseball was something we hadn't heard of, but later there would be baseball games to go to. One time during winter they decided to have a masquerade party in the school. Our family went and brother Rudy and I could go along. They dressed us up. I was a waitress and wore my sister's red dress, a little apron and cap. Rudy was dressed as a girl too. My sisters took their costumes along. Lizzie had a dress with binder twine sewn all over with buttons and flowers. Katie was a flower girl. We had made paper flowers and sewed them all over her dress and brought a basket of flowers. When we got to the school, nobody else had dressed up. So the girls didn't put their costumes on either. I didn't put the mask on and was quite happy to be wearing a long dress, but poor Rudy had a dress on. He sat in a corner on the stage all night. It was a good dance, even if the masquerade was a failure.

Most often everyone would bring a lunch to serve at the dance. For one school dance my sisters made a lunch and coffee at home. We were all in the big sleigh. When we drove over a snow drift the sleigh upset and all the coffee was spilled. So it was lunch without coffee. We all got our overshoes full of snow, but just went on to the dance. The dances in our house or kitchen were easier.

One time we had gone to visit at Jack Haas' farm. Lizzie was sewing at Goehrings[38] and the Goehring boys and girls and Lizzie were going to Shellmouth to a dance. They came past our place to pick us up. Lizzie changed clothes. Brother Rudy hitched up a horse and came to get us at Haases. When we got home, they had already left. Katie and I wanted to drive by ourselves to the dance but Dad wouldn't let us go. We both cried and went to bed.

---

[37] Ante over was played by forming two teams, each standing on opposite sides of the school barn. One team threw the ball over the barn roof. If a member of the opposing team caught the ball, this team would quickly and quietly run to the other side and throw the ball at anyone on the opposing team. If anyone was hit with the ball, he or she joined that team.

[38] Ludwig and Caroline Goehring lived on the S1/2 36-22-22 where they raised a family of 10 children.

Next morning we thought how silly it would have been for us to drive to Shellmouth to a dance.

We always had to ask Dad's permission if we wanted to go someplace. So another time there was a dance at Fred Kitsch's[39] farm. He was still unmarried, so Dad advised us not to go - but if we wanted to go so bad, we could go. Henry picked us up. So besides us three, there were just Lizzie Mensch and Lena[40] Popp, Henry's sister. It wasn't much of a dance. I don't know who had made it. They had bologna sandwiches. Anyway we were very sorry we hadn't listened to Dad that time.

One time Henry Zentner[41] came with a livery team[42] to get us to Langenburg to a dance. It was a bitter cold night. My uncle was at our house and tried to talk Dad into not letting us go, saying that we would freeze the brains in our heads. My forehead had gotten awful cold. I was so scared of freezing my brain, but we did have a very nice time at that dance.

The biggest dances were wedding dances. Weddings were held in the homes, and most homes had at least one big room. Everybody danced. If it was too crowded they would change off - the married people would dance one dance, then the young people would dance one dance. It worked nicely. At these weddings, girls would have flower bouquets with long ribbon streamers to pin on the lapel of a partner they would pick for the wedding. Weddings were usually in the morning; the ceremony in church. Then on the way from church, the young couple would start out first, with a buggy or cutter. Then others would race with them and try to get ahead of them. I was always scared of these horse races. I thought there might be an accident; sometimes there were.

---

[39] Fred Kitsch married ? Anweiler from Melville, Saskatchewan. They farmed in the Landestreu area, near the Manitoba border. They had no children.

[40] It was common among German families to abbreviate women's names so that Carolina became Lena, Augustina - Gustie, Elenora - Laura, Adelheid - Della, Johanna - Hanna, Philipina - Bena, Margaretha - Greta, Elisabeth - Lizzie, and Wilhelmenia - Minnie.

[41] Henry Zentner (1891 - 1971) was fifth child of 21 children born to William and Anna Maria (Lornez) Zentner. Henry married Carrie Andres.

[42] It would seem that a "livery team" meant a team of horses that could be hired from the livery barn owner in Langenburg.

After dinner somebody would get under the table and steal one of the bride's shoes and auction it off. If a young unmarried man would have the highest bid, the married men would bid on it, or women or girls would bid on it. This sometimes went on for a couple of hours, until the groom would buy it back. By then a white shoe would be quite dirty.

Dancing started after supper and lasted all night. The bride's dance was at midnight. Everybody danced with the bride and gave gifts or money. After it was over, one of the women would get on a chair and announce how much money and gifts were collected. Then she would throw a plate on the floor and smash it. My mother was often asked to stand on the chair and break the plate. Usually a cracked plate was used - it would be sure to break and wasn't worth much anyway. The woman would get off the chair and someone would dance with her. While the money was counted, some women would take the bride's veil off and there would be singing, then more dancing. Whiskey, beer, wine and food were passed around all the time. If somebody had a drink they had something to eat with it. Sometimes even breakfast was served.

I remember the first wedding I was asked to. I had just been confirmed and if you were confirmed you would be included in the invitation. I was very young and shy. I had a bouquet and I asked an older boy whom I knew if I could pin my bouquet on him. He told me to wait. I guess he thought I was too young. An older girl, Teenie Rathgeber,[43] saw that all the boys had partners. She got Mac McFadden[44] from Shellmouth for me. (He was later killed overseas.) He was young and just as shy as I was. We sat beside each other at the supper table but we didn't talk, we didn't know what to say. Anyway, I had trouble speaking English and he could speak no German. Even if we learned English at school, we spoke

---

[43] Teenie (Christina) Rathgeber (1889 - 1967) was the daughter of Caspar and Mary (Helm) Rathgeber. Caspar Rathgeber (1849 - 1917) was born in Neudorf, Galicia, Austria. Teenie married John McNair and moved to Neepawa, Manitoba.

[44] Although Mary Popp refers to "Mac" McFadyen, it seems the only McFadyen to serve and die in World War I was Roy McFadyen, son of Daniel and Elizabeth (Hack) McFadyen.

only German at home. So I wasn't happy with my partner, and I don't think he was happy either. That was Maggie Mensch and Fred Kendel's[45] wedding when I was 13 years old.

A month later, Lena Mensch and George Haas[46] got married, so again we had beautiful bouquets. But I was too shy to ask a boy, so they gave my bouquet to an older girl who didn't have one. Later some more boys came. They made some more bouquets, and one for me too. Again Teenie was picking partners and I got John Zentner.[47] He was a lot older and had just come back from the States. He looked so nice. He followed the rules and danced the first three dances with me. I was so proud but I just didn't know what to say, so I didn't enjoy it. After that I was included in the invitations, but I don't remember ever having a bouquet to pin on.

Mother and Dad had taken Latin in school. Since Latin letters are like English letters, they could both read English, but they didn't always pronounce the words right. Writing English was not easy for them, so after I had gone to school a few years Dad got me to write his letters for him. After all, what did I go to school for? He would tell me what to write. Some words I had never heard before and didn't know how to spell, but I wrote business letters about land deals, sometimes even politics.

We all did a lot of reading, English and German. There wasn't too much reading material around so Katie and I ordered the *Needle Kraft* which had good stories. The stories were interesting, but it would take time to read them, so Katie would read one and I would read one. Then we would tell each other. We would take

---

[45] Margaret Mensch (1892 - 1988), daughter of William and Katherine (Haas) Mensch married Frederick Alfred Kendel (1887 - 1969) on November 25, 1910. Fred emigrated to Canada in 1901 with his father, Alfred Kendel and step-mother, Jacobina (Mack). (His mother, Louise (nee Haas) died in Landestreu, Austria.) Fred and Margaret had eight children: Alfred, Winnie, Emma, Margaret, Paul, Katie, Louise and Betty.

[46] Lena Mensch (1890 - 1968), daughter of William and Katherine (Haas) Mensch, married George Haas in 1910. They had 3 children, Ewald, Minnie and Alice.

[47] John Zentner (1886 - 1975), son of William Zentner and Anna Maria Lorenz, married Margaret Haas on January 21, 1917. They had 10 children.

them along when we went stacking hay on the other farm. We would take dinner along and with no dishes to wash, we would read while the men and horses rested. It took us a long time to read them all. Lizzie read them and Mother read them too. They were very good.

If Katie and I didn't read stories to tell each other, we would make them up. We always worked together so we made up stories, either from what we had read or just anything. We worked like men so we became men. Katie was "Jacob", a fellow we knew, and didn't like, and I was "Conrad", his brother. We didn't know any Conrads, but it didn't matter - we were Jacob and Conrad and we made up stories. It seemed to make our work easier - whether it was weeding grain fields, which took days, or picking stones from the field.[48]

We had a wagon to load stones. Sometimes it would take both of us to lift one on the wagon. Sometimes the hired men would come along. Then we would tease him and make up stories about him. They didn't seem to mind. Often they even wanted to hear more.

One time we were on the other farm hauling stones. We would get awfully dirty - our dresses, hands and faces. When we were going home we had to drive on the main road for a piece. Katie and I were sitting on the back of the wagon with our feet hanging down when a wagon came up behind us. We told the hired man to drive faster until we got to our road and turned off, but they turned off too. So we drove faster and faster. On that rough road we bumped around on the back of that wagon, but they caught up to us before we got home - two young fellows from Shellmouth. We jumped off our wagon before it even stopped and ran into the house.

Women didn't wear jeans or slacks and had to do all that work wearing long dresses. One day Katie wore an old pair of Dad's pants. I couldn't wear his because they were too big, and my

---

[48] On March 14, 1998, at the age of 101 years, when Mary Popp was asked what were the best times of her life she recounted the times when she and her sister Katie would make up stories about Jacob and Conrad, their two imaginary friends.

brother's pants were too small. But we had had a boy working for us before and he had left a torn pair there. So I wore them. They were too big, but we wore them over our dresses. We stuck our long dresses and petticoats into the pants so we looked bulky. There was a hole in the seat of the ones I wore. Katie was teasing me and pulled my dress out through the hole. We were cleaning barn when a sleigh drove in the yard. Katie hid in the barn and I hid in the pig barn. Nobody would ever come in there. It was those same two fellows from Shellmouth. They went into the house and got Dad. They had come to borrow our boar and came into the pig barn. Dad was surprised I was in there and was I ashamed for a long time after. I didn't want to go to Shellmouth, or if I did go, I tried to stay out of the way of those two guys.

I hated milking, especially in the winter when the cows were dirty. When the cows freshened they would kick and the new calves would have to be taught to drink. We'd have to put our finger in their mouth and get their head into the pail until they started drinking on their own.[49] That first milk would be so sticky and it got spilled on your clothes even though we wore big all-around aprons. So Katie did the milking during the winter, and I fed the pigs, which was the harder job as we had a lot of pigs. We had a slop barrel in the kitchen so I had to carry pails and pails of slop out to the pigs, then carry chop into the barrel from the granary to soak for next feeding. But I did it. After all the hard work, we would still go out at night, after the wood was cut and split, to play on the ice or on snow banks. We were never too tired and there was no canned entertainment.

Katie and I never quarreled. We worked, slept, played and always went places together. We dressed the same if Lizzie would sew our dresses. Mother would buy material, always enough for both of us, though Katie weighed 160 pounds and I weighed about 115 pounds. Mother bought some light green stripped voile from the peddler. Lizzie made nice dresses, with overskirts, shirred on

---

[49] A new born calf has a sucking instinct but cannot drink from a pail. By putting a finger in the new born calf's mouth it begins sucking. Then the calf's head is lowered into the pail of milk, hopeful that it will begin to drink once it tastes the milk.

the side. We just wore a narrow band of black ruching around our necks. They were nice dresses.

One time I was very hurt, too hurt to say anything. Katie and I had walked miles in the heat to dig senega roots. We washed and dried them. Mother took them to Langenburg and got 75 cents for them, so she bought an umbrella for Katie. I was hurt. But we always went together, so when she used it I could always be under it, rain or shine to save our hats. But it was her umbrella so she could carry it.

One time Mr. Popp (Henry's father) came. We wondered why. Dad took him into the living room. Then Mother came out, smiling, to talk to Katie. He had come to ask if Katie would marry Joe Wagner,[50] a widower with five children and a baby. I don't think Katie was twenty years old then. Well, she said "No." I guess our parents would have said no, but she had to be asked. Well then we had something new to tease Katie about -- she and Joe sitting on the front seat of the democrat and the children in the back to go joy riding. I was going with Henry Popp then so I would have to call her "Aunt Katie", as she would be my aunt.

Henry would always bring Fred Werschler along. He was Katie's age or older. I don't know why he and Katie didn't go together - maybe she didn't like him or he didn't like her - but he always came along. But then Pete Rathgeber[51] started coming. Once in a while, somebody would come over and ask whether Lizzie or Katie would marry him or someone else in the community. Lizzie was getting older then and people wanted to marry her off. With all the young people coming to our place, nobody knew who was going together. One time we were all sitting outside in the buggies in front of the kitchen. When it got dark, the rest went in and Henry and I stayed out, but not for long. Dad gave Katie a

---

[50] Joseph Wagner (January 1869 - October 18, 1943) was a brother to Henry Popp's mother Margaretha (Wagner) Popp. After his first wife, Elisabeth Busch died (1880 - 1913), he remarried a woman from Winnipeg and had six more children, including daughters Rosie (Mack), Frieda (Mensch), Elisabeth and Louise.

[51] Peter Rathgeber (1894 - 1963) was the son of John and Emma (Haas) Rathgeber. His siblings were: Katherine (Adams), Margaret (Matheis), George, Frederick, Emelia (Thompson), Julia (Nerbas) and Emma (Goebel).

mad look so she came out and poked me on the shoulder. I went in - not a word was said.

When we went someplace there were always three or four in the buggy. But one time Henry hadn't brought Fred Werschler along. We went someplace and Lizzie and Katie went with Pete Rathgeber, so Henry and I came home alone in the buggy. That is when he asked me to marry him. I got so nervous I couldn't talk. Once before when we were coming home Fred Werschler had to get off to open the gate at home and when he closed it, Henry drove away and tried to kiss me, but I turned away. I was just scared; I was only 15 years old.

Anyway after he had asked me to marry him he gave me a wrist watch which was something new. Then most women wore watches with chains around the neck or pinned on the chest. So my watch was special. About the second time I wore it the bracelet broke, so I had to give it back to Henry. He had it fixed. Meanwhile, he was going to Chicago for an operation so he had his cousin Phillip Popp give me my watch.

We went to MacNutt to a Christmas concert and I was surprised when Henry's brother, Phillip Popp, called me aside and gave me the watch. When Henry came back from Chicago he brought me a ring with a ruby stone. So we were engaged. Then Katie and Pete got engaged but that still didn't change our social life much. All the young people still came over to our place Sunday night, and often the parents too. Sometimes we would go to Kochs or Mensches, but not often, usually our place. Even if our boyfriends would be there alone, we had our brothers sticking around, teasing us and just bothering us. But then we had a teacher, Mr. Peters, and he wouldn't take hints. Even if we wouldn't talk to him, he would do a lot of silly tricks and just wouldn't go home until the boys left. He was an awful pest. He especially bothered me a lot. Everybody told me he was in love with me. Maybe he was, but he had funny ways of showing it and I disliked him.

In the spring of 1914, sister Lizzie got married to Julius Metz.[52] It was a big wedding. It started in the morning and lasted all day and all night. What I remember most about their wedding is that I had a sore throat and was hoarse. I couldn't sing and could hardly talk. A bunch of young people came to make a chivree.[53] Lizzie was 27 years old when she got married and considered an old maid. By then, Katie was 22. I was 17 and Rudy was 15 so we had a brother to take us places. By then the boys did a lot of the outside hard work. Life was a little easier for us girls, though we still had to help with harvesting. By 1914 Dad's asthma was getting worse so he couldn't help as much. But with the well close, an engine to pump water, coal to burn in the heater, and wood close by for the cook stoves, life was becoming easier. Our social life was still much the same, house dances, ball games, and parties.

Then in the early fall of 1914 our cousin Lizzie Bessler,[54] Dad's niece, came from the old country to our place. After she was there about a week, her uncle Jake Bessler, a bachelor, came and got her. Dad wasn't home and was quite disturbed about it. He scolded Mother for letting her go. He got up real early next morning and went to get her back. She was just about 15 years old so she stayed at our place. She had different ideas than we did - also different ideas than Mr. Peters, the teacher. She would tell him off when we didn't dare as Dad would have scolded us. We called him *Herr Lehrer* (Mr. Teacher) though sometimes I called him *skunk*. Cousin Lizzie stayed at our home about three years until she got married to Fred Nerbas. My folks gave her everything just like one of us. She was a good worker.

---

[52] They were married April 16, 1914. Julius Metz was the son of Jacob and Magdalena (Kullmann) Metz who emigrated from Austria to Langenburg in 1900.

[53] A chivree usually happened the evening of the wedding when visitors greeted the newlyweds with a chorus of banging pots and pans and loud raucous singing. Drinks were served. It was a time of well wishes and merriment.

[54] Elisabeth Bessler (1897 - 1941) was the daughter of Christian and Elenora (Lowenberger) Bessler. She married Friedrich Nerbas (1898 - 1978), son of Friedrich and Dorthea (Mack) Nerbas. Friedrich and Elisabeth had three children: Emma, Richard and Albert.

Later my mother bought a washing machine and my folks would get a wood cutting outfit to have all the wood cut, and even a man to split it all. They also had a cistern put under the kitchen for soft water, so life was easier. This all happened, though, after we had married and left home.

MARRIAGE

The summer of 1914 was a good summer. The crops were good; it was an early fall with good weather so most harvesting was finished in September. Henry and his partner, Fred Housman, bought his father's threshing outfit. Henry also had a half section of land with some buildings. He had been coming to our place for almost three years. His father decided it was time he got married. So he thought it was time to act.

One Monday morning in October, brother Rudy and I had walked to Baumungs to get the cabbage cutter. When we came home Henry's horse and buggy were in the yard. I wondered what was wrong. He had just been there the night before and left after midnight. We had had a little quarrel and had made up before he went home, but I was still a little mad. So I wondered what he had come back for. When I came in the house mother looked at me with a funny smile on her face. She told me Henry's dad was in the living room talking to my dad about us getting married.

So I was called into the living room and Henry's dad[1] said he thought we should get married. I said I was too young. He said his Henry was old enough to get married, that if I didn't want to get married I should have got myself a younger boyfriend. I said Katie was older and that she would have to get married first. He said if she got married in two weeks it would be all right, but we would get married in three weeks. Then my dad said, "Child, this is a serious decision for you to make. Think it over!" Then the tears started coming. I wanted to run out and cry - almost a shot-gun wedding. So I asked Mr. Popp if Henry had sent him. He said he had told Henry he was coming. I told him I would make no decision without Henry and I went out and cried. He told my parents he would go home and send Henry down that night. The next day he would come back to go to the minister with Dad and make arrangements for the wedding in three weeks. Oh yes, I wanted to get married, but not to have it forced on me. I had such sore mixed feelings and Katie and cousin Lizzie were teasing me and I wanted to cry.[2]

---

[1] Johann Philipp Popp (1855 - 1926) and his wife Margaretha Wagner (1853 - 1917) had emigrated in 1892 from Katharinendorf, Bukovina, Austria, to the district of Landestreu, Saskatchewan. Philipp was a native of the German Lutheran village of Baginsberg, just outside Kolomea (Kolomya), Galicia. Margaretha was born in Tereblesti, Bukovina, the oldest daughter of Josef Wagner and Maria Maier. Philipp and Margaretha were married in Berhometh, Bukovina in 1876 and were farmers in Katharinendorf from that time. Margaretha's father, Josef Wagner (1828 - 1906), also emigrated to Canada in 1892 with the Popps and several of his children, having been left a widower in Austria. He was from a well educated family and was a lay leader in the Landestreu Lutheran parish. Source: D'Arcy Hande

[2] An entry in Mary Popp's memoirs on October 20, 1990 reads:

> This would have been our 76th anniversary. Our wedding day was a beautiful day, nice and warm. Everyone wore summery clothes. I can't say I was too happy. My sister Katie, five years older than I was not married yet. Cousin Lizzie Besler teased me saying I'd be an old married woman while they would have a good time. I actually had not wanted to get married yet. I was just seventeen and wanted to stay home with my family. But Henry's father, besides being a matchmaker, was also a very bossy man, used to having his own way. Sure I could have my say, but I was not listened to. Henry had been there the night before and a wedding wasn't mentioned. When his dad

Since Mother was going to make *sauerkraut* that day, we went to the garden to cut the cabbages off and Mother said we would put a barrel full of heads down for *holopchi* (cabbage rolls) for the wedding, so there was no turning back. Henry did come that night and went in to talk to Dad. Then we talked about the wedding. It was planned as a very big wedding as both sides had a lot of relatives, neighbours and friends. Henry told Dad they had a big tent they had used to put the horses in for the night when they were building government roads. It would be used for more room.

The wedding was set for October 20th, 1914, so preparation was started right away. Our house was big. The living room, dining room and kitchen were all big rooms, but a lean-to for the kitchen was built on for a couple of cook stoves. All the cooking was done in there. The ground was leveled and a floor was laid to dance on and the tent was put over it.

Wedding inviters were asked. We gave them a list of who to ask and they drove around to invite all the people. They had a long stick and whoever was asked would tie a long coloured ribbon on the stick. People were always prepared and had ribbons at home in case an inviter would come. How many were invited for our wedding, I don't think I ever knew, but most people from Hoffenthal to MacNutt were asked. The banns were said for two Sundays at church by Reverend Wiegner who had confirmed me and would also marry us. There was so much being done, I often wonder how Mother could do all that planning.

Pigs were butchered, hams readied, a beef was killed, dills and other pickles were made and two orchestras were hired. Then there was my wedding dress. Sister Lizzie was sick and couldn't sew me a dress so I ordered one from Eatons. It wasn't a nice or expensive dress, but I didn't care. Katie made me a petticoat and

---

came the next day to arrange the wedding I was just too young to say what I felt or thought. I did say that Henry had not said anything about getting married when he was there the night before. I was not going to let them arrange a wedding just on my say so. So all right, Henry had to come back that night to ask if he could marry me. But they had already made arrangements to see the Pastor and have the banns read. The wedding would be in two weeks. We were being manipulated.

corset cover, and we ordered white shoes. There was so much to do and so much excitement that I would have forgotten that I was getting married if cousin Liz hadn't kept reminding me all the time that I would be an old married woman soon.

Mother had always planned ahead and had made us feather ticks and pillows and had sheets and towels on hand. She had gone to Shellmouth and bought some things, among them, two lovely tablecloths, one for Katie and one for me. They were still wrapped in paper in a cupboard with other things like an old table cloth with fringes. The cupboard was in the dining room and brother George was looking for something on the cupboard with a lit match. The fringe caught fire and he hadn't noticed. I was setting a sponge for bread. When I looked up the top of the cupboard was on fire. I yelled; everybody ran and tore things down. Our nice new tablecloths were badly burned around the edges, as well as a fur cap that belonged to Dad's step uncle.[3] He had come from the old country and he stayed at our place a lot. He was fussy and cranky and we did not like him. His good fur cap was on the cupboard and got burned. We didn't mind about that.

By then Katie and Pete Rathgeber decided to get married on November 10th, so there was more planning.[4] Dad ordered us fur coats from Eatons. Mine was a mink marmot, a lovely fur coat. Mother bought my veil and wreath in Langenburg. Henry got the wedding ring in Russell. It was a little too big but with the other ring in front, it stayed on. It was expected that I would gain weight but I didn't for many years, so later I had it made smaller. So preparations went on. Our attendants were to be sister Katie, Frank Popp, Lena Popp[5] and Pete Rathgeber. A wagon load of

---

[3] It is uncertain to whom Mary refers. Johann Georg Lowenberger (July 2, 1854 - March 28, 1924) lived in the district. He was a half uncle to Mary's father.

[4] Peter Rathgeber (1894 - 1963) and Katherina Lowenberger (1892 - 1953) were second cousins through the Haas family. They had six children: George (1915 - 1996), Helma (1918 - 1997), Freda (1920 -), Lillian (1923 - 1993), Alice (1925 -) and Rudolph (1927 - 1986). The name "Rathgeber" means "Advice-giver". The oldest son, George, changed his name to "Advice".

[5] Karolina Popp (1898 - 1989), Henry Popp's youngest sister, married Arthur McRae August 8, 1917. They had three children: Margery, Norma and Doris.

kegs of beer, wine and liquor was ordered from Jake Rathgeber who owned the hotel in MacNutt. He also had a new car, one of the only cars around. We asked him to drive us to the church. It was the only car at the wedding - quite an honour.

The wedding day was on Tuesday, October 20, 1914. Weddings were always on Tuesdays. It was a beautiful day, summery warm, so I couldn't wear the fur coat. Then there was a hitch. I was being dressed, everybody was ready, but Frank hadn't come yet. Then Lizzie Mensch came in and said that she had already given Frank a bouquet so he was to dance with her and he couldn't be best man! I shed a few tears. (I didn't wash the powder make-up off because we didn't wear any then.) Well then, what were we to do? Henry's aunt, Mrs. Busch[6] and her daughter and son had come from Winnipeg for the wedding. So her daughter, Minnie Busch,[7] who was engaged to Frank Wagner, also Henry's cousin,[8] and Frank were asked to be our other attendants. Then the problem was solved, but I was hurt about it.

Henry had bought me a lovely silk woven scarf and a heavy embroidered silk handkerchief. I don't remember if I had gloves or not. My dress was floor-length, white silk, with a peplum overskirt with silk lace trimming. It looked nice. The ceremony was at 10:30 a.m. at Hoffenthal Church. I do not remember the text for our wedding sermon or the hymns that were sung. I was in a daze. I was glad nobody could race with us, since we were in the car. But John Zorn later told me that the rest raced and his brother Adam beat them all to our place. It was four miles from the church to our place. Then everybody came to my folks' home for dinner. Everything had been taken out of all the rooms and tables were set

---

[6] Katharine (Popp) Busch (July 6, 1852 - October, 1937) was the daughter of Jacob and Katherine (Hartung) Popp. She was a sister to Philip Popp (Henry Popp's father) and Johann Heinrich Popp.

[7] Minnie (Maria Elisabeth) Busch (January 24, 1897 - May 26, 1966) was the daughter of Michael and Katharine (Popp) Busch. She married Franz Joseph Wagner on November 3, 1914.

[8] Franz (Frank) Wagner was the son of Adam Wagner (brother to Henry Popp's mother) and Eleanor Schappert. Frank and Minnie farmed in the Shellmouth valley.

in the living room, dining room and kitchen. More tables were made and set in the big tent.

I do not know how they managed to feed all those people at once, but they did, both dinner and supper. I had trouble to keep Henry from picking the walnuts off our wedding cake. We had baked the cake, three layers, iced and trimmed with walnuts. There were no decorations then.

Then during the afternoon they followed the tradition of taking my shoe off and auctioning it. This went on for hours. We finally got away from the table and went outside. It was so warm out so everybody was in the yard playing games. They were taking the tables out of the tent so one of the orchestras could start playing. Some guests started dancing. The women were washing dishes, setting tables and preparing supper. Men were passing around whiskey, beer, wine and sweet *Kümel Schnapps*[9] with girls following with plates of *kuchen*, strudel and cookies, which had all been baked the week before. We had baked a hundred pies and about that many cakes, *kuchen* and small strudels. I still marvel at how Mother managed it all.

People stayed, some all night, some for breakfast and some even for dinner the next day. There was enough food for everyone. The bride's dance was at midnight. I danced with everybody, men, women, boys and girls. I liked dancing and didn't mind only so many people kissed me, and that I didn't like. After the dance was over, they took my veil off (it was slipping all the time) and sang *Jesu Geh Voran,*[10] and other songs, some funny ones.

Later the money was counted and gifts valued. I do not remember how much money we received, but we had lovely gifts, so very many. I still have some. Mother stood on a chair and announced how much money had been collected in my shoe and the gifts we had received. Then she smashed a plate on the floor. The dancing continued, both in the big room and in the tent. Henry and I would have liked to have gone someplace for a rest, but there was

---

[9] *Kümel Schnapps* was made by carefully browning brown sugar. Water and dill (*Kümel*) were added. The mixture was strained and added to home brew.

[10] *Jesu, geh voran auf der Lebensbahn, und wir wollen nicht verweilen, dir getreulich nachzueilen. Fuhr' uns an der Hand bis ins Vaterland!*

no place. The beds were full of children, the rooms and yard full of people, and the barns full of horses. There was the smoke house, but John Hofer[11] had gone in there, so all we could do was go sit in the tent and dance, or watch the rest.

Toward morning when people left and took their babies off the beds, we did find a place to lie down but people were still there. Some had even gone home and done their chores and come back. Everybody was eating breakfast. Others, to this day, tell us what a fun or good time they had at our wedding.

[11] John Hofer (1886 - 1948) was the son of Anton Hofer and Maria Elisabeth Lowenberger who came to Canada in 1891. Anton Hofer donated four acres of his land for the Hoffenthal Church and cemetery. John Hofer married Elisabeth Phillips in 1917. They lived on the Peiden place, near Shellmouth until they moved to the NE 6-22-29. They had five children: Edgar, Felicia (Bryer), Lionel, Phoebe (Dowhy) and Raymond.

FARM WIFE AND MOTHER

The wedding was on Tuesday and on Thursday we loaded my possessions, my trunk, bedding, clothes, gifts, food, and started for home. Henry had gone home and returned with a wagon. I don't remember if we took the cow, heifer and calf Dad gave us.[1] I had not been to the house yet but Lena and Minnie Busch and Henry had cleaned it. It had been Henry's cousin Philip Popp's[2] place, which Henry's dad had bought. It had a kitchen, living room, and an unfinished attic. They had prepared the living room and put blue figured oilcloth on the upper part of the kitchen wall, the lower part had V-joint boards, unpainted. The ceilings and floors were unpainted, with two windows in the living room, one in

---

[1] Henry and Mary Popp moved to the NE 21-23-30 W1, five miles south of MacNutt, one mile east of the Landestreu Church.

[2] Philip Popp (1884 - 1964) was the son of Johann Heinrich Popp and Katharina Brandt. He married Elisabeth Schappert.

the kitchen, one door in the kitchen, and a pantry under the stairway with shelves for dishes.

We lived close to Landestreu Church, it was just a mile west of our farm. I didn't know many people there, but slowly I got to know them.

My parents had gone to MacNutt and bought me a bed and dresser, a table, sideboard and six chairs, a cook stove and a sewing machine (which I still have).[3] Lena Popp and Minnie Chittick[4] gave us a rocking chair for a wedding present. Sister Katie gave us silver knives and forks. Somebody gave us two pairs of curtains. What we hadn't received as gifts, Mother went to MacNutt and bought.

Outside the barn was a lean-to built onto a log granary. Henry had four horses, so we were settled. I have wondered what I cooked that first winter. Henry said he had planted potatoes. They were in the cellar. I suppose the folks would have given us some meat and our cow still milked. They must have given us flour because I baked bread - the first batch I got nine loaves.

The first Sunday after we were married, both my folks and Henry's parents came and brought food. Phillip and Jake Zorns came, and I don't remember who else. I didn't know the Zorns even though they had been at the wedding, but got to know them before the evening was over. They had also brought drinks. That was

---

[3] It is somewhat surprising that Mr. and Mrs. Lowenberger had the financial resources to provide so well for Mary and their other daughters who were married in 1914. George Lowenberger, Mary's brother, commented in his memoirs respecting his parents' ability to pay for the weddings:

> How Dad managed to pay for all this I sure don't know. True, the other families all contributed their share. I do believe because there was a war going on prices were higher for the crops and also for cattle so this would have helped considerably. However, Dad had to set up the three girls with house furnishings and cooking utensils, etc. and they each got two or three cows to start them off on their own. I also think there was a good crop that year.

[4] Minnie (Mary Anne) Chittick, who married Jack Moore on June 20, 1917, was Henry Popp's niece, daughter of William Chittick (1864 - 1938) and Rosina Popp (1879 - 1964). William and Rosina had eight children: Mary Anne, William, Clara, Evelyn, Philip, Violet, Arta and Shirley.

called the *No Hochzeit*[5] after the wedding. They stayed until morning.

The weather was beautiful for about three weeks after we were married. In the evenings we would walk to Jack Popp's,[6] Henry's brother. They lived just one half mile away and his folks lived about a mile away. Lena and Minnie Chittick and Jack Busch would come over. We would play cards and we were asked to a lot of weddings. Minnie and Frank Wagner, who were our attendants, got married three weeks after we did. Also Mary Mack and Fred Mitschke[7] got married that day. So we went to Minnie and Frank's wedding first then drove ten or fifteen miles to Macks to Mary and Fred's wedding. We had also gone to a wedding in Beresina at Mundts. It was a long ride and it had turned cold. I nearly froze coming home.

Before Katie's wedding on November 10, 1914, there was a snow storm and very cold weather. Everything was left from our wedding -- the tent and the extra kitchen. Her wedding was not quite as big as ours, but it was still a big wedding. They had put a stove in the tent and everything was much like our wedding. Pete, too, had land with old buildings on it only about a mile from home. So Katie could get home oftener. I would get homesick for home and I guess for Katie and the kids. Helen was quite small. And most of all, I'd miss the Sunday night parties we had at home.

A week after Katie and Pete were married, they gave them a *No Hochzeit*. We went with the big sleigh and took Henry's parents along. There was a crowd there and the older men got Henry to

---

[5] *No Hochzeit* (or in High German, *Nach Hochzeit*) means "after the wedding". It was a party at the home of the newlyweds.

[6] Jacob Popp (June 20, 1881 - July 18, 1957) was Henry Popp's older brother. He married Elisabeth Schoepp, born 1885, (daughter of Jakob Schoepp and Katherine Daunheimer) on July 7, 1903. She died July 18, 1917. Jack Popp lived one-half mile east of Henry and Mary Popp. Another brother, Philip Popp and his wife Laura (Wagner) lived one mile south of Jack Popp.

[7] Fred Mitschke (August 26, 1892 - December 22, 1973) was the son of immigrants from Hamburg, Germany, Josef and Elisabeth (Ramke) Mitschke. Mary Mack (March 6, 1896 - September 4, 1969) was the daughter of Valentine and Katharina (Nerbas) Mack. They were married November 3, 1914. They had six children: Bruno, Elna (Jeske/Baumung), Robert, Benno, James and Morley.

play cards with them. Every time he won he got a drink. They let him win. After they quit he came and sat beside me on the bed and he fell forward on the floor and I started crying so we went home. It was after midnight anyway. When I felt in my coat pocket for my house key, it wasn't there. I had lost it, so we had to stay at Henry's folks for the rest of the night. In the morning they found a bunch of keys to try and we went home. When we came home the key was in the lock. I had forgotten to take it out.

Horses were still the way of travelling in 1914 when we got married. Henry had a top buggy and a cutter too. We also got a foot warmer and a fur robe. We didn't take any long trips to Langenburg or Marchwell. But people would go to Russell a lot or even to Yorkton by horses.

My dad bought a two-seat democrat for the family to go to church and to festive occasions. He also bought a buggy for a single horse and a cutter for easy winter traveling. A buffalo robe and footwarmer kept us warm in the cutter. We would put a piece of charcoal in the stove, get it burning and then put it in the footwarmer. It would burn for hours. That was better than hot stones. Dad always had good horses. But he had one pair of bays who liked running away and often did.

Another kind of winter transportation was a van, a small enclosure on sleigh runners with a window in front for the driver to see through and holes for the reins to go through. They had a little wood-burning heater to keep you warm while driving. There were seats on both sides and a door at the back so you could get out if it upset, which it sometimes did.

Then people began buying cars. In the fall of 1917, we bought a car, a MacLaughlin touring car - pretty nice car. It had side curtains to be buttoned on if it rained. We were always prepared with the fur robe, sweaters, caps and scarves that we brought along. Even driving 30 or 40 miles per hour there would be a cool breeze. It had leather seats which were cold too.

I learned to drive the car. We got it in the fall, but we did not drive it in the winter. So by the next spring, I had forgotten how to drive. I had to ask Henry how to start it and how to change gears. But I had also forgotten how to stop! When I got to the gate I drove right through it! Later we got a second hand Overland.

That one I did not like. It was so heavy we would always get stuck and there was no pushing it out. We also got a second - hand little red truck. It had been Richter's butcher truck. I think George Becker sold us all those cars.

Then one Easter, Fred Busch took us to MacNutt to a dance. It was snowing and raining. He had a sedan and we sat in that car just like in a house and watched the weather outside. We liked that. But people did not know what to think -- that kind of a car was for the farm, taking cream cans, etc. to town and bringing barbed wire or lumber home. It just didn't seem possible.

The roads were very poor. If it rained they were all mud and we would get stuck. We got our clothes all dirty. Sometimes we had to leave the car and walk. It was cold driving in them so we always took toques, scarves, mitts and sweaters along for the children.

That first winter we were married seemed long, not much to do. Lena and I sent for books to read. I ordered some embroidery and worked on that. Then the Hofer boys came and brought us books and magazines to read. We went visiting a lot and often had visitors come over. The spring of 1915 was cold, dry and very windy. I was making a garden. Henry had plowed a piece of land close to the house but it was so hard and lumpy. I raked for days but I couldn't get it like our garden at home. I had started cabbage plants in a box, so I had nice cabbages. Everything grew. When the garden was quite nice, the cows broke the fence and ate most of the cabbages and trampled everything down. That was a catastrophe. Our cow had gone dry during the winter so we had no milk unless somebody would bring us some. By then I was pregnant and I wanted milk and porridge. It didn't really matter though, because as soon as I ate it, it just came back up anyway.

When our cow was having a calf, it died so Dad gave us another cow. The heifer had a calf, so we had two cows, and milk, butter and cheese.

When Henry brought his stuff from home he gave me some papers to put away. I put them in the trunk. Then one day I was looking for something in the trunk and came across those papers. So I looked to see what they were. They were contracts where he bought the land and owed 2,700 dollars and other papers showing where he owed 1,400 dollars for the threshing machine. I just couldn't believe it. His father always said that he gave Henry a half section of land and the threshing machine. Henry told me that as well as my folks and everybody else. I believed it and Henry never told me differently. So I was shocked, just sick. I thought maybe I didn't understand those papers. When Henry came home I asked him. Yes we owed 4,100 dollars. To me this was life-time debt.

We always had debts at home. Dad would buy land, machinery, or had wells dug. Debts were always paid with annual payments after harvest when the grain was sold. We milked a lot of cows, even though the cream cheques weren't so big. We also had a lot of hens. Mother bought the food, our clothes and everything for the house. In the fall we sold chickens, geese and ducks. So she managed. I don't think she ever charged at the store.

Dad did buy a new kitchen range on credit. A man came around with a wagon carrying stoves to sell. He had a beautiful stove with a lot of shiny nickel. It was strong. He would take the ax and hit the lids and they wouldn't break and he jumped on the over door and it held. It was just too good a stove not to buy. It cost 80 dollars so dad bought it. He paid 40 dollars on it; the rest was to be paid in the fall. I would spend hours cleaning that stove. It was malleable steel, black on the top. We used “Bon Ami” on the nickel. I polished and polished that oven door and everybody wanted to sit on it.

Mother, too, would always tell us how much we owed if something was bought on credit. There always were a lot of debts, but I don't think they would amount to 4,000 dollars, as that was a terrible amount. So when I found out about ours I just worried and worried about it. We weren't even married a year.

The first fall before threshing, Henry went to Yorkton and bought a new threshing separator, as the one he had couldn't be fixed anymore. I don't remember how much it cost but there was a good crop that fall and he made a lot of money with it to help pay for it. He also bought his parents' share for the next couple of years, so he owned it himself.

We went visiting a lot that first summer with the other newly weds, or they would come to visit us. All the young wives were pregnant; sister Katie, Mary Mitschke, Minnie Wagner and

Margaret Nerbas. But I thought we would have our baby first, because we were married first and I had gotten very big. I grew taller after I was married and while pregnant, I gained 40 pounds. I didn't go to a doctor. I had figured with Henry's help and a doctor book, that our baby would come in November. But all the others were having their babies and there I sat, getting bigger and waiting. I was sewing, making baby clothes from flannelette, nighties, dresses, little skirts, binders, bonnets and diapers. I had a whole dresser drawer full of baby clothes I made. Mother made me a couple of soft pillows big enough to wrap the baby in. I had also ordered some baby blankets and shirts so I was all prepared.

But Henry was still out threshing. We had his niece, Minnie Becker,[8] staying with me. She was just 13 years old but at least I wasn't alone. Henry started coming home every night. There were no phones and it got colder out. We got some snow and there were chores to be done. Our crop was all threshed so our cattle and horses could be in the fields, but other people's stock would break into our land and come running around the house and yard. There was a government-built dike on our land, across in the opposite corner, over a mile away. The cattle went there for water. I pulled water out of a well close to the house for the calves, pigs and chickens. But I couldn't keep strange cattle away when I watered the stock. They would push me and I was so big and clumsy, I was forever falling down.

It was going on into December. I had churned butter and was taking it down to the cellar on a plate. When I was halfway down, the ladder broke and down I went. I scraped my legs and arms and the butter landed on the dirt floor. There seemed to be so many things going wrong.

Henry had a black spaniel dog called Queenie. She stayed home with me when he was gone. One day she started barking and jumping. I went out to look and there was the threshing machine in the yard. They had moved home and I was glad because I was still waiting for our baby to come.

---

[8] Minnie Becker (June 7, 1901 - July 17, 1983), daughter of Ferdinand Becker (November 8, 1873 - January 16, 1965) and Katherine Popp (December 20, 1876 - December 23, 1918), married Rueben McRae on May 16, 1931.

On December 13th I was having stomach aches every once in a while. I had to lie down for a while, then get up and do things. That night we had just gone to bed when the pain got worse so Henry got up, hitched up the horses and went to get his mother. But they weren't home. They were at Adams, so Henry came back to see how I was. Then he went to get his mother. He brought her home then went to MacNutt, five miles, to get Mrs. Dagg,[9] the country nurse. When she came, she gave me castor oil, ginger tea and an enema and made Henry go lie on a coat on the kitchen floor. I wanted him to help me. I felt very sick. I should have had a doctor but the closest one was in Langenburg. It would have been too late anyway. So our first baby, Arnold, was born on December 14, 1915. Henry took Mrs. Dagg and went to get my mother to stay with us for a week, until I could get up to look after the baby and do the work. I was badly torn when Arnold was born, but was never fixed. So I had trouble.

When Mother went home I was quite worried about looking after the baby, though sister Helen was just two years old when I got married and we all looked after her but not when she was so little. We had no phone and no doctor close by. Arnold got sick with diarrhea really bad. The folks were going to MacNutt. Mother came in and she said Arnold might die. I got so scared, so I looked in the doctor book. It said to beat egg white until foamy and add a little boiling water. So I gave him that, and he had gotten so sore. I put corn starch on him, and it seemed to help. Then we got the minister over and had him baptized Arnold William Popp. He became a very active child.

When Arnold was about ten months old, we left him with Henry's folks. Henry went to a school trustee's convention in Regina and took me along. We stayed at Barkers,[10] his sister

---

[9] Jennie Coleman came to MacNutt as a registered nurse from Brandon, largely through the efforts of Richard Dagg, an agent for the Theodore A. Burrows Lumber Company of Grandview, who became her husband. Jenny Dagg gave nursing care for many years and assisted Doctor Lee when he became the first resident doctor.

[10] Mary Popp, Henry's sister, (January 30, 1885 - February 17, 1981) married Alan W. Barker on November 20, 1902. They had eight children: Gertrude, Florence, Ella, Minnie, Leonard, Lila, Arthur and Doris.

Mary's place. That was quite an experience for me - the electric lights, running water and flush toilet were the most wonderful things! Even the train ride was exciting, though I had been on the train to Russell once. At Regina, they took us to shows. I went along to the convention during the day. Two other men had gone too, Mr. Dietrich and Fred Haas. One person living now who went along with her dad from Langenburg was Heddy Yeske, now Ridgway.[11] She says she remembered me on the train. I wore my new fur coat.

After that Regina trip I was planning - if we would build a house, could we have electric lights? Henry said he could put a steam engine boiler in the basement and we would have steam heat and electric lights. I dreamed and talked about it. Others envied us for what we would get, but with all our debts, the years rolled by and I kept on planning and dreaming.

We weren't married for long when a man came to the door and asked to speak to my dad. I guess I looked young. He talked to Henry. He was from the Department of Education. They were building schools. Before that, an old building by the Landestreu Church was used for school. Sometimes they had a teacher, if not the minister would teach. But there was no regular school. So they were building the Zorn[12] and Landestreu[13] schools. Henry was the first secretary.

Then it was decided to build a telephone line. That must have been the first or second year we were married. Henry went to town with somebody else. I waited and waited; he didn't come home. I did the chores and when it got dark, there was an awful

---

[11] Hedwig Yeske (1907 - 1993) was the daughter of Hugo and Emilie (Bessel) Yeske. She married Ernest Ridgway of Shellmouth in 1936.

[12] Zorn School was named after Philip Zorn who took an active role in its organization in 1916. Zorn School was four miles south and one mile east of MacNutt. Henry Popp was chairman or secretary-treasurer from 1916 to 1928. The school closed in 1962.

[13] The Landestreu School District was formed in March 1916. After formation of the School District, Henry Popp was elected chairman and N. P. Threinen became secretary-treasurer. The school was constructed in 1917. The Landestreu School closed in 1961 and the students were transferred to MacNutt.

noise upstairs. It must have been mice. I thought it was men. I got so scared, I started out to go to Jack and Lizzie Popp's. I hadn't gone far when a buggy stopped at the corner and Henry got off, so I went back home. They had had a meeting to get organized. Henry was elected Secretary-Treasurer. He had bought a club bag[14] to put his papers in. I was angry he had spent money so carelessly and I said some nasty things. But later, when the lines were built, I boarded telephone men nearly all summer and earned a little money.

The second year we were married, Henry's mother got pneumonia and in a few days died on May 19, 1917 at 65 years of age. "Grandma Popp" was short and stout. She had a great sense of humour. When she was dying her sister-in-law, Mrs. Henry Wagner,[15] removed the pillow from under her head. I wanted to put the pillow under her head again but she had stopped breathing. I felt so sad. She hadn't been my mother-in-law for long, but she had been so good to me.

Then a few months after, Jack Popp's wife Lizzie died of tuberculosis. They had seven children, the baby was seven months old. Reverend Predoehl, our minister, took the baby.[16] I missed Lizzie too, they lived so close to us. Jack tried to manage with his children. Mary, the oldest girl got sick,[17] had a ruptured appendix and they took her to Winnipeg. We took the two youngest girls, Margaret and Lizzie to our place for the winter. Arnold was still small.

---

[14] A club bag was a small satchel which served the same purpose as a modern briefcase.

[15] nee Maria Dietrich (1865 - 1940)

[16] Joseph Popp, son of Jack and Elisabeth Popp, born March 27, 1907, related that his mother had been diagnosed with tuberculosis before the child (Elsie) was born. Elisabeth Popp had made arrangements, even while she was pregnant, that Reverend and Mrs. Predoehl would take her child upon her death.

[17] Mary Popp was about 15 years old when her father took her to Winnipeg on the train for surgery. Her incision never healed properly. Upon her return to the farm, Mary and her new step-mother did not get along well. Mary also began to date Fred Busch. Mary's father disapproved of the relationship. Mary eventually moved to Winnipeg and worked as a domestic. She became ill from complications arising from the appendix operation. She died in 1922.

Then Lena Popp, Henry’s sister, got married and Henry's dad decided to come live with us. We really had no say. That was very hard. He drank quite a bit and when he drank he could be very mean. He was spoiling Arnold badly. He told me he had raised more children than I and he knew how. During that winter, Henry would go to the sawmill to get lumber and have boards cut for the new barn we were going to build. He would be gone for a week and his dad would take over. He would go to town, bring a gallon of liquor home, and while that lasted he would yell during the night. I'd get so scared. By then we had the upstairs fixed. Henry had bought the old parsonage and with the lumber had fixed the upstairs. But the upstairs was cold - if I changed the baby's diaper it froze by morning. The downstairs was cold too.

By spring it got so bad I thought I couldn't take it any longer. Jack had taken Margaret and Lizzie home and I told Henry I'd take Arnold and go home to my folks. But I didn't and things went on until one day Henry and his dad came home from town. Henry’s dad knocked on the door until I came down from upstairs and opened the door. He had two paper bags of onions. He threw them on the floor, called me names and went over to Jack’s. He phoned later saying he was sending Ferdinand,[18] Jack's oldest boy, over with the wagon to get his bed, trunk and clothes. He did, and so he stayed at Jack's for a while.

After Henry’s dad had moved to our place, they were on the old farm tearing down their old house and building a new one for Frank, who was getting married in September. The old house was built with layered sods. It had only two rooms - a living room and kitchen. Each room had two beds and all the other furniture and the stove. There were no clothes closets so the clothes were hung on the wall. A small porch was built on the south side. In this house they raised their large family and entertained their friends and relatives. They also had a big summer kitchen near the house. In summer it was used for butchering and storing meat and other food - like a modern-day deep-freeze. Anyway, when they were pulling

---

[18] Ferdinand Popp (1904 - 1997) married Dora Orr from Calder. Ferdinand was a grain buyer in several towns in Saskatchewan. They had two children: Patricia and Terry.

the house down, one of the heavy sod walls fell over and killed a young man (Schneider).

Frank built a new house and married Lizzie Mensch on August 6, 1917. They had a big wedding. Lena Popp, Henry's sister and Art McRae, a teacher at MacNutt, were going together. They just went away and got married and lived in MacNutt.

Henry's dad married again on November 2, 1919 to Mrs. Steffens at Melville. Jack was in Melville and phoned us to come to the wedding. We all went to her son's house. A woman there was very nice to us. We thought she was Henry's dad's new wife. Then the minister came and this real old woman came out of the bedroom. She had a white apron on with crocheted lace. We all got quite a shock. She was too old to do any work and she was sick. Henry's dad had bought some houses in Melville and moved into a small one. She was too sick to do anything. She only lived about six months after they were married.[19] We didn't go to the funeral.

By 1918 we needed a new barn. Henry bought the lumber and hired men to build it. I was pregnant again and not feeling well. We had hired about six men to work at the barn. They and two men painting our church came to eat at our place. I was cooking for them all and doing all the other work.

One day, I started a fire in the stove with chips and shavings. I had a pail of potatoes to peel. I poured half a pail of water on the potatoes; into the other half I put the peeled potatoes. Then I heard something crackle. I opened the upstairs door and could see flames. So I ran all the way to the barn yelling, but they were hammering and sawing and didn't hear me until they say me. Then I ran to the well house with pails. But the trough was empty. Then I thought of the rain water barrel. I saw the fellow from Germany who was working for us run upstairs and throw his suitcase, clothes and shoes out of the window. Henry had run in. There was no water except a big pail full of slops, chop, dishwater and milk. The pail was full. He took it upstairs and threw it on the fire. Then the other men carried rain water up and got the fire out.

---

[19] Matilda Steffen (nee Ruecker) was in fact just 62 years old at the time of their marriage. She died on May 19, 1920.

When I saw the fire was out, I sat down and couldn't breathe. I moaned - I had to clean up that mess. The pail full of slop came running through the living room and kitchen ceilings. I felt sick.

We had our well drilled before we built the barn. Before that I used to carry water for drinking and cooking from a well in the field, about one-half mile away. In the winter Henry would bring it with a barrel. We drilled a deep well, 105 feet deep and bought an engine to pump water. The water wasn't so good, but we got used to it.

Arnold was a very active child. If Henry was home he would always be with him but when he was alone outside, I'd often go see where he was. One time he was yelling in the barn. There was a calf tied up and he had got himself tangled up in the rope. He and the calf were wrapped together and he couldn't get loose. Another time I was going to churn butter - I had a barrel-type churn with a hook on it to keep it in place. I poured a milk can full of sour cream into the churn. When I turned around, Arnold had unhooked the barrel and all the cream went on the floor. I guess I gave him a slap. He ran out. While I was cleaning up I went to look once where he was. He and his pup were across the road. I thought he was getting the cows home. When I had finished cleaning up and went to get the cows, he wasn't there. I looked all over. I called and called. Then I got scared. It was in the fall. Henry was away threshing. There were stooks around the house and I wondered if he had fallen asleep behind a stook. It started getting dark, so I phoned Jack Popp. His son, Joe, got on a horse, rode through the field and came in the yard. Then the pup barked under the granary and Arnold started crying. He had crawled under the granary, fallen asleep and woke up when the dog barked.[20]

Another time Arnold had gathered up a pile of hay and straw at the corner of the barn and lit it. He said he was making a smudge for the calves. When I looked and saw smoke, I took a pail of rain water and ran. Two men were on the road. When they saw

---

[20] Joe Popp, (born March 27, 1907), in 1998, at the age of 91 recalled riding his pony, King, looking over the prairie for Arnold. He recalled the dog, Queenie, running out from the granary disclosing Arnold's whereabouts.

the fire they came walking in. When Arnold saw them he ran in the house and crawled under the sofa. The men helped put the fire out.

Shortly before Dick was born, Henry was out doing chores with Arnold. He had the pump engine going. Sometimes the pump jack would get stuck and Henry would give it a push. Arnold noticed that so he tried it. His mitten got caught in the cogs and pulled his little hand into the gear. Luckily the engine stopped. When it stopped Henry went to look what had happened and found Arnold screaming. He brought him into the house. His hand and fingers were all bloody and looked crushed. A piece of one finger was off. I felt sick all over. I put a clean cloth around it and we drove into MacNutt to Mrs. Dagg, the nurse. He was whimpering all the way. The nurse took scissors and cut the ragged edges off while Arnold screamed. She bandaged it and we took him home. I had to dress it every day. The other fingers came back but the one with the tip off got stumpy with pieces of nail growing on both sides.

I was very worried about my pregnancy. So many things had happened to me. After the barn was finished and the men left, I went to see Mrs. Dagg and she told me to be very careful and to lie down when I wasn't feeling well or I might have a miscarriage. But how could I lie down? Fall was coming with so much to do. Then more men came to help fix up the threshing machine. And when threshing started, Henry was gone all the time. There were cows to milk, calves, pigs and chickens to be fed and cared for. The garden had to be looked after, potatoes had to be dug. I'd hitch a horse to the stoneboat,[21] get the potato bags on and haul them home. Then I would throw them down through the cellar hole.

The cows would be a mile away near the dike. I'd have to get them. Arnold was not quite three years old. I would make him walk, but when he got tired I would have to carry him. The prairie was so rough, I'd fall down and get up and go on. Then I would have to milk the cows. I would try to keep Arnold as close to me as I could.

---

[21] A stoneboat was a flat, open sleigh built on two runners. Stoneboats were commonly drawn by a team of horses and used to haul manure from the barn.

In the fall of 1918 the Spanish Influenza broke out.[22] The weather was very nice that fall but nearly every morning the church bell would ring. Somebody had died - young, strong people. Carl Erhardt (the fellow who had thrown his suit case out the window earlier that summer when we had the fire) was working at the machine and got the flu, so Henry brought him home. I had to look after him. It was getting late in the fall. The doctors were very busy that fall. They came out by horses from Russell. They were on the road most of the time and would hire drivers to drive them from place to place. Often they slept in the cutter as they made their way from one patient to the next.

One day we went to MacNutt and I heard people talk how others had died of the flu. Some had been found dead in their hotel rooms. Others had walked across the street and dropped dead. They said you should wash all fruit, but I had already bought and eaten some grapes. When we went home, we went past Kitzs where the threshing machine was. Henry stayed there, and I drove home. I wasn't feeling well but went for the cows. Arnold fell asleep so I had to carry him all the way. After I had the chores finished, I felt quite sick. I couldn't eat supper and I was very cold. Then I got scared - what if I should die during the night, what would happen to Arnold? I left the door open to the bread box and put some milk out. I phoned Lizzie Popp, Frank's wife, and asked her to call me in the morning. But the next morning I was fine. That was the only time I was really scared of the flu. Later, Henry

---

[22] An estimated 20 million people worldwide died from the Spanish Influenza. The virus was prevalent among the young and hardy, ages 25 to 34. In August, 1918 the virus appeared and in four months had spread across the globe. Victims literally drown as fluid filled their lungs. When the Influenza broke out, MacNutt was quarantined and the pool room was closed at 6:00 p.m. No strangers were allowed to stop in the village and all houses containing persons infected with the Spanish Influenza were to be quarantined. A fine of $50.00 was to be imposed for any infringement of this regulation. (Source: *Those Were the Days: The History of MacNutt, Calder, Dropmore and Surrounding Districts*) The Hoffenthal Church Registry shows four deaths of the Spanish Influenza within a three week period: George Burkhart, 27 years old, on November 25, 1918; Emma Haas, 2 years old, on November 29, 1918; Elisabeth Haas, 37 years old, on November 30, 1918; and Jacob Mack, 32 years old on December 13, 1918.

got it and Arnold and I slept with him, but we did not get it that year. And when we went places where people had it, I wasn't afraid. Then people started warning me not to go places as it seemed to take pregnant women.[23]

The day before Christmas I was melting a lot of snow for bath water. We used to bathe in the big round wash tub, but by Christmas the tub was too small for me so we got a big barrel in. I had it half filled with warm water, when the phone rang. Henry's oldest sister Katie Becker,[24] had died of the flu. She was pregnant and the baby didn't live so her brothers, Henry, Jack, Phillip and Frank, went to Beckers at Zorra[25] that night. I went on with my

---

[23] Mary Popp's brother, George Lowenberger, in his memories also recounted how the Spanish Influenza struck Hoffenthal:

> Then the Flu broke out... I believe George Burkhardt was the first one that died of the Flu in Hoffenthal. He was just a young man. We went to the funeral but did not go into the house. In those years there was a short service held in the home before the casket was taken out. The Flu was hard on pregnant women and they were really worried. I know sister Mary was one of them. Mrs. J. G. Haas was also one and she gave birth to a baby girl but died after, but the baby survived. Mrs. Busch, a sister of Mrs. Haas, adopted the baby and raised her. [The baby, Elisabeth, was two days old then her mother, Elisabeth (nee Adam) died on November 30, 1918.] We were on the yard at Mrs. Haas' funeral but did not go into the house so as not to be exposed to the Flu germs, but we went to the church service at Hoffenthal. Then I can remember when Jacob Mack died on December 13, 1918. I was at sister Katie's place when somebody phoned her that Jacob Mack had died. He was considered being related to us because his wife, Amalia was a cousin of ours. Pete and Katie went to the funeral. I stayed at home to do the chores. Jacob was a strong man, only 32 years old so his death left his wife a widow with three small children to look after. [Amalia Kendel married Jacob Mack in May, 1910. They had four children: Katherine, George, Alwina and Othelia. Amalia married Joseph Rosner in April 1920 and had five more children: Erwin, Ewald, Gertrude, Erna and Adeline.]

[24] Katherina (Popp) Becker (December 20, 1876 - December 23, 1918) married Ferdinand Becker on November 26, 1896. At the time of her death, she was 42 years old and expecting her 12th child.

[25] Zorra was a community north of MacNutt named after Zorra, Ontario, the home of one of the first settlers, John Ross. The Zorra school was built in 1907. In 1908, a Lutheran Church was also built. It was demolished in 1949 and a new church which still stands was built.

bath. I had just got into the barrel when the phone rang. So I got out and answered the phone. It was Reverend Predoehl. He had heard about the death and asked me not to go to the funeral in my condition. It didn't matter where you went the flu bug was everywhere. Well I got back into the barrel and had a good bath after melting all the snow.

By January 1919 my time was getting closer and I did worry because so many things had happened to me during my pregnancy. One Sunday, we went down to my folks. I told Mother I was having pains. She told us to get home quick. We got home and Henry went for Mrs. Dagg. Then he took Arnold to my folks and brought Mother back. There were no complications. Our second son, Richard, was born January 20, 1919. He was a small baby. Everything was fine. Later that winter Arnold and I got the flu. It was not as severe but we took a long time to get over it.

My dad did not have the flu bad, but his asthma enlarged his lungs. He could hardly breathe and he died November 22, 1919, at the age of 54 years.[26] About that same time, Jack's children got

---

[26] George Lowenberger, Mary's brother, who lived at home when his father died, commented on his father's death in his memoirs:

> About 8:30 in the morning on November 22nd, Mother called us to the house. We were in the barns doing the chores. Mother said Dad had asked for us. We went into the room and stood by the bed. Dad spoke to us. I do not remember what he said then. He was quiet for a while and then he closed his eyes and passed silently away. We all stood there stunned and wept for some time. Then we went back to do the chores; the work had to be done.
>
> The rest of the family was notified and they came and helped to make the funeral arrangements. When the casket arrived the body was laid in it and set up in the room where he had passed away. It remained there until the day of the funeral. Many relatives and friends called at our home to pay their last respects. Then on November 25th, after a short service in the home, the casket was taken into the Hoffenthal Church for the funeral service with Reverend Wiegner officiating. He was taken into the church he had helped to build and in which he worshipped regularly. He was buried on the Hoffenthal cemetery. By the time the service was over at the cemetery the weather had turned cold and later on turned into a snow storm. I am quite certain that this was the last trip that was made with the Dodge car that year - the car that Dad had purchased three years before.

diphtheria. By the time he got a doctor from Saltcoats it was too late. He phoned to tell us little Lizzie[27] had died, and a half hour later he phoned again, Margaret had died.[28] We felt very sad but we had children and were afraid to go over there. Poor Jack - he had lost his wife such a short time before. He was alone there. But Mrs. Henry Zorn got her husband to drive her to Jack's.[29] She stayed and looked after the other children and prepared the dead ones for burial. When she went home, she left all her clothes outside before she went into her house. Later when Reverend and Mrs. Predoehl moved to the United States they took Jack's daughter, Elsie,[30] as had been arranged by Jack's wife before she

---

From the four families that arrived in Langenburg some time in 1889, Dad was the first one to depart. He was a good father to us and a good provider for this family. He did not want to die; he was only 54 years old and had many plans for things he wanted to do. But his Lord and Savior in whom he believed with all his heart and loved, had other plans. He called him to his heavenly home.

Dad's passing put a heavy responsibility on Mother with the farming operations. Rudy was home for the funeral and since he was oldest, close to 21 years old, I believe he was prepared to stay home and help Mother run the farm. I do not know how it was decided but he went back to Yorkton to continue with his business course. This left Jake at 19 and me, 18 years old, to carry on with the farming. Adolf was 14 and going to school so he was not much help. He was determined to get an education. Sister Helen was young and going to school.

[27] Elisabeth Helena Popp was born October 6, 1914. She died November 17, 1919.

[28] Margaret Wilhelmina Popp was born June 12, 1913. She died November 17, 1919.

[29] Joe Popp, brother to Elisabeth and Margaret, recounted in 1998 that Mr. and Mrs. Henry Zorn drove to their house and brought Mrs. Brandt who tended to the preparation of the two deceased girls. Joe Popp also related that the bodies were taken to the Landestreu cemetery and buried. Later a funeral service was held.

[30] Elsie Popp was born January 8, 1917. She and the Predoehl family left Landestreu when Elsie was four years old. She was raised in Kansas, Missouri. In 1935 Reverend Predoehl and Elsie came back to Landestreu to celebrate a church anniversary. She lived her entire life in the United States. She married once (Donahue) but had no children. She died February 9, 1980 in California. Her body was brought back to Landestreu for burial beside her mother and sisters.

died. So Jack had lost his wife, two daughters to diptheria and one daughter who moved to the United States.

After Dick was born I wasn't feeling well. I had seen doctors and they told me I had to have an operation. In the winter of 1920, when Dick was a year old, we took the boys to Mother's and went to Winnipeg on the train. I went to see Dr. Hiebert. He took me to the Misericordia Hospital, removed my appendix and did some repair work on me. He also said I needed a nose operation. I had catarrh but he couldn't do it all at once. I was very sick after that operation. Henry went home and came down again to get me when I was out of the hospital. I had to take it easy for a while, but by summer I was able to do all my work again, go berry picking, and go to sports and dances.

PROGRESS DURING THE TWENTIES

So time went on. We enjoyed life and worked hard. We reduced our debts and made new ones. We bought a quarter section of land close to our land. The threshing engine was getting old, so Henry bought a new one. Other machinery had to be bought.

Henry got sick in the spring of 1920 with severe stomach aches. It was seeding time and he couldn't work. After three days he told me to phone Dr. Bates at Russell. He came and examined Henry and said he had to take him to the hospital to operate to remove his appendix. While I was getting Henry ready, Frank and Lizzie Popp came over and told me to go along with Henry. They would take the boys and look after the chores. So I went along. They operated on Henry that night. He had a ruptured appendix and was very sick. I stayed at McKay's in Russell for a few days until somebody came and got me home. Henry's brothers and neighbours came and did our seeding. I could do the other work.

Henry was in the hospital for about four weeks. When he came home he hired a man. It took some time to get his strength back.

When Arnold was about four years old he got a bad toothache. We took him to MacNutt where two young dentists had set up a practice on the third floor in the hotel. We took Arnold in and they put him in the chair. Henry was holding the lamp. When the dentist started pulling the tooth, Arnold let out a yell and kicked the lamp. The chimney fell off. He said "Where's my cap?" He grabbed it and away he went. We all ran after him. He ran down one flight of stairs and the next and out the door. We couldn't catch up with him. When he got out he ran down the sidewalk. Mr. Fishman, one of the store keepers, picked him up and tried to quiet him down. We didn't get him back to the dentist even though the tooth had been loosened. He was so scared of those dentists. One Sunday night there was a dance at our barn and a wagon load of people came out. Those dentists were along. All at once we didn't know where Arnold was. He had run in the house and hid under the couch.

We would visit back and forth a lot. There was no age barrier - young or old. We visited with my sister Lizzie and Julius Metz, Katie and Pete Rathgeber, Frank and Lizzie Popp, Philip and Laura Popp.[1] They all had children. Wherever we went, we had to take our children along. In the winter we had surprise parties, one or two a week. All would take lunch. If you hadn't been surprised, you could expect a party any night. The men would play cards, the women would take care of the children, gossip and make lunch. Those parties would sometimes last until 3:00 a.m. At the party, the next party was usually planned.

Our front room was probably the largest, so often a *Fastnacht* party dance was planned for our place. The tin heater was taken out leaving a mess of soot and ashes to be cleaned. The furniture that could be taken out was put outside or upstairs, and the dancing started. The bed was left in to sit on and lay the

---

[1] Philip Daniel Popp (December 3, 1888 - October 24, 1974) married his cousin, Eleanor (Laura) Wagner (February 15, 1892 - March 13, 1991) on October 29, 1911. She was the daughter of Frank Wagner and Margaret Gulman. They had five sons: Ewald, Frank, Alvin, Edgar and Morley.

children on. Sometimes the babies would wet our bed. One night it was so bad the bedding was soaked through. I had to get different bedding from upstairs. Before they left, they would set the stove up, which meant more ashes and wet snow. What a mess. It was usually so late we would just go to bed in all that mess and clean up the next day. Sometimes I got disgusted with the mess but I would get over it and they would come again.

Then I painted the floor and varnished it, and we bought a base burner heater. It was a big fancy stove with nice windows on three sides. It was a self feeder for hard coal which had to be bought in Langenburg. The red hot coals would glow through the nice windows. When we came home late at night the light of the stove was always on. That stove could not be lifted out and so there were no more dances in our room. But then we had a hay loft in the barn so they made Sunday night dances in our hay loft. That went on for some time until the boys were getting bigger.

A bunch of us used to have picnics at Hawkins Lake.[2] We would take a lunch or roast wieners there and make a fire to boil coffee. We would go in swimming. Yes, we made our own entertainment. Nearly every Sunday in the summer a group would play ball at our place. If I felt well enough, I would play too and so would Henry. Later those ball games would develop into picnics. Jack Moore[3] would bring a can of ice cream and confectionery. He would set up a booth and they would have races and games.

Often people would come to our place after Landestreu[4] Church services. I would bake about five pies and a big cake and

---

[2] Hawkins Lake is a shallow lake three miles east of MacNutt, on the border of Manitoba and Saskatchewan. The lake was named after Harry Hawkins, an American settler.

[3] Jack Moore married Henry Popp's niece, Mary Anne (Minnie) Chittick, daughter of William Chittick and Rosina Popp.

[4] The majority of settlers in Landestreu area had emigrated from the village of Katharinendorf in the Austrian province of Bukovina, about 100 kilometers southeast of Landestreu, Galicia. As land became scarce in the German villages of Galicia, some settlers began to look to buy land in the northwesterly part of Bukovina. Baron Alexander V. Wassilko made land available for settlement. The first settlement was called Alexanderdorf, named after the Baron; the second settlement was called Katharinendorf, named after his wife, Katherine. Immigrants came to Katharinendorf during the 1860's from many

cook a ham on Saturday. I was always prepared. Some people came without being asked and often that irked me, but I did not want to offend them so I said nothing. They would even stay for supper! Those picnics went on until we left the farm.

Other big occasions were mission festivals. We were close to the church so we would ask people to come to our place. The last year we were on the farm, there was Synod Convention in Landestreu. We had four pastors staying at our place for a week and two more came for meals. For the Sunday mission festival we had between 50 and 60 people for dinner. I don't know if they all got something to eat. I had baked twelve pies, cakes, a milk can full of cookies, cooked a ham, and had a twelve pound roast besides other things. It was all eaten up. We had fewer people for supper. We had a gallon of fried down sausage and fried pork. I could always find something to eat but I didn't even get time to think. I had Millie Aasen there for a month to help me that summer.

The fall of 1922 was a very wet fall. It rained a lot. Then we had a lot of snow and in spring we had a fast thaw. The fields were flooded, the roads were under water and grades were washed through.

One day that spring Henry was breaking in a new colt. He hitched it up with an older horse to go to town. I needed some things so I went along. I had a box of eggs in front in the buggy. Arnold was in school and I had Dick on my knees. When we got to one of those washouts, the colt didn't want to go over it. It backed up, then made a jump. With that egg box I couldn't brace myself,

---

Galician villages: Baginsberg, Landestreu, Josefsberg, Ugartsthal and Konstantinowka. Some of the first settlers in Katharinendorf were: Heinrich Lindenbach, Christian Adam, Alfred Geib, Wilhelm Gross, George Peter Mayer, Heinrich Popp (Henry's uncle), Johann Mack, Philipp Brandt, Georg Zorn, Georg Kitsch and Valentine Schappert. Many of the first settlers to the Landestreu area of Saskatchewan came from Katharinendorf, Bukovina. It is believed Joseph Wagner named their new district "Landestreu" in honour of the village in Galicia to which many traced their origins. Joseph Wagner (Henry Popp's grandfather), Andreas Lindenbach, Adam Kitsch, Philipp Hautz and Philipp Brandt were some of the first settlers to settle south of MacNutt and preserve the namesake of Landestreu. Source: *Alexanderdorf und Katharinendorf von 1863 - 1949*, Konrad Gross.

so I went over the dashboard, taking Dick with me. When Henry stopped the horses, I was under the buggy. Dick was under me and the wheel was on my hip. I yelled "Drive!" By the time he got the horses to go again, the wheel was sliding down my leg, skinning it. I managed to get up. We were all mud but went on to town. By then, Dr. Lee[5] was there. I went to see him. I was a few months pregnant then and was afraid. He examined me and I went home. My whole body ached for some time and my leg was very sore, but it got better.

That fall, when Henry was away threshing and I had to do all the chores, Arnold got sick. He had a few pimples, but just for a couple of days. Then he went back to school. Then Dick and I got a very high fever and just felt sick all over. But I still had to milk the cows and carry the milk by half pails to the well house. It was so hard to pour it in the separator bowl, but I did it as well as feed the calves, pigs and chickens. Then we would lie covered up on the sofa. That lasted for a week. When I later told Dr. Lee, he said it had been scarletina, a form of scarlet fever that was going around. We should have been quarantined. We were lucky nothing else developed from it.

In the fall of 1923, Henry had taken a load of grain to MacNutt and was bringing a load of coal home for Reverend Baumans. I knew he wouldn't be home early. Arnold was in school when there was a knock on the door. I opened it and there stood a strange, well-dressed man. He asked if Henry was home. I told him he was in town. Then he asked if I knew him. Well, I didn't. He couldn't understand why I didn't know him. Anyway, he wanted to see Henry so he went to unhitch his horse. I tried to think who he could be. He put his horse in the barn and came in, took his coat off and again asked if I knew him. Then he took his glasses off - now I should know him - but I didn't. So he told me his name - Charlie Eftoda. The name didn't mean anything to me. I was getting a little scared. Dick wasn't quite five years old then. So the fellow sat by the heater and fell asleep. Before that, I asked him why he thought I should know him. Well, in 1904 he had worked for my dad, and in 1919 he worked for my brothers. He seemed to

[5] Dr. John Howard Lee moved from Deloraine, Manitoba to MacNutt in 1920.

know our family. When Arnold came home from school he was so friendly with the boys. I got more scared, so I got dressed and went to carry in wood. He thought he should do that and patted my shoulder saying, "Mary, you are getting very fat." Well I was very pregnant with Ella at the time. Then I took the boys and we went to do the chores. We stayed in the barn until Henry came. We went to the road to tell him. He said he would take the coal to Reverend Bauman's, which was just a mile away. We were cold but we stayed in the barn. Then this fellow came in the barn to water and feed his flea-bitten horse. So we stood beside the barn. Finally we heard Henry coming, driving very fast. He came in the yard, jumped off the wagon, and asked us, "Where is he?" The fellow heard him come and came out saying, "Hello, Henry!" Henry said, "What do you mean by coming here, scaring the wife and kids?" He said "I'm sorry, I'm sorry." Henry told him to get the hell off our place or he would be sorry. He ran for his coat, hitched up his horse and left. After he was gone I thought I shouldn't have been so scared, though he had acted and talked funny. Sometime later we heard that he had just been released from the mental institution. Then I got scared all over again.

About that same time, earlier maybe, a man was at large who had shot a woman in the MacNutt area.[6] It was during threshing time when the men were all away. I didn't think of being scared until he was captured and the women told me how scared they were. He had been seen just about three miles from our place. I was glad he was captured.

I used to get quite scared at times. If I looked out the window on a bright moonlit night and something moved in the yard I would be so scared. But I would try not to show it so the children wouldn't get scared. We would go upstairs to go to bed then I'd open the window and look outside. I would take our .22 rifle

---

[6] William Marteniuk of Calder has recounted to Mary Mostaway that in 1917 Alex Schulman was shot by his wife and her alleged lover, Mr. Rutko. As Mr. Marteniuk recalled the story, Mr. Rutko loaded a gun and pointed it through the house window and allowed Mrs. Schulman to pull the trigger. Apparently Mr. Rutko escaped punishment but Mrs. Schulman was penalized in some way - either sentenced to prison or ordered into custody in a mental hospital. Three Schulman children were left without parents. Social Services took the children.

upstairs beside the bed. I had no bullets in it, as I don't think I would have shot it anyway -- but nobody knew there were no bullets in the rifle.

We had a little black dog, Queenie. She was Henry's dog when we got married. She was small, but she could put up quite a fight. There was a man who would come to our place a lot. One day he came in without knocking. Queenie was under the table and she went after him. First he thought it was fun and teased her. But then he got scared, stepping from one foot to the other. She was biting his legs. We had a time getting her away from him, but it served him right. He was such a big smart alec.

Then a stray dog came home from school with the boys. He was big, I guess part St. Bernard. He stayed around our place. I fed him and I liked that dog more than I liked any other dog we had. He slept in front of the door and he would not let anybody in during the night or even in the day time if he didn't like somebody. But he was a bum. He wanted to follow the boys to school everyday and wouldn't come home until noon. Then he would take our other dogs along too. We would tie him up, but as soon as he was loose he went to the school. We had him for about six months. Then one day he didn't come back - nor the next day. The boys found him dead. He had been poisoned. Guess somebody didn't like him, as there were people he didn't like. I don't remember what we called him.

On January 15, 1924 Ella was born. Henry got my mother and then had to get Dr. Lee. He gave me ether which put me to sleep. It was like not having a baby. But I worried all the time with the different things happening to me, that the baby wouldn't be right. When I came out of my sleep I wanted to see her. I was very happy she was all right and a little girl. Henry had taken the boys to Mother's place since we just had the living room with our bed in it. We had a big crib - both boys slept in it. Dick was not too happy about the baby, as I would have to wash the diapers then bake bread and pie. But when he saw her he thought we should keep her anyway.

That spring, Ascension Day morning, we were getting ready for church when Jack Popp came driving around the house yelling, "The barn is on fire!" As he came over the hill from his place, he could see the fire had just started in the hay loft. Our hired man came running downstairs saying "I didn't do it, I didn't do it." We ran out. There were no horses or cattle in the barn. The men got the harness and everything out. I went into the barn to try and chase the pigs out. They wouldn't go. The men came and threw them out. I picked up clucks with chicks under them, then went into the hen house trying to chase the chickens out. By then the roof was on fire and Arnold and Dick were standing there and screaming. In just a matter of minutes, the barn was gone. By then the neighbours were coming. It was very dry. We had to keep the fire from spreading since the car shed and separator shed were close to the barn. We drove the car away and tried to push the separator away. The sheds didn't burn. They carried water to keep the fire from spreading. It all went so quick. The fire was out so we went to church. The hired man stayed home to watch. If Jack hadn't seen that fire start and come to tell us, the car in the shed and the separator would have burned. And we were all in the house not knowing a fire had started. We had no window facing those buildings.

I had been in the lean-to of the barn maybe an hour before the fire started, feeding chickens and looking after the setting hens. One had left the nest, and I thought the little red mites were very bad in the chicken barn. So Henry was reading his big book to see what to do for mites. We didn't have to worry about those mites in the barn - they were burned. But the mites were still under the granary or wherever the chickens were.

There had been a dance in our hay loft the Sunday before the fire. There was hay in one corner into which all the dust was swept. A match must have been dropped, maybe that Sunday, or at any other time. We guessed that a mouse had gnawed on the match and started the fire.

Our fire was on Thursday, May 29, 1924, and on Friday night, MacNutt burned.[7] The fire started at the corner at the

---

[7] It was thought the fire began in the board sidewalk in front of P. W. Wagner's Hardware and Service Station (owned by Henry Popp's cousin). Nearby gas barrels soon caught fire and exploded, sending flames hundreds of feet high, and setting the entire block on fire. In less than two hours, the whole block of wooden buildings burned to the ground. Although many residents believed the

hardware store and went both ways. It took the whole block. We couldn't phone.[8] Somebody came and told Henry so we took the car and went to see. Jack and Minnie Moore lived at the hotel which had burned. They had a baby boy Ella's age. Well it was a sorry sight. It was such a big fire. During the night people couldn't save much. We went home and had dinner. Then Henry thought we should go back to MacNutt. I wanted to go but I hadn't given Ella a bath that morning, so I decided to stay home. Henry's dad was there, so he went along. He lit a cigarette before they left and threw the match in the wood box. After they were gone a while I sat with my back to the wood box, nursing the baby, when I heard something. I turned around and the whole wood box was on fire. There was a wash basin full of water nearby. I threw it on the fire and put it out. The boys had torn up a catalogue and had thrown that paper in the wood box. Paper was always thrown in the wood box to start the fire. The fire had given me a terrible scare and if I had gone along to MacNutt, our house would have burned down with everything in it. We would have never known what had happened or how. It was still the old house, but the only one we had.

After the barn had burned, we had a window put in the north wall facing the buildings. It was a hard job, as it was a log house, and a very messy job. But it was done. Then we again had to get lumber for a new barn. We had some insurance on the barn but not enough to build a new one. Henry went to Shevlin[9] to make arrangements to buy the rough lumber. We built a barn, just like the other one, on the same place. I don't remember who built it, maybe Christian Schaan - he had put the window in the north wall.

Then one day in the summer of 1924, just before noon, one of the boys from school brought Arnold home. He had gotten sick in school. He had vomitted and was in pain. I put him to bed thinking perhaps he had eaten something, or that he had asked one

---

fire was the work of an arsonist, no evidence supported this belief. Source: *Those Were the Days: A History of MacNutt, Calder, Dropmore and Surrounding Districts*

[8] Presumably the MacNutt telephone exchange had been burned or damaged.

[9] Shevlin is a small village on the Shell River east of Roblin, Manitoba.

of Jack's boys for snuff. He seemed better for a while. Then during the night he worsened, so in the morning we phoned Dr. Lee. I washed Arnold and changed his bed before the doctor came. He examined Arnold and told me not to give him any milk. I don't remember if he left any medicine. Arnold seemed better. The next day, Sunday, they were playing ball at our place. We had a lot of people over. Arnold got out of bed. He wanted his clothes to go to the ball game. We put him back to bed. Then Dr. and Mrs. Lee were out car riding and called in. He came in to see how Arnold was. He told us Arnold had to be operated on and to bring him in right away. He phoned Dr. McKenzie[10] at Langenburg to come and assist. We took Arnold in and he was operated on right away. It was a badly ruptured appendix. Lees asked us to stay at their place overnight. Dr. Lee was afraid Arnold might not pull through, but he did not tell us that until the next day. But Arnold woke up the next morning and was hungry, wanting to eat. So Henry and I went home.

When Ella wasn't quite a year old, she got very sick. We got Dr. Lee. He said she was near pneumonia. He gave me some medicine as well as therogene and alcohol to put on her chest instead of mustard plaster and some medicine. From our place, Dr. Lee went to Jack Wagner's[11] who had a little girl Ella's age. When he got there they thought she was better, but she was dying. Dr. Lee had a little girl about the same age. Mrs. Lee said when Dr. Lee got home he walked the floor nearly all night. He worried about those babies.

The well we had close by the house was dangerous. The well cover was ground level and it just held seepage water in the spring or if it rained a lot. So when we had our other well made, we filled that one in with stones and dirt. One sunny spring day I went out to see where Ella was. She was about two years old. She was by the old well playing with the cats. Snakes had come out of the well and lay there, coiled in the sun. I took a stick and killed

---

[10] Dr. MacKenzie practiced medicine in Churchbridge from 1920 - 1924. He then moved to Langenburg where he practiced for fifteen years before moving to Esterhazy.

[11] Jack Wagner lived in the Landestreu area. He married Minnie Schaan. Jack and Minnie moved to British Columbia.

some. They were very stiff and couldn't move fast. I could kill three or four at a time. More snakes came out every day until it got warm enough for them to all leave. This happened every spring. I'd have a stick there ready. After that I watched Ella until I got her to understand not to go there. I was not afraid of snakes as they had been all over the farm at home.

One time I was sitting, sewing with my shoes off. The dogs barked. I was going to see who was coming and nearly stepped on a little snake right in the living room. That scared me. I took the broom and swept it out. Our door was ground level. It was the Raleigh man who had come while I was sweeping the snake out. He told me their baby was in the cradle and didn't want to go to sleep, kept on fussing. When they lifted her up, there was a snake in the cradle. That scared me.

Snakes would get into the cellar too. The cellar was a hole in the ground and when the trap door was open there would be enough light to see some - there was no light or flashlight. If you saw something move it was a mouse or a snake.

The only time I was really scared of a snake was when I was small. My brother Rudy and I were going for the cows across the field and we saw this great big snake. We didn't have a stick so we picked up stones and threw them at it. It didn't go away, but just lay there and was mad. It lifted its head about six or eight inches, wagging its tongue; its eyes seemed red. We kept on throwing stones. All at once it came for us. We started running as fast as we could, not daring to look around if it came after us. That was the one time I was afraid of a snake.

After the barn had burned and we had that north window put in, the children could watch me while I was doing the chores in the yard. One morning when Ella was a little over two years old she was sitting on the window sill watching me. She was playing with Henry's big meerschaum pipe which his brother-in-law, Allan Barker, had brought for him. Henry would just smoke it in the house as it was too big to carry in his pocket. Ella was sucking this pipe for maybe a couple of hours by the time I came in. I was washing dishes when she started screaming. She had swallowed the saliva that had gathered in the pipe. She was crying and all at once seemed to be dying. She went cold and passed out. I started screaming. I rubbed her, took her outside and shook her. Then she started vomiting. After that she seemed better, but I couldn't rouse her. Then I phoned Dr. Lee. He was not home, so Mrs. Lee, who was a nurse, told me to let Ella go to sleep. But it didn't seem like sleep - she seemed to be dying. My mother was at my sister's, so I phoned her. She said that I shouldn't let her go to sleep and should keep her awake. So I got the kitchen stove going strong and got her warmed up. She was so cold. I kept rubbing and working at her until she started singing and acting like she was drunk. Then I pulled the rocking chair in the kitchen and wrapped her up warm. I put her in the chair and she slept and slept. What a scare.

When we went to Shevlin to buy lumber for the new barn, we brought home twenty young spruce trees and planted them on the west and south sides of the house. A year or two later, Henry went to Togo and brought another twenty bigger spruce trees. I planted eight lilac trees in front of the spruce trees. Behind that were five hundred caraganas and some maple trees we had planted. Did we carry water to keep them watered! The well was close to the trees but it took a lot of work to keep them watered. Most of them grew and we were bound to get a wind break for that new house we were going to build - and never got. The trees weren't much shelter yet when we left the farm.[12] Every time we would go to Joe Popp's, the first thing I would do was walk under those trees. They had become a big bush and I seemed to remember each tree separately. Some needed more care than others.

We worked hard to make the place a home. I would sit and plan that new house. Knowing no other life, I liked the farm even though it was hard work. In the spring Henry would get up at five o'clock to feed, clean, curry comb and brush the horses. Then he'd come in to call me and I'd be so sleepy. Maybe I'd had a poor

---

[12] When Henry and Mary left the farm in 1928, Henry's nephew, Joe Popp, began farming the land. He married Wilhelmina Andres, daughter of Rudolf Andres and Elisabeth Daum, on March 20, 1928. Joe and Minnie bought the half section from Henry and Mary Popp in 1945 for $6,000. Until then they lived in Henry and Mary's log house. They resided on the farm until 1964. Joe and Minnie built a new house in 1947. Joe and Minnie had six children: Loverna (Kentel), Voughn, Merceda (Love), Eunice (Baumung), Karen (Charlet) and Marilyn (Antony).

night because I had not been feeling well or the baby had been restless and I just wouldn't wake up. Henry would get up and go milk his cows and come into the house real angry at me because I was still in bed. Then I'd wake up in a hurry, go milk my cows, separate the milk, feed the calves and pigs, then have breakfast. Henry would get out to the field by seven o'clock. When the boys were going to school, I would fix their lunches and get them away to school. Then I would go out to look after the chickens, maybe to set clucks or look after young chicks. Since we had no slough close, we never had ducks or geese.

In spring there was meat to cure by putting it in brine then smoking it. We would have to make good smoke in the smoke house early in the morning before the flies were around. Then I would wash dishes. Later we had our separator in the well house, so we would take water out there to wash it and the cans, pails and strain cloth. Often there was a baby to bath, baby clothes to wash, floors to sweep. Sometimes I could catch a little rest while nursing and putting the baby to sleep. Then I'd go work in the garden while the baby was sleeping, and always check on the smoke in the smoke house so it didn't go out or get too hot. Then I'd start a fire to cook dinner. Sometimes it just didn't want to burn, especially if it had rained and the wood was damp. And if I couldn't get the fire to burn, I wouldn't get dinner ready in time. Again Henry would be angry at me. I tried so hard. I had to bake bread at least once or twice a week, churn butter, make cheese and do other baking.

Saturday was always a hard day - clean the house thoroughly, wash all the floors and bake about four or five pies and a big cake in case we got visitors on Sunday. If we didn't get visitors, we had baking for part of the week. I did a lot of sewing for us - dresses, shirts, underwear, pants for the boys, and a lot of mending. If we had a hired man, I would have his to do too.

If Henry went to town, I'd sometimes go along and spend the afternoon in town. Then I would have to work at night. Maybe I would get rhubarb ready for jam, darn, mend or sew. I could sew better at night by the coal oil lamp, with no children or meals to worry about. But when Henry heard the sewing machine going, he would yell down from upstairs and tell me to go to bed.

Work was seasonal. During the summer I would help with haying if there wasn’t a small baby. I liked raking. It wasn't easy but what work was? Henry would do the summerfallowing. I would do canning and tend the garden, weed and hoe potatoes. If work was not quite as pressing, we would go to sports days. Sundays were free, outside of milking and feeding the animals.

Then in fall, there was harvesting. When the grain was ready it had to be done in a hurry to beat the frost or bad weather. We often had a hired man then. He would stook; Henry would binder and change horses. He would eat quickly and I would get the other horses ready. Then at four o'clock I would again get the horses ready. He would bring the others home. I would water, unharness and feed them and he would binder as long as he could see. I would get the cows and milk and do all the chores. Then we would have a late supper.

Sometimes Henry would get more men to binder and stook and he would start getting the threshing machine ready. I would have to cook for them all. There was no freezer full of food. We had ham and bacon. Sometimes I had some canned sausage. By then there were young roosters. So after a long day I'd have to kill a couple of roosters and get them ready for the next day. Sometimes I would buy some fresh meat in town, but I had to use it right away as there was no way of keeping it for any length of time. Sometimes Henry would shoot some ducks, which I hated cleaning.

In the fall I'd also have the potatoes to dig and get down in the cellar, dill pickles and *kraut* to make. I'd have peas and beans to thresh out and dry, a lot of onions to braid in loops to hang up to dry, and jams to make. Maybe Sundays we would go picking cranberries or chokecherries and make jars of jams and jellies and wine. Sometimes I'd find wild pincherries or raspberries on the farm and do them. So there wasn't too much time to spare in the fall either.

Winter wasn't easier. If only our house hadn't been so very cold. It was a log house, plastered with clay which had come loose from the logs. There was unpainted siding on the outside, that the wind would just blow through. The kitchen floor was so cold, that when I scrubbed it the water would freeze on the floor. We would keep the fire on all night. On the coldest evenings we carried the bread box and the slop pail and other things into the living room so they wouldn't freeze. In the living room we just had a tin box heater. It would throw a lot of heat. All three of our babies were born in that house during the winter, Dick and Ella in the coldest part of January.[13]

During the winter I did a lot of crocheting, which I learned the first year I was married when Minnie Becker[14] stayed with us before Arnold was born. Mother could crochet but she wouldn't show us how. She said it was hard on the eyes. You could buy such nice laces. When I did learn, I did an awful lot of crocheting, knitting and embroidery, all by the coal oil lamp. It was hard on the eyes.

Making wine was a lot of work, but what wasn't? So if there were a lot of chokecherries, Henry would help pick and put them through the food chopper. Sometimes we'd make a 10-gallon cider keg full and have it sitting in the kitchen while it was still fermenting before we would put it in bottles or jugs. One of those times Ernie Hande[15] was at our place. He had been in the MacNutt hospital with an appendix operation. When he was discharged we got him to our place until his folks came to get him. He was lying on the couch in the living room and I was scrubbing the kitchen floor. When I moved the wine keg, the cork blew out and the wine went shooting up to the ceiling while I stood there yelling. Ernie got such a kick out of that - he would mention it for a long time after that whenever he saw me.

One time the wine wasn't sweet enough so I emptied it into a cream can and put more sugar in. On Sunday a bunch of people came and since the wine was in the cream can, they drank it with

---

[13] At this point in her memoirs, Mary Popp stops and notes on April 12, 1972, "I notice it's nearly two years since I wrote last, and I'm 75 years old now. I've just read over what I had written." Then Mary Popp resumes her story.

[14] Minnie Becker (June 7, 1901 - July 17, 1983) was Henry's niece. She married Rueben McRae on May 16, 1931.

[15] Ernest Alfred Hande (December 12, 1911 - May 15, 1977) was Henry Popp's nephew, son of Halvor Hande (1870 - 1936) and Elisabeth Popp (1887 - 1973). Ernie Hande married Vera Isabel Bennett on August 6, 1936. They had five sons: Barrie, Boyd, Clair, D'Arcy and Dirk.

the dipper. We had some very silly people around. I never liked wine, still don't.

At house parties in those early years there would be no alcohol to drink, but at the weddings there would be every kind of alcohol. Beer was just bought in kegs. The first few years I would make barley beer in big beer bottles. Because our well was so far away, I would catch rain water and make beer. But it was an awful lot of work and sometimes the beer bottles would blow the corks and the beer would run away. When we got a well close by, I didn't make any more.

When prohibition[16] came in, and you couldn't buy liquor, people started making home brew. Henry and Frank decided to each set a barrel of mash. They were going to borrow a still and make home brew. Someone must have reported them to the police. We got phone calls that the police were coming. The men weren't home. The police went to Frank's. Lizzie didn't want to let them in but they got in and Frank had to pay a fine. Henry came home, loaded our barrel of mash on the stoneboat, drove out to the field and dumped it.[17] The police did not come to our place but we never attempted to make brew again. Before that our brother-in-law told us how to make brew. He gave us some recipes - one with wheat, one with potatoes. He told us how to make it: put mash in a pot, set a cup in the mash to set a bowl on to catch the steam

---

[16] Prohibition refers to laws designed to prevent the drinking of alcoholic beverages. Generally such laws forbid the manufacture, sale, or transportation of alcohol. After World War I began support for prohibition increased in Canada. In 1918, the federal government passed a law that banned the manufacture and importation of all alcoholic beverages until a year after the war ended. By 1918, every province except Quebec had adopted a prohibition law. Between 1921 and 1948, all Canadian provinces repealed their prohibition laws.

[17] In the early 1930s, the RCMP were searching the Village of MacNutt for "moonshine". Two jugs of this brew were sitting in a cutter in front of Charlie Wolf's store. Instructions were given to a certain boy to remove the jugs and carry them across the street and place them on the steps of Haberstock's store. It worked just as they figured, the RCMP walked right past them, not even glancing down, believing the jugs to be full of coal oil. (Source: *Those Were the Days: The History of MacNutt, Calder, Dropmore and Surrounding Districts*)

dripping. Then cover the pot with a big bowl of ice or snow, and boil. We tried it. It worked, but the stuff was sour. We didn't know just how long to boil it, but it sounded so believable we had to try it.

The hotel served beer and sold it in small bottles and cases. We started getting kegs of beer, especially for the thresher parties. When they finished threshing, there would be a party with beer and whiskey, with mostly just the threshers, but sometimes the families too. A lot of the men weren't married. Often some would get too much to drink. After one party someone who slept in the caboose vomited all over the fur robe. We got it cleaned but I hated to touch it as long as we had it. I was glad when someone stole it from our car. Those parties weren't all fun.

There were always two or three months of threshing in the fall. Even in rainy weather there would be two or three men who had no place else to go, so they came to our place. They always had a very good gang of hard workers. There was a lot of teasing, playing tricks, and if anyone couldn't take it he would have to quit. While Henry and Fred Housman were partners, Fred's brother Ted would come out in the fall to run the separator and stay at our place. When Henry had to buy a new separator, then a new steam engine, he bought Housman's share and paid it out himself. I was always so worried about making more debts.

The threshing gang were all neighbours. For years after if we got together with any of them, they would talk about those days. They would remember this or that and maybe that's why so many of their stunts have stayed in my mind. Some men were young and married, but most were single boys with lots of energy. They knew how to work hard, but were fun-loving and full of tricks. Henry was just 24 years old and was their boss. He got along fine with them all.

It was often my job to feed the threshing gang. The first year, 1915, I was just 18 years old, pregnant, and had to prepare for this gang of 20 to 30 men. We had no portable granaries, just enough space to keep seed wheat, oats and barley for seed and feed, so the rest of the grain had to be hauled to MacNutt to the elevator, right from the machine. That meant eight to ten men hauling grain to MacNutt. So to prepare for a gang of men like that without fridges or freezers - we had to prepare ahead. Henry's sister Lena helped me that first fall. She was 17 years old. How I did it or how the food tasted I wouldn't know, but I guess I managed to cook and bake enough. I was used to cooking for extra men all the time. Then there was the milking to do and whatever other chores were to be done.

That first harvest Arnold wasn't born yet so I was pretty clumsy getting around. One time Lena had come over with the horse and buggy. After supper the men lifted her buggy on the wagon with the double box on. Rudolf Werschler[18] sat on the buggy playing a clarinet and Adam Andres[19] played the violin. The rest pushed the wagon around the house and sang while Uncle Joe Wagner walked ahead like a leader. It was all so very funny. We went out to watch but had to go in and wash dishes.

We would most often set the table at night for breakfast, as there would be meat and potatoes for breakfast too. We did not serve lunch in the forenoon. While we, the cooks, would eat, some of the men would "serve us" and bring everything from the kitchen onto the table. There was no use getting mad, it wouldn't help.

One night they pushed the caboose in front of the kitchen door with the wagon tongue stuck into the kitchen. While they were playing and singing we had to step over the tongue every time we went from the living room into the kitchen. One time they pushed the caboose right under our bedroom window and were so noisy. The boys were small. Dick woke up and got scared and cried. I told him it was just the threshers. He asked, "Will they bite?" A fellow who worked for us a lot got on the roof of the caboose and danced and sang. So I went down and got a pail of water and threw it on him. That quietened them down.

---

[18] Rudolf Werschler was born in Landestreu, Austria in 1892. He married Carolina Busch, daughter of Friedrich and Dorothea (Schappert) Busch of Beresina in November 1913. Rudolf and Carolina first lived in the Beresina area and later moved to a farm west of Shellmouth beside German Hill where they raised ten children: Albert, Paul, Martha, Walter, George, Benhart, Richard, Milton, Lorraine and Betty. In 1942 Rudolf and Carolina moved to Winnipeg.

[19] Adam Andres was the son of Adolph and Pauline Andres. He married his cousin, Annie Andres. They had two children.

We had hardly gone to sleep when someone was calling my name, "Mary, Mary, don't get scared." It was my Aunt, Lizzie Baumung. They had gone to MacNutt to take their baby to Dr. Lee. My Uncle Jack had gone partying with some men and had quite a bit to drink. He couldn't keep the car on the road, so she begged him to drive into our yard. She didn't know we had threshers and thought I was alone. That's why she kept calling me, telling me not to get scared. So Henry got up and coaxed Uncle Jack in to lie on the couch. Henry sat in the corner and slept. Aunt Lizzie and the baby, Gustie,[20] slept with me but by then the night was nearly over. I don't think I slept any more that night. I got up and made breakfast. The threshers were moving some place else that morning. I don't remember who my helper was that year, but she moved too, to help at the next place. We washed all the dishes before she left. Aunt Lizzie helped too. She had changed her baby and hung the diaper up to dry. Our tea towels were all re-used flour sacks. When the dishes were done, Aunt Lizzie looked for the diaper. It had been used to dry dishes. She looked at it and didn't say anything; I didn't say anything.

After they were all gone, I went to milk the cows and do the chores. Then I came in and washed all the dishes over again as I did not know which were dried with the diaper. Washing dishes then was different than now. There was no detergent. Soap would curdle in the hard well water, so we just used water. The dishes were hard to wash, as we served a lot of beef and beef gravy. So I had the dishpan sitting on the stove to keep the water real hot all the time and the teakettle of hot water to rinse them.

The last fall we were on the farm, Henry's nephew, Buddy Barker[21] from Regina stayed at our place. He was about 11 years old. His dad had sent him some fancy watch fobs.[22] He sold them

---

[20] Gustie Baumung was born September 28, 1916. She married Eitel Zorn (1915 - 1997), the son of Philip Zorn and Margaretha Wagner (Henry Popp's cousin), on June 17, 1941.

[21] Arthur Herbert Barker, born April 7, 1917, was the son of Alan Barker and Mary Popp. He married Wynne Cheeseman on March 9, 1940.

[22] A fob chain is a watch chain hanging free from a pocket and usually carrying a seal, key or other ornament.

to the men. Adam Nerbas[23] had bought one but lost it while he was loading stooks. When his load was full, he went looking for the fob and Frank Popp got on the load and started driving. Adam thought his horses were running away with the load of sheaves. He started running after them calling, "Whoa, Whoa." When he finally caught up with them, he got a hold of the back of the rack and climbed on. There sat Frank driving while the rest killed themselves laughing. Poor Adam got such a scare.

That night they got to Frank's place and when they were having supper, Frank told them a trick that had been played on a farmer. Some fellows had taken the bell off the cow and went in the grain field in the dark. The farmer heard the bell and tried to chase the cows out of the grain but couldn't find them.

After supper Frank had to go to MacNutt and when they saw him come back, a couple of them took the bell off the cow and went into the stook field. When Frank came home, the gate was open and he heard the cow bell in the stooks. He got out of the car and called the dogs and said, "Sic 'em" and started running, but they just ran farther with the bell. The dogs would catch up with the pranksters and greet them with their tails wagging. Finally Frank thought he'd go back and get a horse. When he got back, there was the cow with no bell on. Then he remembered he had told them the story at supper time. He got as much a kick out of it as the rest, but they said Adam Nerbas was rolling on the ground and laughing because Frank had pulled the runaway trick on him in the afternoon. That was the kind of things they would pull all the time - our threshing gang was never too tired for a trick.

Henry would seldom take part in their shenanigans. He had the responsibility to see that the machine kept running and often had repairs to do after supper. When the machine wasn't running, if the flues would leak, he would sleep for a while until the engine was cooled off. Then he'd maybe fix flues all night and get up steam again or there would maybe be a drive belt to replace, so he needed his rest. If they were close enough to home, he would walk

---

[23] Adam Nerbas was the son of Philip Nerbas. He married Lena Dietrich. They had three daughters: Agnes, Rosie and Arlene. After Lena's death he married Minnie Esslinger. They had one son, Maynard.

home after supper. But if they were farther away, he would sleep in the caboose. Then he wouldn't even bother washing his face. It would be all black for maybe a week. His clothes, overalls and jacket got so covered with grease they were stiff. Sometimes it got late in the fall. There would be snow and it would be very cold, maybe too cold to sleep in the caboose. Later when we had the little truck he would take it, but if they moved, he would have to do the moving. In the wet years they would get stuck with the engine or the separator, and it would take hours to get out.

These were all his worries. Perhaps the fun-loving gang helped make it easier for him. Also everybody wanted to thresh first and people would bug him. They did have an arrangement - thresh wheat first and go on, each with their turn. If somebody new came in, they had to wait until last.

I'd always get one of the neighbour girls to help me when we had the gang at our place. Lena Popp got married, so there were Lena Wagner, Lony Andres, Mary Popp (niece), Mary Kentel and Mary Andres, all young girls, but they knew how to work. If it was a rainy fall the threshing would drag on and on. It was hard, hard for everyone, especially the people who didn't get their grain in early. It was also hard for the gang, as most had fall work to do at home.

Our farm buildings were close to two main roads as we lived on the northeast corner of our quarter section. One road went north to MacNutt, the other west to Landestreu Church so many people came for help if they got stuck or ran out of gas or were lost. We had a two-gallon gas can in the well house for the pump engine. Many mornings the can would be empty. Once there was some money on the can to pay for the gas. When the fur robe was stolen out of our car, there was a quarter of a bottle of liquor left in the car shed.

One stormy January night before Dick was born, we were up late and some people came. Their horses were played out. They asked if they could come in. They were Ukrainian people - a man, two women and two children. So Henry went out to help put the horses in the barn and feed them, and I made something to eat for them. But then what should we do for sleeping arrangements? The upstairs was too cold, so we got blankets down and they got their blankets in. We made beds for them on the floor in the kitchen where we had a good fire going. I wasn't feeling well and thought maybe we would have the baby that night with all those people in our kitchen. Henry thought it would be all right - if he had to go for help, I wouldn't be alone. Perhaps those people were a little scared. They got up real early. Henry made them breakfast and they left. He had put a bowl of canned plums on the table. He liked plums. I had put them on the table after and he wouldn't eat any. I asked him why. He said when those people took some, they licked the spoon and put it back in the bowl. I was angry because he hadn't told me.

One time a car load of people from Neudorf got stuck close to our place. They were Jack Moore's parents and family, five of them. We had never seen them before. They came to the house. We had no tractor. The horses were all in the pasture. We had to get them, harness them and go pull the car out. It was noon so I made dinner for them all. They never forgot the kindness.

One Saturday, just before supper, a stranger came. His car had broken down and he asked if he could phone the garage at MacNutt. They could not come to fix the car until Monday. So again Henry took a team of horses and pulled the car into our yard and the man stayed. His name was McKay. He was a painter who had done some painting in MacNutt. He painted signs and names for business places. He was on his way to Minnedosa. So we left him home on the Saturday night with the children. We went to town to shop. On Sunday we visited. He was a very interesting man and had been around a lot. On Monday, he got his car fixed but he didn't leave until Tuesday morning. He asked what he owed us. Henry had seen that when he paid to fix his car, he didn't have much money left, so Henry said, “Nothing”. We were willing to help him and enjoyed having him. Well he thanked us so much.

Little did we know that years later he would repay our kindness. After our house fire in MacNutt, we had a brand new dresser which needed repair. The mirror was broken and the pane was damaged. We went to Yorkton to McKay's paint shop to ask if he could paint or varnish the dresser. This man thought he could make a good job of it - when he was in Scotland he had painted a carriage for the German Kaiser so he thought he could paint a dresser. All the time he and Henry were looking at each other. All at once they started shaking hands. He was Mr. McKay who had stayed at our farm. We were all glad to meet again. And he had been so poor then, driving an old truck, going around painting. By then he had a good business in Yorkton. He asked us what had happened to the dresser. We told him about the fire and that we had just bought that dresser. He said to bring it in. He asked if we needed any paints or varnish. We needed a lot. He gave it to us, as well as good brushes. He didn't charge too much for fixing the dresser. Then every time I'd go for paint, he wouldn't charge me for it.[24]

We were still living on the farm when Dr. Lee first came to MacNutt. One of his first patients was a little girl with a ruptured appendix. He told the parents the girl would die. He could operate but it was too late. He operated and the girl died.[25] The parents were bitter about it and so were other people. But most people were glad to have a doctor in town. Mrs. Lee was a nurse and he got another nurse, Miss Perrin.[26] That was the hospital Arnold was in and a lot of other patients.

---

[24] At this point in Mary Popp's memoirs she has several notations saying she had reread her writings in 1981, 1987, 1990 and 1992. In 1990 she wrote, "Things that were out of my mind came back and what happened during that time period. Maybe some good times, but also sorrow, sadness. I'm 93 years old now and getting very tired. Life is getting harder all the time." She concluded in 1992 at the age of 95, "I feel as if I am reliving it all."

[25] This child may have been Laura Nerbas, born June 24, 1915, daughter of Philip and Margaret (Kitsch) Nerbas. She died April 26, 1922. Or it may have been Athalie (Dolly) Schepp, daughter of George and Kathrina (Esslinger) Schepp who died February 24, 1925 at the age of eleven years.

[26] Miss Perrin came to MacNutt in 1922. She married Ted Allbright. She wrote of her first impression of MacNutt:

> On my arrival, the Doctor met me at the Station and told me a room was ready for me in the hotel where I would be staying for a short time. I gasped at him. "Me stay in the hotel! Why?" He then explained that he had not found a suitable house to live in, and that he and his family had the third floor of the hotel rented, and from here was carrying on his practice. At this point I was about ready to catch the next train for another four-day journey back to where I came from or anywhere else where conditions looked better than this.

Dr. and Mrs. Lee had one child when they came to MacNutt. Then they had two more and it became too hard for Mrs. Lee and the family. Then Dr. Lee got an idea. If they would sell 500 ten dollar shares, they could rent a house next door to his,[27] furnish it, and people who had shares would get free hospitalization. So they organized and formed a Hospital Board. Henry was Secretary-Treasurer and started selling shares and buying furnishings. All the women's groups made pillows, comforters or collected money and bought sheets and blankets. As soon as some rooms were furnished they started taking patients in, even before they had sold the 500 shares. Before that, all the women had their babies at home, but with a deal like that they all bought shares and went to the hospital. Other people got upset and would not buy shares. Some people who had been in the hospital wouldn't buy shares for another year. So with no money they had to close up. They had an auction and sold everything. It was Dr. Lee's dream which didn't work.

But MacNutt would try things. They decided to have a Chautauqua[28] come to MacNutt. They had to guarantee them so much. So they got about twenty men to each pledge or deposit 50 dollars and then they came. They had very good shows, afternoon and evening, for three days. We lived on the farm and would rush home to do the chores and rush back to town. The first year it went over big. I don't remember if it went for two or three years, but the last year it didn't go over and the people lost their money. We lost our 50 dollars. That finished it.

When MacNutt burned in May 1924, Schwartz's store burned. Years before, Mr. Schwartz Sr. had been a Jewish peddler. He would walk around from house to house with one leather case

---

(Source: *Those Were the Days: A History of MacNutt, Calder, Dropmore and Surrounding Districts*)

[27] The old Peppler home apparently was vacant in MacNutt. With a few changes and temporary partitions, it served as a hospital for four patients and, if an emergency arose, a fifth bed could be used.

[28] Chautauquas or Tent Chautauquas were travelling groups that operated in Canada and the United States from 1903 to 1930. They moved from town to town giving lectures, concerts, and recitals in a tent. Their popularity decreased with the development of radio and other forms of entertainment.

strapped to his back and he carried another. He was like a Woolworth store. He carried small things that the stores maybe didn't have, and he sold a lot. Later he had a small wagon with a cab built on, drawn by one horse. He would carry dress materials, like a little store. People bought a lot from him. When MacNutt was built, Schwartz built a store with living quarters. Now here I'm not too sure - maybe he bought that store. His son Isidor helped him run the store. The night of the fire, I don't know if somebody woke Isidor or if he awoke by himself. His store was already on fire. (By then the father was dead.) He did not have much time. So all he took was a trunk. He pulled it out the back door and pulled it as far as he thought it was safe, then he sat on it and watched his store burn.[29]

Another idea MacNutt had was when Jack Moore got his brother Johnny and four of his college classmates down from Neudorf to form a baseball team. They were a very good team and played at Russell, Yorkton and Melville. They got big money if they won. But they often lost. They borrowed 100 dollars from Henry and he never got it back. Henry played with them and I'd take the kids, pack a lunch and go along. I was upset about Henry losing that money. I worked hard and tried to save, made all our underwear and his, too, out of flour bags. And I kept on dreaming about that new house which never came.

Henry didn't seem to be able to say "No" to any salesmen, even when we were first married. One day he was working in the field and I took Arnold in the carriage, locked the door and went over to Lena's, Henry's sister, to see if she had got any new books to read. While I was gone, a fellow came around to enlarge pictures. He went to the field and Henry went home with him and crawled in the window. We didn't have any pictures. He had a postcard from when he had been to camp Sewel, dressed as a soldier,[30] and a post card of his sister Katie which he gave to the man. They cost 30 dollars each. When I came home and he told me I was so mad.

---

[29] Isidor Schwartz left MacNutt and no one followed his whereabouts.

[30] Henry was in the Langenburg District of the 16th Light Horse Cavalry, a training Reserve, ca. 1912.

Another time a fellow came around to sell trees and shrubbery. I told him we didn't need any, but Henry came home from the field and while he was watering the horses, the fellow sold him five hundred caraganas. Did we plant caraganas, and give a lot away!

Then another time a fellow came to sell books. I told him we didn't need any books, but he went to Henry who ordered a Rural Efficiency Guide for $7.50. It was a good book, but who had time to look in a six inch thick book when you wanted to do something?

I was afraid when somebody drove in the yard -- what would they sell to Henry? And they kept on coming. Once a couple of fellows came from Winnipeg. One's name was Doern. He claimed to be related to me. He even turned the wringer for me and stayed for dinner. They were selling shares for a clay tile factory in Winnipeg they were going to build. After they had it built, the tile would come out of that machine like sausage out of sausage machine. I was against it. I fought, scolded, cried, but Henry bought 500 dollars worth. The next year a fellow came out again. Henry bought another 100 dollars worth and drove him around for a couple of days to sell to others. A lot of others bought shares too. Well it never developed, and the 600 dollars was lost. Henry was also going to go to Winnipeg to a convention and see the factory. I was afraid they would sell him more. I was very mad. He didn't go. It would have just been more money.

Henry also bought a life insurance policy when we got married. We had so many debts so we dropped it. But later we bought a 20-year policy for 5,000 dollars on his life and 2,000 dollars for each of the children. While we were on the farm we could pay the high premiums, but later we ran into problems.

But we never did get a new house on the farm. The old house had unpainted siding. The clay had come off the logs when I papered the living room and it was so drafty I'd have to make holes in the paper to let the air out. There was no foundation so the floor was rotting in places. We had to put a new floor in one corner. The cellar had been boarded out with slabs, but they had rotted. The ceilings were unpainted. We had put some nice linoleum on the living room floor. But it broke up from the dampness of the floor, so we put it upstairs and painted and varnished the floors. With the papered walls, lace curtains on the windows, and at first when all our furniture was new, it was a nice homey room. We had made extra boards to extend our dining room table to set for twenty-four. We needed it that long for the threshers. We had bought a white oil cloth to cover it.

A curling rink was built in MacNutt. We had a farmer rink - Henry, Fred Busch, Ferdinand Popp and myself. We had a hired man to leave the children with and we went in two or three times a week, no matter how cold it was. They had ladies curling but I could not go in for that. Then when the bonspiel came, I sprained my ankle on the ice and had to stay home.

When Dick started school, Arnold was old enough to drive a horse. Henry had made them a narrow toboggan - five or six could sit in it. So the Wagner girls and Frank Popp's daughter, Katie,[31] would go along. In the summer they went with the buggy. One time Katie Popp, Rosie and Frieda Wagner and our two boys were coming home in the buggy. They had a quiet horse, but some dogs came running out of the bush and scared her. She ran into the fence and threw all the kids against the fence. The harness broke and the horse got away, but not far. They were a quarter mile from home. The first to come home was Dick, moaning and crying. His arm was hurt and swollen. Then the girls came. Katie's clothes were all torn and she had body cuts. The Wagner girls had some cuts. I didn't know what to do. Arnold came later. He had a sprained ankle. He took a stick to walk and caught the horse, got on it and rode home. He put the horse in the barn and came limping in with a stick. Henry was in town and so were Frank and Lizzie Popp. I phoned the doctor and he came out. Meanwhile, some neighbour boys saw the buggy and came in to see what happened. By then I had put blankets on the floor. I got the neighbour boys to get a pail of cold water. I used old sheets to put wet cold cloths on them all. I had to wash the blood off Katie and get her torn clothes off. I had a hospital shirt from when the kids were sick which I put on her. She had deep gashes on her body.

---

[31] Katherine Popp, born May 26, 1918, married Norman McKinnon on July 24, 1941.

When the doctor came I had a row of kids lying on the floor on blankets moaning with wet cloths on them all. He thought that was all right. He looked at them all. I think we had to take the boys in for X-rays the next day. He did a little bandaging and left. Then Frank and Lizzie came. They had heard the news and came tearing home so worked up. After the doctor left, the kids quit moaning. Frank took the girls home. It had given me a terrible shock.

Farm life was very hard work at times, quite dangerous at times, sometimes lonesome too - but also very interesting. In the spring there was young life, calves, pigs, colts, chicks, often pups and kittens. There were green grass, birds, frogs and also things that were not so nice - flies, mosquitoes and hard work. But it seemed like more freedom than town life.

My brother Rudy had bought a store in Shellmouth[32] with living quarters upstairs. Mother and Helen moved upstairs. Jake and Fantie[33] got married on December 23, 1925 and moved to the farm home place for a while. Later they joined Rudy in the store in Shellmouth. Eventually Jake and Fantie moved to Winnipeg and brother George married and lived on the farm.[34] Adolph went to Concordia College in Edmonton. Later he, too, moved to Winnipeg. In 1928 he moved to California. Mother bought a house in Winnipeg and she and Helen moved there.

As long as Mother was on the farm, we would still all go home to the farm for Christmas. We never went to Shellmouth for Christmas - Mother either came to our place or Katie's. We were

---

[32] The Lowenberger brothers bought the store from Garnett and Gerrard. They eventually sold it to Mr. Hamilton. Their store was one of two stores. The other store was operated by George Busch whose family also came from Landestreu, Austria.

[33] Stephana Bell's father, Martin Bell, came from Prince Edward Island to Shellmouth in 1904. In 1905, he returned to Prince Edward Island and came back to Shellmouth with his wife, Melvina, and their nearly three year old daughter, Stephana, nicknamed Fantie. She and Jake Lowenberger were married in the Presbyterian church in Shellmouth which in 1925 had just amalgamated with the Methodist Church to form the United Church. In 1927, Jake and Fantie moved to Winnipeg. They had two daughters, Sybil and Melva, and one son, Robert.

[34] George and his wife Adelheid lived on the Lowenberger farm until 1945. They lived in the log house built by George's father in 1902.

getting to be too many and often wondered how Mother could have us all, prepare meals and stand all that noise, we and all our children.

Reverend Predoehls left Landestreu and Reverend Baumans came. He baptized Ella. They had a car and came to our place a lot, often unexpected. They would catch me bare foot and in dirty clothes. I'd be so embarrassed but I got used to it. They never stayed too long. Then Reverend Millers came. They would come unexpected a lot too.

LEAVING THE FARM

My brother Rudy started talking to Henry about going into the garage business in MacNutt. I was very much against it but that didn't seem to matter. Rudy sold the store in Shellmouth and in 1928 they bought the garage in MacNutt. I was told I could stay on the farm, but we had a sale and sold everything except the land, including the threshing machine which Henry never got the money for. Just when we were getting ahead we put all our money into the business. The only place we could find to live in was a building that had been built for a hotel. Mr. Mensch owned it. I guess Haymans had lived in it before. It had small rooms and a very steep stairway outside where everything had to be carried up and down. We kept our kitchen stove. We had a cupboard made for dishes. The house was not laid out for living quarters, but it was just across from the garage.

The first Sunday in the fall of 1928, after we had moved, we went back to Landestreu church. We had Rudy's new coupe. Our car was a fairly new Chevrolet, but it wasn't right for a Ford dealer to drive a Chevrolet. We went to Fred Kitsch's for dinner and on the way home the roads were very icy. Henry braked. He wasn't used to a four-wheel brake. The car flipped upside down. I must have been knocked out for a minute. When Henry asked if I could open my door I reached down - I didn't know the car was upside down. We had Ella along. I saw a hole in the windshield and got Ella out. When she got out she stood and screamed and screamed. When she was out and I could turn a little, I saw Henry's face was covered in blood. He thought he was pinned under the steering wheel, but when he tried, it moved. It was broken off. He still thought he was holding the car up with his feet, but he wasn't. With the car being upside down, the cushions and things were on us. I thought his window was open but the door was broken off. So he got out, then I got out. We were all turned around then a car came and took us to MacNutt to Dr. Lee. Henry had a cut across his nose and other small cuts. I had a bump on my head and my ribs were very sore. We got taped up. Ella was just terribly scared. Somebody came and took us to our place after Mrs. Lee made us hot tea. And we had to climb up those steep stairs. I didn't go down for a few days. Our bodies were sore all over.

That was the beginning of our town life. It was also the beginning of the Depression years. The men were busy. Henry went out selling cars, they handled some other machinery and twine. People bought cars and every thing, but on credit.

I don't remember just how long we lived upstairs, but I think less than a year. Then we got a house that used to be Kerr's house. Again Mr. Mensch owned it and we rented it. It was old but nice. Haymans had lived in there before too. It had a bedroom downstairs with a small clothes closet, a living room, dining room, and small kitchen. It had a small cistern, an upstairs with no closets, and a small cellar. But what I liked most was a well in the yard, with a squeaky pump. Everybody got water from that well, so sometimes I was not too happy about it. Also there was a garden. Oh, and a big verandah, glassed in, the length of the house. It was maybe the best house we had lived in. But it was cold. The pail under the sink froze hard during the night, but we were used to that. We got a nice heater, furnace style. The heat came out the top. It was nice but there was no place to warm your feet when they were cold. The heater burned coal.

I missed the farm. Our next door neighbour, Mrs. Selkirk, was very kind or tried to be. Next to them lived Dr. Lee. It was close to the stores and to everything. We did have fun there too. We would have surprise parties, dinner parties, lake parties. We had a lot of fun. But I felt an undercurrent of unhappiness all the time. The children were hard to keep track of. I'd sit at home and wait until it got dark then went out looking for them. Henry was away all the time. Sometimes he would come home late when I was asleep and get up and leave early, before I was awake. We bought some lots. And again I was planning a house, not the kind I planned before, but still a three-bedroom house. It was on the north side of town, not too far from the garage. But I had a feeling business wasn't so good. My brother, Rudy, stayed at our place. Then he got married to Tug Keay[1] and they moved into a house. We made them a chivree. Tug did the books at the garage..

One Saturday evening I had told Arnold to come home to stay with Ella while I went to shop. He didn't come. She was asleep so I thought I would go quickly and come back. There was a group of people standing around and Arnold came from them and told me Dick had crushed his foot. I asked where he was. Well they had taken him to Yorkton. I could feel the blood drain from my face. I thought I'd faint. My voice got rough. I couldn't talk. There had been a ball game. After the ball game some boys sat on the back of somebody's car to ride to town and Bill Miller backed into the car and crushed Dick's foot. They took Dick to the garage and Henry put him in a car. Margaret Schaan went along and took him to Calder. A quack doctor called Dr. Berry[2] looked at him

---

[1] Beatrice Keay was the daughter of Richard and Margaret (Longheed) Keay who farmed on Section 19-23-28 in the Rochedale District near Dropmore, Manitoba. Mr. Keay was born in England; Mrs. Keay in Ontario. Their daughter, Beatrice, or Tug, married Rudy Lowenberger on December 21, 1928.

[2] The following notation appears in *Those Were the Days: A History of MacNutt, Calder, Dropmore and Surrounding Districts*:

> On October 11, 1911, Mr. John Berry, an English immigrant, was appointed Sanitary Inspector in Calder for a salary of $10.00 a year. Mr. Berry, who was frequently called Dr. Berry, was noted for treating

there. He gave Dick some aspirins and wrapped a dirty old sweater around Dick before they took him to Yorkton. It was about two o'clock when Henry came home. He had left Dick in the Yorkton Hospital. I walked the floor. I was so worried and hurt that they would do this to me, rushing Dick away without telling me. I imagined the worst. We went to Yorkton the next day. The foot wasn't badly crushed - they thought it would be all right. They put it in a cast. We had crutches made for him when he came home. His foot got all right again. I thought I'd never heal from the shock.

On the Labour Day weekend some time in the early 1930s there was an inter-provincial picnic in the Assiniboine Valley when the Saskatchewan and Manitoba highways were joined. Everybody was to bring their lunch and they had barbecued buffalo and beef. They held an inter-provincial baseball game and other entertainment. There were lots of dignitaries from all over. When Premier Bracken from Manitoba was speaking, Joe Pirt, a big Irishman RCMP constable shot and killed Mrs. J. Light, an American citizen. We were close enough to hear the commotion and the shot, but the crowd had gathered around so we couldn't see. Both the woman and the policeman were rushed away in cars. It put a damper on the festivities. I don't even remember if we got any of the buffalo meat. Everything was hushed up. We didn't hear what happened to the policeman and nothing came out in the newspapers.[3]

---

minor ailments of many of the settlers as he had some medical training in England. "Dr." Berry was actually an engineer who built steam engines in a factory before emigrating to Canada from England in about 1910.

[3] R.C.M.P. records relate that Joseph Pirt was born at Seaham Harbour, England. Prior to emigrating to Canada in 1928 he worked as a miner and was a member of the Borough of Hartlepool Constabulary. Pirt was engaged in the R.C.M.P. and posted to general duties at the Yorkton Detachment. On September 1, 1930 he was assigned to carry out policing duties at an Inter-provincial picnic held in the Assiniboine Valley near Roblin, Manitoba. While details relating to the event are missing from the R.C.M.P. records, it is known that he became intoxicated and subsequently shot and killed Mrs. E. J. Light. Information respecting criminal charges or any disposition is also missing from the R.C.M.P. file.

March 1, 1931 was a very cold, windy day. The snow was half gone. There were ponds of water frozen. I couldn't get the fire to burn in the heater. Snow had drifted into the shed and wet the coal so it didn't want to burn. Everyone had been home for dinner and Henry was going to Roblin to curl. I told him the fire didn't want to burn. He said to shake it down and he left. I shook it down and sat in the kitchen looking at the paper. Then I heard something pop. It was just three steps to look into the living room. The ceiling was on fire. I ran through the room to the phone, rang, but didn't wait to answer. I dropped the receiver and ran out to call but that day nobody was at the well. By then I couldn't get back into the living room. I threw things out of the verandah. Then I broke our bedroom window and tried to reach for my coat. I was getting very cold. By then some men came and pulled me away. They put an old sweater on me but my head was cold so Mrs. Schneider took my head under her arm. She was a big woman. She held me.

Then Mrs. Selkirk came and got me but when I looked out their window and saw how they threw our stuff out, I went back. I had ironed all morning. The clothes were on the dinning room table. They were all thrown in the snow. It didn't matter because they were pouring water all over the inside of the house. They had trouble getting the fire out behind the piano. Everything was soaked. They asked me how it started. I didn't know. I was drying clothes. I had the clothes horse[4] around the stove but the sides of the stove didn't get hot and there was no smoke in the room. The ceiling and walls had sponged paint on which burned like gas. There was black smoke coming out of the chimney so they figured the gassy coal exploded and blew the pipes apart. One

---

Superintendent Spalding, as cited in the Commissioner's Report. described that Pirt while under the influence of liquor, shot and killed Mrs. Light in "an absolutely purposeless crime, committed without provocation". Pirt, who had been a member of the Force for less than a year, and had spent about five months at Yorkton, presented excellent testimonials and until the occasion on which he committed his crime, seemed an efficient policeman and was well thought of by the public.

[4] A clothes horse is a folding wooden frame upon which clothes are placed to dry.

lay on the floor, the other leaned against the wall. They thought the ceiling caught fire first. Then I wondered if our insurance was paid. Some people asked me. I just didn't know until Henry came home. Somebody phoned Roblin so he could come home right away. I went to Rudy Zorns[5] until he came home. The children were in school. They said Arnold looked out the window and started running. He got in the house to put the hose behind the piano to put the fire out.

We couldn't touch anything until the fire inspector came nearly three weeks later. We stayed at the hotel at Moore's and told the children if anybody asked them to stay at their place, to go.

The fire damage wasn't as bad as it looked. It took a lot of rubbing and washing, but the dishes were all right and most of our clothes could be cleaned. My good coat and sweater were burned, but the clothes closet door was closed. The clothes were wet, smoky, and very stinky and brown. The piano was open so the keys were burned off and the sound boards and posts were burned. They shot the hose upstairs too and soaked everything there.

It would take too long to fix the house so again we were looking for a place to live. There were rooms above the bank which had been closed so we moved there. I liked it there, but again there were such steep outside stairs. But it was across from the garage and I could watch what was going on over there. There was a cistern and Lindenbachs across the street had a well for drinking water. I made a garden on the lots we had bought. I had the bushes pulled out and I worked so hard pulling roots and carrying sods off.

We didn't get any new furniture when we moved. I scraped the burned chipped paint off the chairs and dresser, desk and table. The wicker chairs we got new in the other house were burned.

I still wondered if we would build a new house and buy new furniture, but the business was going from bad to worse. We got full insurance for the fire, 800 dollars. One day Henry came home. They needed money. He wanted the insurance money so I gave him 400 dollars. Not long after, he asked me to sign a mortgage of

---

[5] Rudy Zorn married Pauline Propp from Rhein. Rudy was a brother to Adam, John, Henry and Philip.

the farm. I cried and wouldn't sign. Then Rudy came over and got after me. So I signed the mortgage against the farm.

Another misfortune happened to us while we were still in MacNutt. We were going to Yorkton in a new Ford car. Mr. and Mrs. Grassie, Mr. Kerr, Rudy Zorn and Adolf Kendel came along. We had a load. There was another car on the road just like ours, a new Ford that Henry had sold to Schulman. We passed him once. It was a Ukrainian holiday and they were stopping along the way. Then they came behind us blowing their horn. We crossed a bridge then Henry slowed and pulled to the side. They passed us and pulled in too soon, hitting our car. Our car nose dived on a steep grade and kept on rolling. You can think while you roll, I'm still alive, and again, I'm still alive. And the other car went on, never even stopped. Mr. Grassie was thrown through the window. The rest of us stayed in until the car stopped rolling. There were some people on the road taking horses to Yorkton. They saw it all happen and came walking back to see if there was anybody alive in the car. And there we all came crawling out of that wreck. Nobody was hurt too badly. Rudy Zorn had a cut on his forehead. Mrs. Grassie had a sprained elbow. My legs had abrasions, and I thought my face was skinned but Mr. Kerr spit on his handkerchief and wiped my face. It was just dirt. The police car came and took some of us to the hospital to get bandaged. The men got a ride in and went looking for the car that hit us. It had a Lowenberger-Popp tire cover on. They found him later. The police said Henry should sue and he did which didn't help. The driver had no money and hadn't paid for the car. They had to repossess the car and we had to pay the lawyer and have our car fixed. I think it cost 400 dollars to have it fixed. We kept that car but I never liked it because we had such a bad accident with it.

OUR CALDER SOJOURN

One day in July 1932 Henry came home and said we were moving to Calder to buy grain at the Pool elevator. We went to Calder to look at houses. We wanted a three-bedroom house so we took a big house which had been built as a doctor's house. We used the small examining room for Ella's bedroom. Our bedroom was downstairs. The house had a furnace which didn't work too well and a cistern which leaked, a big basement and a verandah. There was a garden. It was a nice place but big.

They gave us a farewell party from MacNutt with nice speeches and a clock which we still have.

Henry was about forty years old when we moved to Calder, and he started buying grain for the Pool. I was 34 years old. I did not want to join the Willing Workers, but joined the Bridge Club, helped with other activities and curled. Henry belonged to the Board of Trade and curled. The boys belonged to the Young People and Ella to the Smiles.

After we had moved, I still had 400 dollars. So I went to Winnipeg to buy furniture on sale. I did an awful lot of looking. My brother took me to a wholesale house where I bought our dining room suite and two wicker chairs. I had our old table redone. We still used our old sofa. We bought two linoleum rugs for the living and dining rooms and 17 pair of curtains at Eaton's sale for all the windows. I thought I had done well. We cleaned our brass bed. We had our dresser redone at McKays in Yorkton and we ordered a mirror for it.

So we got settled in Calder. Henry was getting 100 dollars a month which I thought was very good. It would have been fine only MacNutt's debts followed us. Rudy left the garage too and went into the Case business in Yorkton so they tried to collect from us. Mr. Burkhardt owned one of the garage buildings or had an interest in it. He wrote letters. Henry sent him 25 dollars a month. He tried to give the buildings back to him but he wanted money. Then the Traders Finance Company started repossessing cars. The cars weren't worth what was against them so the difference was charged against us. Then there was the loan at the bank. Henry and Rudy gave the bank Promissory Notes from customers who owed money to the garage, but the bank couldn't collect on them either. Henry had borrowed 500 dollars on his Life Insurance Policy and they wrote to pay some on it or it would be lost.

Moving to Calder at the time we did, wasn't so good.[1] There was a quarrel on in the area. It seemed the town folk were against the country folk. But even the town was divided. We tried very hard not to take sides as the town had no grain to sell. But we lived in town and were asked out a lot. I belonged to the bridge club. When they had school elections I tried to hide so they wouldn't find me and get me to vote. We weren't interested and did not want to get involved. Later the feud died down.

They had such different customs in Calder. They put the chicken on the table, whole, not cut up, or jugs of cider on the table with just one glass to drink from.

---

[1] Whereas Germans had arrived in the Langenburg and MacNutt areas as early as 1889 the influx of Ukrainians into the Calder area did not start until 1897. Many Germans, however, spoke Ukrainian since they had emigrated from Galicia where Ukrainian and Polish were the prevalent languages. The site for Calder was surveyed in 1908. In 1911 Calder was incorporated as a village. The Village was a composite of various ethnic origins. The rural community, however, was mainly Ukrainian.

We learned how to behave at their weddings. They would serenade you when you got there. We didn't know we were to put money in their instruments. We knew some of the Calder people before we moved there and got to know the others. There were still differences. The Ukrainian people would have their own parties, dances, etc. and the town, a mixture of origins, would have theirs. They were all very active people.

The Bill Davis family came to Calder the same fall we did. He was a school principal. They had a daughter, Doris, who was Ella's age. The girls became close friends. They would fight too but were together all the time, and slept at each other's house.

In the summer we would go to MacNutt or Zorra church but in the winter we would sometimes go to the United Church in Calder [2] or one of our Lutheran ministers would come.

The second year Henry got a raise to 125 dollars a month. That helped some but there were still all those debts against us that worried me a lot.

There was old Mrs. Hartz (Höfer) who had moved to Calder a little sooner than we. She was my dad's aunt.[3] I went to see her. She was very independent and touchy. She wasn't well so Rose Schrader[4] and I sort of looked after her. One Christmas we made a little tree and took it over to her and sang Christmas carols. She did not appreciate it. In fact, she looked annoyed and threw the tree out the day after Christmas. So we didn't know how to please her. Then there was Mrs. Dill across the road from us who told me she was so glad when we moved there and that we would become such good friends but I wanted to be careful.

Calder had an active Willing Workers club and they were always planning something. They had no movie theatre but it was just 35 miles to Yorkton if people could afford to go. The Willing Workers got the hall free and had a lot of bridge drives and socials, some very good ones. The last year we were there the crops were

---

[2] The Calder United Church Mission was built in 1931. Later a church was built.

[3] Maria Elisabeth Hartz (October 1, 1855 - April 22, 1939).

[4] Rose (Zorn) Schrader was a daughter of Henry Zorn and Katharine Schappert. Rose married Chris Schrader. They had the telephone exchange, post office and store in Calder.

rusted and Henry's salary was cut to 70 dollars per month. We couldn't even use our gas lamps. We had to be very saving.

For Henry's birthday, I made a surprise party. I wrote little invitations. The men were to dress as women and the women to dress as men. I had fun planning it but when it came closer I began to worry about it, but they were all very good sports and came. Francis Rombough[5] had a red wig and a big bust. Well they were all so good. Henry got the surprise of his life when Ferd Popp came in dressed as a woman. Henry did not know him. We played silly games and had baked beans, brown bread and ginger bread for lunch. That party went over well. Then the teachers had a party at our house in the form of an amateur hour and everybody planned to have a different party. There were no alcoholic drinks. It showed that it didn't take a lot of money to have a party.

One time I was writing a letter to mother and crying. I got up and got a handkerchief to blow my nose and was going to put the handkerchief behind me on the chair while I was sitting down. The third finger on my left hand got caught in the rungs, got bent back and broke. By the time I got into the living room to show Henry, it was all swollen. I had set a sponge for bread so I had to knead the dough next morning. My finger was very sore. The doctor in MacNutt came to Calder one day a week. The next day I went to see him. He asked me what had happened. I told him I sat on my finger and broke it. He wanted me to show him how. He saw patients in the hotel parlor. I was sitting on the piano stool so I couldn't show him and there wasn't that kind of a chair in there, but I explained what happened. He put a splint on, but so loose, it would always slip off. I would take it off, wash the dishes or whatever I did then put it on again. Did I ever get teased about that finger. Since the splint was so loose the finger grew a little crooked.

Dick got confirmed while we were in Calder. The first year he had some confirmation instruction in MacNutt from Reverend Leininger. Then that summer Dick stayed at my brother George's

---

[5] Francis Rombough was a teacher in Calder from 1937 - 1939. He was the son of Jack and Jessie Rombough who owned the Kalass and Olson store in Langenburg.

on the farm. He got more instruction and was confirmed by Reverend Fuhr at Hoffenthal. Arnold had stayed at MacNutt the first fall we moved to Calder. He trucked grain but then came to Calder and went back to school.

While we were in Calder I had to have a mastoid[6] operation. I had been to see Dr. Houston.[7] He told me I should have a nose operation which I had been told many years before in Winnipeg but thought we couldn't afford it. That year we went to Madge Lake for holidays. The first day there I went down the slide and got water in my nose. I blew my nose and got a terrible earache. There was no doctor there. I used hot salt and aspirins but was sick for the week. On the way home it got worse so we went to Yorkton the next day. I had to go to the hospital right away. I had Dr. Whittaker. It was a terribly painful mastoid operation and I had to have nearly half my new permanent shaved off. I thought I could do my own work when I got home but I couldn't. Hilda Mack[8] came for a couple of weeks to help me.

Then in the spring of 1934 Arnold got in trouble so he went to Winnipeg. My brother Jake got him a job at City Dray and later Arnold got married.[9] There was so much trouble. He was just eighteen years old and all that to me was more painful than the mastoid and that pain didn't seem to want to go away.

While we lived at Calder, Dick decided he would go to Edmonton[10] to study for a Lutheran minister. It was difficult to get him all the things he needed but he went in the fall of 1935. That year on September 28th, my mother died in Winnipeg of tuberculosis at the age of 68. Reverend Wiegner came along from Winnipeg to bury her at Hoffenthal.

---

[6] The mastoid is the projection of the temporal bone behind the ear.

[7] Dr. Clarence Houston was a doctor in Yorkton. His wife was also a doctor.

[8] Hilda Mack, born July 23, 1916, was the daughter of Fred and Kate Mack. Hilda married Lawrence Jira on March 6, 1942.

[9] Arnold Popp married Meta Kendel on May 28, 1935. Meta was born October 22, 1914, the daughter of John and Margaret (Wagner) Kendel. Meta's mother was a first cousin of Henry Popp, making Arnold and Meta second cousins.

[10] Dick went to Concordia College.

Also while we were in Calder, Ella got confirmed. She took a confirmation correspondence course and Reverend Lucht[11] came up to instruct her and Alice Zorn. They were confirmed with the class in MacNutt in English.

Drinking was a problem. Henry liked drinking. The first years when he drank too much he would be loud and funny. Only I didn't see it as funny. One Easter while we were still on the farm we and Frank Popps had been asked to Fred and Maggie Kendel's for Easter dinner. There was a lot of snow yet. We each went in our own cutters, starting out gaily and happily. Maggie Kendel had a lovely dinner. Then all afternoon the three men were drinking home brew and getting drunk, telling each other how much they liked each other. Henry was buying a purebred from Fred, which wasn't born yet. As we were leaving for home Fred liked Henry so much he got their hired man to hitch up our horses. Frank had to hitch up his own team.

We started for home. Once on the road the horses went by themselves. We were over half way home when Henry started vomiting. He was real sick. When we got home he unhitched the horses, went into the house and laid down on the sofa, with his coat and overshoes still on. The boys were asleep. I carried them into the house. Then I went and put the horses in the barn. When I went in I put the boys to bed and tried to wake Henry but I couldn't. So I changed my clothes, lit the lantern and went out, unharnessed the horses and fed all the stock. By then they were very hungry. We had fresh cows so I got the pails and milked, separated the milk, fed the calves and pigs. By then it was pretty late. So again I tried to wake Henry to go to bed but by then he got real angry. So I left him and went to bed and cried myself to sleep. Before then I didn't have time to cry.

Sometime during the night he awoke, undressed and went to bed. In the morning he acted as if nothing had happened. He did the chores. It was Easter Monday, we got dressed and went to church.

There was another time while we were still on the farm, the fall before Ella was born. The threshing was all finished. It had

---

[11] Reverend Lucht came to MacNutt in 1933 and left in 1936.

rained so Henry went to town. I always wanted a little bench to sit on, to peel potatoes, or to shell peas or do work like that. So I found a board and built a little bench. I couldn't find the right kind of lumber and nails I needed but I built it anyway. I was quite proud of it. I waited for Henry to come home. When it got late, I went for the cows. When I came back and went into the house, the boys had peeled the window frames and the sill with their new knives. (We had been to Yorkton and bought the boys each a little knife.) I felt so bad. But it was getting dark so I milked the cows and fed the pigs and calves. I made supper for the boys and put them to bed and waited for Henry. He came home very late, very drunk. He sat on my new bench and squashed it flat. His face was bloody and swollen and he started telling me what had happened.

They were drinking and Henry said he could shoot a certain dog through the tail. Somebody got a rifle and Henry shot and missed - he shot the dog dead. It happened to be Faustman's[12] dog. They had a fight and Faustman bit Henry on the face. I had cried some before but when he told me that, I went outside and lay in the grass and cried out loud until I got cold. Then I slept on the sofa. Next morning Henry was very sorry and promised never to drink again, which he remembered for about two months.

There were other times but these two stand out in my mind. In MacNutt on certain occasions he would get drunk, but not too often. When we moved to Calder there was a lot of home brew around. They would bring it in to him. When he got drunk from home brew he would get angry and very nasty.

At times Henry would be very busy. Often in the fall I'd fix his dinner and take it over to the elevator and he would always go back after supper. Whenever it got late I would worry - was he working or drinking? Sometimes it was both.

Jack Moore, who had moved to Yorkton, came down to Calder and opened a beer parlor. Sometimes I really disliked Jack. He liked to get people drunk and after that Faustman episode he phoned me next day to see how I was, if I was still living. I told him I wished I wasn't and hung up. So the same things were happening at Calder. Not only would Henry came home late and

---

[12] Adolf Faustman farmed northeast of MacNutt.

toss and moan all night, but I was so afraid he would lose his job, especially when they took homebrew to the office.

One time while we were in Calder we went to the Regina Exhibition for a holiday. Lena and Art McRae had left MacNutt and had moved to Regina. Then Bill Davis had moved to Regina as well as the Rueben McReas, Art's brother who had worked at the machine for Henry and stayed at our place on the farm. Rueben drank a lot. He was married to Minnie Becker, Henry's niece. So we had a lot of people to visit and party with. One evening the men went to a ball game. Rueben came home and brought a dog along, a cocker spaniel that had come to them at the game and stayed with them. Henry insisted we take that dog home. Rueben said he'd get it for him and brought him to Lena's place. When Henry came they put the dog in our car. I was mad about it. Jim Montgomery[13] had gone to Regina with us. He asked me if he should go open the car door. I said "Yes." He did but the dog wouldn't leave. He had no collar and had no licence. Rueben said he knew the owner. He said it was a show dog, but a bum. The dog wouldn't stay home. He would get on a street car and go for a ride or get into anybody's car. They never knew where he was.

Anyway, that night Henry and Lena made a bed for the dog (they called him Spot), in the basement. He wouldn't stay. He came upstairs into our room and slept on Henry's pants. He growled if he heard a noise. During the night I woke up and he was on the bed. I tried to push him off, he growled and nearly bit me. We brought him home. I would like to have lost him on the way home but he just stuck to Henry and wouldn't leave him. He was Henry's dog. Wherever Henry went, Spot would go. He tried to sleep on our bed but I wouldn't let him. So he slept on the mat in front of the bed. Later he would sleep in the hall or even outside. In the summer Ella slept on the verandah and Spot slept on her bed. After running through the wet garden he was a nuisance. He would follow us wherever we went and stand outside the window and look in. If we put him in the basement he would gnaw at the door and walls and kick up a fuss. On Sundays or evenings when Henry would lie on the couch and fall asleep Spot would nudge him and

---

[13] Jim Montgomery taught in Minerva School, five miles from Calder.

whine and bark to wake Henry. He wanted to go out. He would go along to the rink and wanted to look out the window when Henry was curling. So people complained. Henry would leave him at home. He would get on the couch, scratch on the window, mess up the curtain and scratch at the door and bark. I wondered how I could get rid of that dog.

Then we got a radio and I would write down the quotes from the grain market. There was no phone at the office, so I would keep Spot at home until two o'clock then write the market prices on a paper and tie it around his neck. He would run straight to the elevator. That worked for a while. Then, since Spot was such a big eater, he would go through some garbage first or go to the Chinese Restaurant where they had a box of dry bread in the kitchen. He would have a few pieces of dry bread before he would go to the elevator and somebody would take the paper and write something else on it. So I had to quit sending the market with Spot.

Spot loved being in the car. If we forgot to close the car door he was in. He had long white and black silky hair which was everywhere in the house, in the car, on our clothes. He had such long hair on his feet and loved going through puddles and mud before coming into the house. That was Spot at Calder.

The Insurance Companies would write wanting money. Henry's life insurance policy had been paid about ten years at 160 dollars a year. Then when we left the farm the premiums weren't paid, then we had taken a 500 dollar loan on the policy. They wrote for interest on the 500 dollars we had borrowed. One time when I was in Winnipeg I discussed this with my brother Jake. He got an agent from Sun Life to come to his place to discuss this. I couldn't see where we could pay off the loan or pay back the premiums. So he advised us to reduce the policy from 5,000 dollars to 2,000 dollars. That would pay off most of the debt and Henry was that much older then so the premiums would be 10 dollars a month. We did that and paid the premiums for a few months.

When Henry took me to Yorkton for my mastoid operation, he told me he had bought another policy from Geo Alerdyce, a friend. I was too sick that day to listen. Some months later I found a letter from that company. He had missed his payment. It too was 10 dollars a month. I asked him to let the new policy go, even if he had paid 60 dollars and try and keep the old policy paid. But we couldn't keep that policy up either. Then there were the children's policies. Arnold and Dick got some money back but Ella's was just four years old and was lost. Henry's policy, even with just paying premiums once in a while, carried but they charged six percent interest on the unpaid premiums. We eventually paid it up.

When brother Rudy left the garage, Bill Lupul, who had been their mechanic took over. I don't know what arrangements they had with him, but the business was still known as Lowenberger and Popp. The Ford Co. sent Bill Lupul a new V8 car to sell, but he couldn't sell it. So we decided we would take it. Henry had a chance to sell ours, so he drove to MacNutt to get the new car. But Bill had just returned it to Winnipeg. Bill had got married so he decorated and used this new car for his wedding at Inglis, perhaps even for his honeymoon. Anyway, the Ford Company took the car back as second-hand and we lost about 300 dollars or more on that. It just went against us with the rest of our debts. Henry didn't seem to mind much, but to me, who expected some day to pay off those debts, it was a lot. Later, I saw in some papers that the bank had a mortgage against the car and had sold it for 300 dollars to the garage owner Bill Lupul.

Bill was in the garage for some time then he left too. After Henry had made some more payments to Jake Rathgeber, he took his building back. We wanted him to take it back right away but he wouldn't. The other building they had bought from Fred Kendel. Henry had borrowed some money from Mr. Burkhardt and had not paid it back. That was why he was writing us for money. I don't know who got that building. I know Henry didn't pay any more on it.

One time some fellows came to the house to take our car to go to Yorkton. I was not going to let them take it but one fellow said, "I'm John Tournaway. I have a lot of grain to thresh yet and the machine broke. I have to get a piece for it and Henry said I could take the car." So what could I say? They took the car and didn't come back for three days. It was all a lie. He had finished threshing. I guess Henry knew, but he was a good customer, so let him have the car. They brought it back. It wasn't damaged but had a lot of mileage on it.

People also borrowed money from Henry, five dollars, ten dollars, or as much as he could let them have. He wrote it all down in a book (which is still here). They never paid it back -- never intended to.

Henry gave me 25 dollars a month. With that I bought the groceries, school books and our clothes but I would never charge at a store. Then one day I was at Gorbacks store and he asked me when we would pay our bill. I asked him, "What bill?" Well Mr. Bishop had bought flour and groceries on our name. Mr. Bishop owed a big bill on the garage which we couldn't collect. And there he was charging groceries on our name! Then I found out that somebody had charged at Egelsons Hardware. So I went to all the stores and told them not to let anybody charge on our name.

Steve Sopko also owed money at the garage and then had borrowed money from Henry. He would charge our radio battery. I paid him every time for it. When I found out he owed us money I didn't want to pay him, let it go off what he owed us. So he wouldn't charge our radio batteries anymore. I guess they didn't like me very much, but they all liked Henry a lot. No wonder.

Dick wrote home from Edmonton saying he needed a jacket to play hockey. I had no money. I had an old coat of Arnold's. I ripped it, turned it inside out and made Dick a jacket. He wrote home that the button holes were on the wrong side.

I couldn't buy Ella a winter coat. I made her an outfit, jacket and breeches from a coat of mine. It was nice for skating. When she got confirmed it was still cold so I put a little fur collar on her summer coat. And all the while, and often without me knowing it, other people were borrowing and spending our money.

There was no hospitalization or insurance. We had to pay our doctor bills to have our teeth fixed. For my mastoid operation we had to pay a little at a time. Then Dr. Houston wrote about a bill. When Dick's leg was hurt in MacNutt we just couldn't pay. Dick had a bicycle when he went to Edmonton. We sold his bike and I took the money and paid the bill. Dr. Houston asked me if we had to sell the bike to pay him. I said no, we sold it because

Dick was away at college. I guess Ella was using that bike but we sold it to pay the bill.

By 1930 a lot of the cars were converted to Bennet Buggies. It was a Bennet government then and during the Depression people could not afford to buy gas. They were selling gopher tails to the municipality. Ernie Kutnick said he tore some tails in half and even had some catkins from trees among them. But when someone had a couple of hundred gopher tails, could you blame a municipal councillor for not sitting and picking over and counting them? It brought in money. People would catch the gophers, pull the tails off and let the gophers go to breed more with tails. That was unbelievable as gophers did so much damage to our crops. But then the crops weren't worth anything and gophers were plentiful.

They had a Ladies' Bridge Club in Calder. I played bridge but wasn't too good at it. They weren't all too good either but some played as if their life depended on it. I was asked to join and was scared. They played auction bridge. I guess I had a run of poor cards. I don't think I was all that poor but I seemed to win the booby prize all the time. They wrote down the scores and in the spring had a final bridge and gave first and second and booby prize for the season. I won the final booby prize - a box of nice stationery. Lily Jira won the first, a silver tray which she said was tin. She didn't want it and gave it for a bridge prize and I won it. So I had the first and booby prizes for that year. Then the next year I had a streak of luck and won first very often. Rudy Zorn said, "They must have poor players." Then men played bridge a lot, but mostly just one table at different houses.

One year we went to Waskesieu for a summer holiday. We borrowed a tent and took bedding and food. The first night we pitched the tent in a field. In the morning we found a cow and milked enough milk for cornflakes and coffee. It was a very interesting trip. Coming home we stayed a night at Emma Lake, went past a sawmill, a strawberry field and some salt lakes. We were gone nearly two weeks and didn't see anyone we knew until we came back to Yorkton. Dick and Ella were along on that trip.

One year we went to Madge Lake. If we didn't go away Henry wouldn't get holidays. The people would come, maybe with a bag of grain or to borrow money. One year we went to Watrous. Dick and some other students had got work there. They had a cottage and a couple to housekeep for them. That was a real holiday.

Then one Sunday in July 1938 Mr. Lapp, the superintendent of the grain company, came to ask if Henry wanted to move to Langenburg. He did. We were very happy about the move. The first reason was we didn't have our church in Calder. There were other reasons, though we enjoyed living in Calder the six years we were there. Only we could hardly afford to move. The year before the grain was rusted and Henry's salary was cut from 125 dollars a month to 70 dollars a month. That year we had no holiday and had saved no money.

LANGENBURG

We went to Langenburg to look for a house. There was just one - where the former pool buyer had lived. It was too small for us but we rented it. The house had a living room, small kitchen and a little hall. Upstairs was a small room you had to go through to get to our bedroom. We had to leave some of our stuff at Calder. Ferd and Dora Popp[1] moved into the house we were in. Anyway as soon as we knew we were moving I started packing dishes and washing curtains and all washables because there was no cistern or well at the house we were moving to. I had to carry water. Then there were parties and good-byes. I was glad we were moving but still wanted to cry.

We got a truck to move. Henry helped to load the truck and hurt his back. We moved on Saturday, and on Monday there was a terrible hail storm. Windows were smashed and the crops which had been very good were hailed out. Henry's salary was raised back to 125 dollars a month but with moving expenses and Dick's first year at St. Louis, Missouri, we needed a little more

[1] Ferdinand Popp and Dora Hoar were married November 4, 1933.

money. And Henry wasn't well, his back and leg were sore, getting worse. The first year we were in MacNutt Henry lifted a battery and strained his back. Then he got lumbago. After that once or twice a year he would get it and sometimes he would need bed rest. I'd rub him with liniment and put some belladonna[2] plaster on him.

Since we were short of money, Dick and I drove to Geo Burla's farm, a man who had bought our threshing machine and hadn't paid for it. We would go collecting every year, but sometimes all we would get is a drink of homebrew. So when we went to see him I must have begged. He promised us 35 dollars by Sunday. We had to go back on Sunday and get it. He was sorry he had promised it. We had notes from him for about 1,000 dollars. He used the machine in the fall for threshing, used the engine all winter for sawing logs, but never paid for it. He was just a very dishonest man. I wonder if he is still alive. We never went back to collect.[3]

Those first few months in Langenburg were frustrating. After Dick was gone, Henry's back and leg got sorer. One day Dr. McKenzie brought him home with a kink in his back and unable to walk. The doctor said we should have his teeth checked. So I put him to bed and sent for Dr. Hallet, the dentist.[4] He looked at Henry's teeth and said there was one he would pull. When he stuck the needles in he told me to come and look. Pus was coming out. The doctor left a prescription. At the time Henry had Lloyd Kohnen[5] as a helper, but the superintendent came and had to get a different buyer. Bill Scheible came and stayed at our place. Ella slept on a Toronto couch in our room. Bill slept in the other room.

Henry's leg worsened. We knew a few people in Langenburg and everybody was friendly and helpful with advice.

---

[2] Belladonna is a poisonous plant sometimes called deadly nightshade. From the plant the drug, belladonna, is used to relieve pain or spasms.

[3] On February 13, 1973 Mary made the following note in her memoirs. "Will try to do some more writing. I am now 76 years old and not really in the mood. Notice when I last wrote we had just left Calder."

[4] Dr. Hallet was the dentist in Langenburg during the 1930's. He married Veronica Kohnen. They later moved to Saskatoon.

[5] Lloyd (Alois) Kohnen, born March 20, 1908, married Freida Becker. He died at the age of 46 of Bright's (kidney) disease.

They told me to make him fomentations. Some suggested I rub his leg with turpentine and some said hot salt with vinegar. Nothing seemed to relieve his pain except heat. So I made fomentations. Mrs. Berger sent word with Mr. Lepp the superintendent to put saltpcter in the water for the fomentation. I had to carry every drop of water from Caul's livery barn well.[6] I took the biggest pails I had. At first I had to rest five times then only four. Then I could carry all the water with just resting once. I saved on water. I would empty the hot water bottle and save the water to rinse out the chamber pot. I had to carry the water for washing too and often the sheets would get wet and I would have to change the bed. During the night Henry would start moaning. I would go down and start a fire in the wood stove and heat water for the foments and the water bottle. We did have electric lights which we had never had before and I was very thankful for that. Then Mr. Jacobs came and said Henry should take Tempeltons (T.R.C.) pills. They had helped him so we tried them. Henry took them until he was getting dizzy spells. Then one day Ella came home from school with a pain in her stomach. So she was in bed and I carried food up for them both and the pot down.

When Henry felt a bit better I packed him in the car, made a bed in the back seat, took Ella along and took him to Yorkton to a chiropractor. I thought we might have to stay in but he examined him and said to take him home, continue with the foments, but instead of putting them on the leg I should put them on his back and massage his back with oil of wintergreen. Then George Beckers went to Winnipeg. Henry went along to see Mrs. Cramer, a special chiropractor. Arnold lived in Winnipeg so Henry stayed there. He was putting his shoes on, sat on the side of the bathtub and got a kink as bad as the first. They brought him back lying on the back seat and I had to start all over again with saltpeter foments.

---

[6] Caul's livery barn was on Carl Avenue across from the present post office. It was owned by Wilfred Caul from 1933 to 1946. Wilfred Caul (1894 - 1974) and his wife Edith (Barker) (1895 - 1943) came to Langenburg in 1916. They had three children: Stanley, Merril (Rathgeber) and Esther (Boreen).

On Thanksgiving Day Arnold Zinke[7] brought us a barrel full of soft water. I was so happy and thankful. I had such a big washing and when I put those sheets with the saltpeter on in the machine with homemade soap, the water curdled and got gummy. It was awful washing. I was ashamed to hang it up. One time Mr. Caul came and brought us some pieces of ice. People were so very good to us. But I still had to carry a lot of water.

After the first month Henry didn't get his cheque. Bill got his and I don't even remember if he paid me board, but we had no money. I couldn't pay the rent and had to charge groceries at Patrick's.[8] I said I'd pay next month and next month came and still no cheque. That was the beginning of December. I'd go to the post office every day, but it didn't come. Ella wanted skates. I ordered them C.O.D. but I had no money when they came. Dick wanted a jacket for Christmas and I wouldn't go back to Patrick's store because I had promised to pay. Everyone had told us how the Pool agent before us had charged everywhere and left town and never paid. We had left no unpaid bills in Calder. But we still had those thousands of dollars against us from the MacNutt Garage from bills people owed to the Traders Finance or from parts they had bought. Sure we had thousands of dollars worth of notes. I still have them, but they were no good. The debt was against us.[9]

By December 1, 1938, we had moved into the Burkhardt house.[10] I was so very glad. It had a cistern, a well next door and two bedrooms downstairs. We bought an old stove. I thought maybe Noah had used it in the Ark. It was very fancy. We paid

---

[7] Arnold Zinke's parents immigrated from the United States to Langenburg. Arnold was one of fourteen children.

[8] Patrick & McAfee was a general store on Kaiser Wilhelm Avenue. In 1945 Eitel and Gustie Zorn bought the store and it became known as the "United Store". In 1948 they sold it to Morris Berman who ran the business until 1964.

[9] It is unclear exactly how the garage was involved with Traders Finance. Most likely customers bought vehicles on credit from the dealership. Traders Finance took an assignment of the customer's debt and paid cash to the dealership on the proviso that if the customer defaulted on the loan it would have "total recourse" against the dealership.

[10] The Burkhardt house was at 105 Wells Avenue.

eight dollars for it and freight from Yorkton. Henry got it from Chris Ness. In the other place we had only a tin box heater.

Henry felt better so he could go to work, but we still had no money. One Monday he came home, lay on the sofa and couldn't get up. He had terrible pain. Ella came from school and ran for the doctor. He came and said he would take Henry to Russell to X-ray his teeth but Henry was in too much pain. He couldn't move. The next day Mrs. McKenzie came to give Henry a needle, but he was feeling better. Henry had his teeth X-rayed at Russell. They all had pus pockets. He came back and went to Dr. Hallet and had them pulled. When he told Dr. Hallet he was a bleeder, he wouldn't pull them without Dr. McKenzie there. They packed Henry's mouth. He bled for a while but fell asleep. Dr. Hallet said he worried all night.

On December 14th two Pool cheques came. Henry cashed them and paid bills. He was back to work with a helper. Mr. Lepp came and said he hoped it had not inconvenienced us that the cheques were late. I did not tell him how much it had and how I had worried.

Well, by Christmas things were smoother. Henry ordered a bottle of rye, opened it at the Lumber Yard office, gave everybody a drink and had about an inch of it left in the bottle when he came home late for supper. He brought a neighbour bachelor (Hantz Suethel) home for supper. Ella was in the church program. We made it but should have stayed home.

Christmas Day Carl Langer[11] came and asked us over for dinner. People were so very good to us, still are. There weren't the lonely times I sometimes felt in Calder. We had relatives and friends close by and we got involved. I joined the bridge club and we curled. We were asked to a lot of dinner parties. So we had to entertain more often. Food wasn't so expensive and maybe we would buy a bottle of rye and pass a drink around before the meal. Then we would play cards.

---

[11] Carl Langer (June 30, 1894 - April 16, 1963) operated the Reliance Lumber Yard from 1922 to his death. He married Anna Walz (May 28, 1900 - October 28, 1994) on April 6, 1922. They had two children: Delmarie and Charles.

They had a lot of big surprise house parties. We would go into the country. Paul Mitschke[12] had a team of horses and a big sleigh. We would take a few cases of beer and all pile in the sleigh and go. We would have fun on the way, but I wasn't feeling well, would have continued colds, a pain in my back, stuffed nose. I would have preferred sitting by our ancient stove, with my feet up on the nickel trim and a cushion on my back. But Ella would tell me, "You better go or they will think you are snooty." So I went and since I wasn't feeling well, did not enjoy the parties, not at first anyway. The men would sit at the tables, play cards and drink beer. The women would sit on boxes or beds or stand. Some would have beer. I didn't like beer. Then we would make lunch, wash dishes and go home.

I would get so cold and the fire would be nearly out when we got home and that house was cold. Otherwise I liked the house a lot. Only there was no place for a bathroom or even for a sanitary closet, but we lived in that house for 14 years until we built ours. We had some very good times in it, and some not so good. We did some fixing on the house while we were there, but it was not ours. We had got a big truck load of shavings to insulate it. John and Alfred Hofer worked for a week, but they did not finish, so I worked on it. Henry would help in the evenings until he got too busy.

The wind had torn a board off the top of the roof on the verandah and a bird had gotten in upstairs. So I got a ladder and the board and crawled up and nailed on the board. When I started to go down I got scared. I tried to slide down on my seat. The shingles were so rough and when my foot hit the ladder I nearly knocked it over. I was so scared and so glad when I was down. Then we got cardboard boxes and nailed them inside the attic roof. We nailed tar paper around the outside and banked it with snow to keep the cistern and cellar from freezing. A lot later we got an oil

---

[12] Paul Mitschke (1878 - 1964) was born in Germany (now Poland), the fifth child born to Josef and Elisabeth (Ramke) Mitschke. He married Eleanor Schappert in 1908. In 1920 they moved to town and operated the hardware store purchased from Adolf Becker. Their daughter, Irene, married Henry and Mary Popp's son, Dick, on January 1, 1943.

heater, which gave an even heat. We had never lived in a warm house, so it was fine.[13]

Henry found it hard at first to build up the business. He had strong opposition. Also some of his Board members were against him. We worried about it. There would be busy times in the fall when trucks would haul grain nearly all night. But then there were slack times too, when he wouldn't be busy.

We had our piano which had been repaired after the MacNutt fire. Bobsie Cornelius,[14] Eileen Richter[15] and Ella would have some giggly sing songs. Or if a gang would be there somebody would play the piano and everybody would sing. There was a lot of singing at those first parties in Langenburg. Everybody would stand and sing in our big kitchen.

One year curling, everybody picked their rinks. So Mrs. Caul asked if I would curl with her. She made up a rink. We had Alvina Miller.[16] Mrs. Rombough[17] was going to curl then couldn't get away, so we had Mrs. Mitschke. We were rated very low and all the other rinks had to spot us so many points, some as high as

---

[13] Mary Popp's memoirs contain a note from the fall of 1973. "We walked over there [the old Burkhardt house] one day this fall. The August VanCaeseeles bought it and fixed it up so very nice."

[14] Bobsie Cornelius was the daughter of Henry Adam Cornelius and Millie Becker (whose father, Adolph Becker, was the original owner of the Rex Garage in Langenburg). Bobsie graduated from nurses training in 1944.

[15] Eileen Richter was the daughter of John Richter and Emilie Exner who emigrated from Russia. John operated a butcher shop in Langenburg. Eileen was born April 21, 1922.

[16] Alvina Miller (born October 14, 1900 and residing in the Langenburg Centennial Care Home) was the daughter of Robert and Emilie (Bucholz) Miller. She married John Pawliw in 1948. They had no children. In 1908, Alvina's father, Robert Miller purchased a store in Langenburg, on the north side of the railway tracks. His children, Alvina, Ella and Robert Jr. continued to operate the store, eventually located south of the railway track, until 1978.

[17] Jack and Jessie Rombough ran a hotel in Churchbridge in the early 1920s. Then they moved to Langenburg and went into partnership with Henry Rudy. They bought the Kalaas and Olson store - a diversified hardware store located just north of the current Wallin's Grocery Store. The store was called "Rombough and Rudy - Hardware and Implements". Mr. Rombough died in the early 1930s. Mrs. Rombough and Jake Baumung formed a partnership and operated the Langenburg Hardware Store until 1945 when it was sold.

eight points, so we could beat most rinks but not the Norman Aasen rink, all young boys. Then the Yorkton bonspiel came up. Mrs. Caul said, “Let’s go.” I couldn't afford the train fare and hotel. I could only go if I could stay with my brother Rudy. So we went and we had a streak of luck, just kept on winning until we got up against a strong Melville rink. They were known to win wherever they went. We were way up on them. Then Mrs. Caul missed her shot. We were lying five and she raised them in for one. They beat us but we had won big jars of coffee, cups and saucers, and pyrex casseroles. I was very pleased as I hadn't expected to win at Yorkton. We were very happy coming home.

The summer of 1939 Dick had gone back to Watrous, working for Mrs. White, running concessions and the swimming pool. In September he came back to return to the Lutheran Seminary at St. Louis, Missouri. So I planned a party for him before he left. I had seen in the *Country Guide* how to plan a hobo party. Ella wasn't too taken with my idea but it was different and Dick did not know the Langenburg young people too well. So we made a list of all the young people. In the *Guide*, it said how to word the invitations which I wrote on pieces of brown store paper, torn off and rolled up and tied with twine, and passed them around. Ella took a lot to school. I left some at the Korner Lunch. The invitations told everyone how to dress as hobos and to bring a stick with a red handkerchief or bundle to look like lunch, and to meet at our place at eight o'clock in the evening. I had asked Ruthie Schoepp[18] to be the leader. For lunch, we went to a farm close to Churchbridge which had a field of corn and got a tub full of corn. We had sandwiches and two big cakes.

When Dick came home he wasn’t too pleased about the party. I guess he had other plans, but there was nothing to do about it at that stage. I got him to put a couple of lights up in the yard. There were two vacant lots next to our place with some bush

---

[18] Ruth was born in Winnipeg on October 19, 1921 to Ludwig and Frieda (Scholz) Schoepp. Ludwig was born in Neudorf, Austria in 1888. He moved to Langenburg in 1924 and established a business known as Schoepp and Scholz. He owned the Central Hotel and the John Deere machinery dealership. Ruth married Erwin Bessel in 1944. They had three children: Sandra, Valerie and Wesley.

on so we built a big pile of dry sticks for a bonfire and I painted "SOAP" on a strong box to stand on for speeches. So everything was ready. Then I got nervous. Will they come? It took nerve to walk through town before dark dressed as a hobo. But they all came - real hobos. Ruthie had made herself a big map, where they would go. She had it rolled up and tied it around her neck with a string. When they were all there she got on the soap box and spoke to them. Then they all left and walked around town, in one door and out the other at the Korner Lunch. She would have to stop under lights to study her map. Then they all sat in front of the hotel and sang *How Dry I Am*.

When a train pulled in they all ran for the train. They were tired when they came back. I had Ida Davis[19] to help me. We had the boiler on to cook corn, make coffee and get the lunch ready. When they came back they lit the bonfire and roasted corn on sticks. They ate lunch and all sat around the fire and sang. Ruth was such a good leader and kept things going. Later Mrs. Rombough came over to see them. About 40 young people were there. After they were gone Smitty[20] from the Bank and one of the teachers came back to say how much they enjoyed it. I had not noticed them until they came back. I don't remember the teacher's name, but she wore a shirt open at the neck and fox tail stuck in for chest hair. I was glad that they came back and told me how much they had enjoyed it

I had troubles with Jacobs' turkeys. They would come in our garden and pick holes in the cabbages and I would chase them away. They would leave, but when I turned to go back, they would return. When the young people had left the party, they left their sticks behind. So I picked up one of the sticks and I threw it and hit one of the turkeys on the head. If I had I tried to do that, I couldn't have. But I hit that turkey and it fell over. It was still kicking. I let it lie but the other turkeys came back and started picking at it so I threw it in the grass. When Henry came home for

---

[19] Don and Ida Davis came to Langenburg in 1938. Don Davis operated and worked for several businesses in Langenburg. They had nine children. Ida died May 1, 1990. Don died August 6, 1996.

[20] Smitty was a male teller at the Toronto Dominion Bank.

supper I told him about it. He took the turkey to Jacobs and told them what had happened. He offered to pay for it. They said it was all right. They chopped its head off and said they would use it. I was so embarrassed to have killed somebody's turkey.

Next I had to get Dick ready to leave. It cost a little more to send him to St. Louis. It seemed harder to send him that far away but it really made little difference because we would just hear from him by letters while he was in Edmonton. Dick went to St. Louis for two years. He would get odd jobs and had to study hard, but he liked it.

October 20, 1939, was our 25th wedding anniversary. When the time came closer people were hinting about a party . One man told Henry he was "sorry, but they couldn't come." I could not figure out what they could do. Our house was too small and the hall was rented to a travelling orchestra. The posters were up for that. So I was puzzled. I baked bread and *kuchen*, but still couldn't figure it out. Well Millie Aasen[21] and Mary Baumung[22] made some agreement with the orchestra. About eight o'clock Aunt Lizzie Baumung came to the house and told us to come to the hall. Luckily I had bought myself a pretty green dress with a bustle. They brought me a corsage. When we got to the hall there was such a mob we could hardly get in. It was a very good orchestra. They had a mock wedding. Mrs. Rombough was the minister, Mrs. Farthing[23] was the bride. It was very funny. They had a mock wedding cake and presented us with a silver tea service. We were so very pleased about it all.

Spot came with us to Langenburg. If we left him home he would follow the car as far as we could see but he would be home when we got home. The first Christmas we went to church and left him in the house. When we got home he had got on the dining room table and had got deep scratches on it. He must have walked on the buffet to look out the window. He knocked dishes over and

---

[21] Millie Aasen was the daughter of John Aasen and Mary Kendel, Mary Popp's cousin.

[22] Mary Baumung was Mary Popp's cousin, daughter of Jacob and Lizzie Baumung. Mary married Rudolph Zorn.

[23] Hugh Farthing had the blacksmith shop on Carl Avenue. Everyone called his wife Auntie Farthing. They had no children.

broke two crystal goblets I had gotten from Calder as a going away gift. I was so mad at him. I chased him out and told him never to come in the house again. I told Henry and Ella not to let him in. But Mr. Schnell[24] came in the afternoon so he sneaked in with him. Anyway I couldn't let him freeze.

Another time we got a rope and tied him to the stove leg. He got around the table leg and pulled the table up to the stove and was all tangled up. One year we went on holidays so Henry left Spot with Mr. Proux[25] at the station. He liked Spot.

One day Spot went to the hotel with Mr. Proux. At noon he got into a fight with a smaller dog. Someone poured a pail of cold water on them. Spot walked across the street, lay down and died. Henry and Ella were heartbroken. I felt bad about it. He was a very nice dog but I liked him better when he was gone. Henry brought him home and after supper Henry and Ella buried him on the vacant lot next to us. End of Spot.

---

[24] William Schnell (1907 - 1978) married Marjorie Houck in 1933. He was the Manager of the Saskatchewan Co - op Creamery in Langenburg until 1972.

[25] Jack Proux was the station agent.

THE WAR YEARS

When the war broke out in 1939 they started conscripting men up to age 23. Dick and three other students were 23 years old. In the early fall, when they went to Regina to get their visas to go to the States, they were told they could not get them and could not go back to the Seminary. It was quite a shock to the boys. Some of our ministers started working to get exemptions for the boys, as they needed ministers. They arranged for a parochial school for Dick in Winnipeg. When Dick came before the parole board they asked his reasons and were going to give him another postponement but then Dick enlisted in the Air Force.

Arnold had enlisted in the Army almost as soon as the war started. He was sent overseas and got more training in England. He was anxious to go active. Well he got it as he was in Italy, Egypt and Holland. He was very glad when the war ended.

In the fall of 1942 Ella finished high school and went into nursing training in St. Boniface Hospital in Winnipeg. We were where we started, alone. I'd get very homesick and had to depend on letters from the children. Ella didn't like training. She feared the

Augusta and Jakob Lowenberger and their children: Rudolf on Augusta's lap, Mary standing between her parents, standing at left-Katherine and behind-Elisabeth. Circa 1900.

Lowenberger family, Circa 1911
Back row: George, Mary, Katherine, Rudolf, Elisabeth.
Front Row: Jakob Sr., Adolf, Augusta and Jacob Jr.

Elisabeth and Katherine Lowenberger standing, Mary Lowenberger seated. Circa 1911.

Seated: Henry Popp's parents: Philip and Margaret (Wagner) Popp. Back row: Frank, Henry and Philip Popp. Girls: Lena Popp and Gertrude Barker.

Landestreu, Austria, circa 1907. Man with hat: Johann Friedrich Baumung and to his right, his wife Marie Elisabeth (Haas) (Mary Popp's grandparents) Adult male foreground left and woman behind him, Johann Friedriech Baumung Jr. and wife Elisabeth (Haberstock). Child in arms: Johann Baumung and Elisabeth Baumung. Remainder uncertain.

Mary Popp's maternal grandparents: Johann Friedrich Baumung and Maria Elisabeth (Haas), Landestreu, Austria. Granddaughter Elisabeth Baumung, grandson Friedrich Baumung in foreground.

Elisabeth (Nerbas) and Jacob Baumung (Mary's maternal uncle). Elisabeth holding Emilie, Jacob holding Fred.

Mary's mother, Augusta (Baumung) Lowenberger

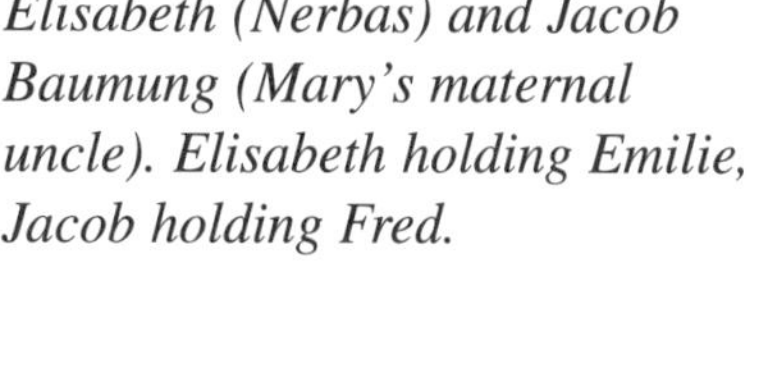

Henry Popp's brother, Philip Popp and Laura (Wagner) with son Ewald.

Henry's brother Joseph Popp and wife Elisabeth (Schoepp), children (left to right): Mary, Ferdinand, Katherine and Joseph.

Halvor Hande and Elisabeth Popp, January 1, 1906.

Johann Rathgeber Family. Back row: Peter (future husband of Katherine Lowenberger) and Margaret. Fred, Johann, Julia (in front of father) Amelia, George, Emma (Haas). Lena on Emma's lap.

Peter Rathgeber on the binder; grandfather Peter Rathgeber standing.

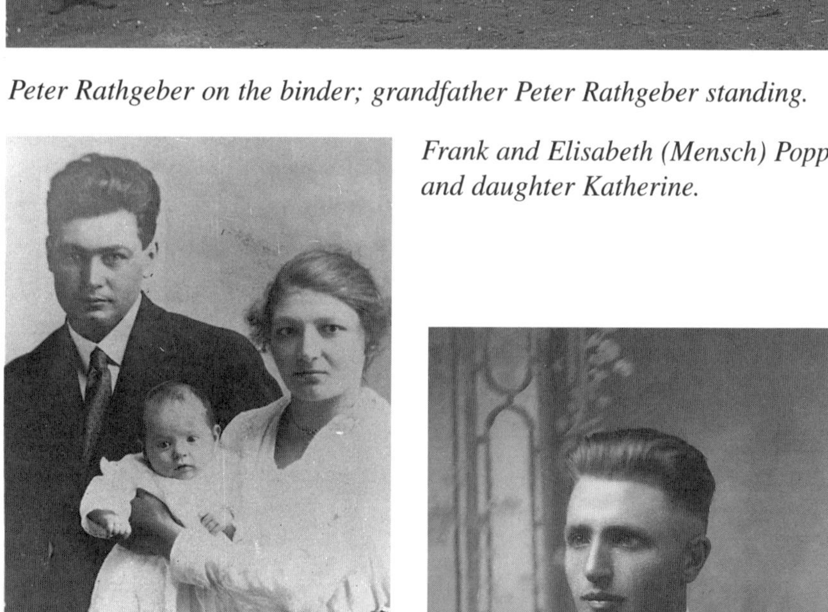

Frank and Elisabeth (Mensch) Popp and daughter Katherine.

Jacob Lowenberger, Circa 1920.

Jacob Lowenberger and Stephana Bell, December 16, 1925.

Rudolf and Beatrice (Keay) Lowenberger.

Hoffenthal Church where Mary was confirmed and married.

Rudolf and Dorothea (Dressler) Baumung. (Mary's maternal uncle) .

Mary and Henry Popp, 1920.

Arnold, Dick and Ella Popp.

Threshing gang, 1927. Front row, seated: Jacob Popp, George Andres, Henry, Dick, Joe and Frank Popp. Ella Popp in foreground, Arnold standing on left. Back row: unknown, unknown, Ewald Kitz, George Wagner, Philip Wagner, George Poier and Fred Busch.

Landestreu, Austria 1939

The Lowenberger farmhouse, 1927.

Arnold, Dick, Ella Popp and Wagner children going to school.

Julius and Lizzie (Lowenberger) Metz.Children (left to right): Elsie, Arthur, Frieda and Gertrude.

Henry and Mary Popp with Spot.

Henry and Mary Popp with children by Kerr house in MacNutt. Circa 1930.

George and Adelheid (Mack) Lowenberger and family-1945

Henry, Ella, Dick and Mary Popp.

Henry and Mary's house in Calder.

William and Helen (Lowenbgerger) Hauser. May 15, 1932

Back row: Ottomar, Alma Wiegner.
Front row: Mrs. Wiegner, Meta and Reverend Wiegner.

Mary and Al Lowe -Mary's brother.

Jacob, Dorothea, Elisabeth and Rudolf Baumung. Jacob and Rudolf were Mrs. Lowenberger's brothers.

Ella, Henry, Mary and Dick Popp.

Ella (Popp) and Ernie Parkinson's wedding, June 16, 1946.

Dick Popp and son, Brian-1946.

Henry Popp, Bill Schnell, Harold Schoepp and Leo Hartung.

Mary and Henry Popp.

Sisters and she said if it hadn't been for what it cost us for clothes, uniforms, books, and the entrance fee, she would have quit. She had two good friends there, Eileen Richter, a year ahead of her, and Yvonne Ryckebosch.[1] My sisters and brothers lived in Winnipeg. Ella went to see them often, but the hospital had such strict rules at that time. She had to be in at a certain time and she didn't know the city too well. She was so afraid of missing a bus or street car or being late if they got stalled. She wrote me about these things and I worried with her. One time a patient became violent and tried to strangle her. Her nerves got bad. She came home for Christmas the first year.

Dick married Irene Mitschke on January 1, 1943, a very cold day. They had a small house wedding. Meta came, as well as other relatives and close friends. I wore thin nylons. When we were going home our car wouldn't start. We sat in that cold car when it wouldn't start, then started walking. I could feel my legs freezing by the time I got to the railway track. I thought I could hear my legs rattle. I began to run. That hour of the night nothing was open. I made it home. I had frozen my legs badly. They were sore for a long time. I do not remember where Dick was stationed when they got married I think he had a week's leave.

Those were sad days. Arnold was overseas at the front and so many of the young boys from our town and around had left, some never to return.[2]

When Ella left, nobody played the piano. Oh, I could play with one finger. I had taken some lessons and liked picking at tunes. It was such a big piano and we had so little room for it. We still had our sofa from when we were first married. It had been re-covered several times. When we went through the fire we had it re-covered again. We also had a good cash register from the garage.

---

[1] Yvonne Ryckebosch, born August 30, 1925, was the daughter of Florent (Rickey) and Susana (Zentner) Ryckebosch. The Ryckebosch family left Langenburg in 1935. Yvonne entered nursing at St. Boniface Hospital in 1942. For notes respecting Eileen Richter, see footnote 15, page 127.

[2] Veterans from Langenburg who died in action included: E. J. Berger, Ernest Degryse, Albin Feusi, Harold Fuhr, Quinton Johnson, Wilbert Schultz, Raymond Vermeersch, Albert Wotherspoon and William Zentner.

Jakie Baumung[3] thought he might buy it and then we could order a new chesterfield suite. We heard that the MacNutt school was looking for a cheap piano. The sound on our piano was good, the keys were wooden. I had taken them out and put good white enamel on them several times. The school bought it. I don't remember what we got for it, but with that money and the cash register, we bought the chesterfield and chair.[4]

We were still getting letters from the Traders Finance. They wanted money. The bank took the crops from our land. The taxes weren't paid and they had taken brother Rudy's land. We were out driving with Mrs. Rombough and Jakie Baumung one time and we talked about our troubles. They said, "Times are better. Why don't you try and collect some of your old debts?" But Henry had lost all interest in that business and there was so much against us. Rudy was in the Case business in Yorkton and had no time. We were still hard up. So I got Henry to bring some old books home with carbon paper in them. He was going to burn them anyway. We got the garage ledger from Rudy and some notes the Bank was holding in our favour but were uncollectable. I started writing letters by the hundreds. The amounts on those notes had doubled or more with compound interest. I wrote people that if they would pay the note value, we'd forget about the interest. I wrote maybe twice a year. Some notes were outlawed by then.[5] Some people had moved away. Some said they had paid Bill Lupul. Then when Henry had a day off, Thanksgiving or other holidays, we would go see people and maybe collect enough for the gas, perhaps a few dollars more. It was not until 1943 that we started collecting again.

---

[3] Jacob Adolf (Jakie) Baumung (1907 - 1978) was Mary Popp's cousin, the son of Jacob and Elisabeth Baumung. Jakie was involved in numerous businesses in Langenburg. In 1953 Jakie married Elna (Mitschke) Jeske. They had two daughters: Pamela and Susan.

[4] When Mary Popp left her house in 1993 and moved to the Langenburg Centennial Special Care Home, Don and Jan Layh bought the chair and chesterfield. The re-upholstered chair sits in Don Layh's study; the chesterfield in Jan Layh's art studio.

[5] In Saskatchewan law a creditor has six years to collect a defaulted loan. After six years a statutory limitation period provides a complete defence to a creditor's attempts to collect a loan.

One year, while Ella was still training, Mabel Venn[6] asked me if I would come to Clear Lake with them for holidays. Mabel's mother, Mrs. Hughes, was going with them. I asked Henry and he said "Sure, go." He didn't like to go for holidays. So I did some baking and cooking, some to take, and some to leave for Henry. I had never been to Clear Lake before. It was a lovely holiday. They had a nice cabin with a bathroom. During the day, Mrs. Hughes and I would go out sightseeing. At night we would stay home with the girls, Carole and Shirley, and play cards. One night we all went to a spooky show.

On Sunday, Carl Langers and Louis Schoepps came down and brought Henry along. We all went to a café to eat. It was a very nice holiday for me. We stayed there a week, then went to Winnipeg. Mrs. Hughes had a suite there so they were going to stay another week. I went to my sister Helen's. I had written Ella saying we would come that day. Ella phoned Helen. I answered the phone. Ella talked to me and asked if her mother had come yet. I said, "No." We talked for a little while before she realized she was talking to me. Helen's voice and mine were much the same.

Jakie Baumung was in Winnipeg so I went home with him. I brought Elaine,[7] Helen's little girl, home with me for a while.

In November 1943 some of us started planning a surprise birthday party for Mrs. Rombough. It was to be women dressed as men, and men dressed as women. We had some fun planning it. I was feeling so well. Henry had got a truck load of big blocks of wood. He dared me to split it. The day before the party I had finished it. When he came home at noon I told him I had done it. I tried one of my biggest dresses on him. It didn't fit too well. About three o'clock Mae Aasen[8] walked in and I asked if her mother knew about the party. I told her I was just writing Ella about it. I didn't even give Mae a chance to talk. Finally she said, "I came over to

---

[6] Mabel Venn was Carl Venn's wife. Mr. Venn managed the Toronto Dominion Bank.

[7] Elaine Hauser was born April 30, 1939 in Winnipeg. She married Lawrence Miller on July 6, 1957 and was divorced in 1975. They had four children: Donald, Timothy, Sherry and Melanie. Elaine married Michael Rigby in 1978.

[8] Mae Aasen (Rombough) was the daughter of Jack and Jesse Rombough. She married Norman Aasen (whose mother was Mary Popp's cousin).

tell you Mr. Popp broke his leg." I couldn't believe it. I asked her how. She said, "He fell off the annex roof." I didn't give her a chance to explain. I went in the bedroom and put on my coat. When I came out Alex Aberhart[9] came in, looked at me and said, "Don't take it so hard." I started walking, my mouth was so dry I couldn't talk, but I could think. When we got to the Bank corner we saw Dr. Claire's[10] car and a small truck coming. When I passed the doctor's car he called, "Mrs. Popp, come here." I didn't listen. I went to the truck and stepped up on the side. Henry was lying in there. He looked up and said, "I broke my leg." I said, "Is that all?" He was hurt because I said, "Is that all?" But I had imagined so many things while I was walking. They stopped at the Hardware Store where Jakie Baumung stopped to get a cover for the truck. It was snowing. I went in and asked for a drink of water.

How it happened - it started snowing and Henry had some air vents open on the annex roof. He went to close them, something he had done dozens of times, but with the fresh snow he slipped and slid down between the annex and a box car. Big bolts stuck out on the wall but he missed them. Some men were in the elevator. When he didn't come in, they went out to look for him. They found him and called the doctor. He came, took his belt off, strapped Henry's legs together and gave him a needle. That's why they could not move him right away. They also had to get a truck. I went along to the Russell hospital. They X-rayed him and set his leg and put him in a new fracture bed they had just got. When Jakie and I went to see him, Henry said to me, "Now you don't have to worry about a dress for me." Jakie looked and asked, "What did you say, Henry?" Henry said, "Now she doesn't have to worry about a dress for me for tomorrow night." Jakie shook his head and looked puzzled. He went home and told everyone that Henry was hurt worse than just the broken leg. He didn't know about the party being planned. I stayed and came home later with Dr. Claire. When I came home some people came over and said that they

---

[9] Alex Aberhart (1908 - 1978) and his wife Lydia Lesser moved to Langenburg in 1933. They worked as farm labourers and operated a livery stable and dray business.

[10] Dr. Claire was a doctor in Langenburg during the 1940's.

would call off the party. I thought they should go ahead with it. I was going to Russell next morning with Mr. Tapp[11] and if Henry was doing fine, I would go to the party but I wouldn't dress.

That party was a complete surprise and so funny, especially the men. Mr. Farthing, with his long mustache, wore Mrs. Farthing's dress which was too big for him. Farmer Hertlein[12] had a flowing bridesmaid dress and fancy hat. Dr. Magill[13] wore a nice red dress, stuffed bust, high heeled shoes and nylons. Lorn Miller had a big stomach (was built that way). George Becker[14] was a flapper with a short full skirt, tight sweater and big hat. Albert Yeske[15] wore a dress and with his curly hair looked a natural woman. Hugo Yeske[16] was stout. He wore a dress I had made for a masquerade for Henry. I don't remember if there were others. The men played cards and had to lift their dresses up to get their money out of their pockets. It all was a lot of fun and how I would have enjoyed it had I not had a sore feeling inside me.

Henry was in Russell hospital for about two months. The superintendent came and hired a temporary Pool agent. Henry was not in a cast but he had sand bags around his leg and a sand pail weight to keep his leg straight. He didn't suffer too much after it was set.

---

[11] Mr. Tapp was a teacher in Langenburg.

[12] John Hertlein (1895 - 1983) was the son of Lorenz Hertlein and Bertha Bauer. Better known as Farmer Hertlein, he was a bachelor who was known as everyone's friend and an excellent curler.

[13] Dr. Magill was a dentist in Langenburg.

[14] George Becker (September 5, 1899 - January 19, 1995) was the son of Adolf and Karoline (Ruckeman) Becker. He married Margaret Baehnisch on May 23, 1922. In 1925 George joined his father in business at the Rex Garage. They had one daughter, Dorothy, born June 4, 1929.

[15] Albert Yeske (1887 - 1972) was the son of Wilhelm and Emilia Yeske. He married Bertha Severin (1895 - 1993) on November 19, 1914. Albert and Bertha operated several businesses in Langenburg, including the Langenburg Theatre from 1940 - 1956. They had three sons: Norman, Hubert and Woodrow.

[16] Hugo Yeske (1880 - 1945) was Albert Yeske's brother. He married Emilie Bessel. They farmed and retired to Langenburg in 1936. They had five children: Walter, Hedwig, Oswald, Alfred and Ardena.

Seventeen days after Henry broke his leg, Ellie Wohlers[17] and I went to Russell with Dr. Claire. He measured Henry's leg. He wasn't too satisfied. He had the leg X-rayed and sent the X-rays to a specialist in Winnipeg saying two heads were better than one. He went to Binscarth while Ellie and I waited at the hospital where he was going to pick us up. When he came to pick us up, he had been drinking. On the way home he often stopped "to see if he had a flat tire." By the time we got home he was very drunk and insisted we go to the Chinese restaurant. Ellie had her own cafe then so we sat there. I wanted to walk home. He wouldn't let me and said what a juicy piece of gossip it would be that we were in the cafe with him at two o'clock in the morning.

Then Dr. Claire went on a drinking spree for about ten days. We didn't hear about the results of the X-rays all that time. Finally he went to see Henry. He walked in with the X-ray results, just as if he had been there the day before. Everything was fine; nothing to worry about.

One Sunday night while Henry was in the hospital, Mr. Draper[18] came over asking if I would come and stay with Mrs. Draper. She was expecting a baby and he had to look for Dr. Claire who was out in the country for supper. The doctor came, examined her and said it could be two hours or two weeks. The Drapers had moved to Langenburg from Calder and had intended to go to Yorkton for the delivery but he was threshing and couldn't stay home so she said the baby would be delivered by Dr. Claire. A few days later she came over asking if I would go to the doctor with her. Dr. Claire was staying at Ma Berger's hotel[19] then. Ma said, "He can't see you, he is too drunk." But Mrs. Draper wanted

---

[17] Eleonora (Ellie) Wohlers and her widowed mother, Anna, ran a restaurant in Langenburg. Ellie and Anna bought the Korner Lunch Restaurant from Gustie Zorn and Thelma Hartung. In 1945 Ellie married Walter Mack (1917 - 1978). They had five children: Joan, Linda, Joyce, Paul and Thelma.

[18] Mr. Drake was a teacher in Langenburg.

[19] Richard Berger (1873 - 1916) and his wife Mary Ann McKay (1880 - 1974) built the Imperial Hotel on Kaiser Wilhelm Avenue in 1902. After Richard's death Ma Berger continued to run the hotel until 1953. She died in 1974. The hotel is now owned by C.R. Properties. Richard and Mary Ann had five children: Eleanor, Ethel, Elsie, Edward and Charles.

to see him so we went upstairs and woke him. He came downstairs, asked her where the pain was. He wanted to take her to Russell. Ma Berger told us, "Don't you go with him in that condition." Our car was in the Rex Garage[20] so I went and asked George Becker if he would drive us to Russell. She was in the hospital for two weeks. On Christmas Day 1943, Dick and Irene came home and we went to Russell and took Mr. Draper and their little girl along. When we got there she wanted to come home with us. Dick was very scared to bring her home, but we got home fine. Next morning Mr. Draper knocked on the window to say they had a baby boy during the night. The doctor was sober and Mrs. Brown[21] was the nurse.

Henry was in the hospital until about the middle of January 1944. The doctor had been down and told him he was ready to come home but had not discharged him. The doctor came home and got drunk. I went to Russell with Walter Scholz. Henry was in quite a state. He wanted to come home and told me to go see the doctor that night and tell him. So I went to the hotel. Ma Berger called Dr. Claire downstairs. He was very drunk and asked what I wanted. So I told him that he had told Henry he could come home but he had not discharged him. "Oh," he said, "we can fix that." He phoned the Sister at the hospital and said "Henry Popp is discharged as of right now. I have his loving wife here who craves her husband." I was so mad at him but there was nothing I could do. Henry came home the next day on crutches. In about a week the doctor came to see him. Not a word was said about how Henry got home. Nor were any questions asked. He was a very good doctor but had a drinking problem.

After Henry was home, we were still writing collection letters. We told them Henry was laid up with a broken leg. We asked people if they could pay the principal debt without interest. Quite a few people came and paid. One man came (I won't mention

---

[20] In 1918 Adolf Becker and August Welke Sr. built and operated the Rex Garage on Kaiser Wilhelm Avenue. Adolf's son, George, continued the business until 1965.

[21] Mary Brown and her husband, Jack, came to Langenburg in July, 1943. She was a registered nurse. Mrs. Brown resided in Langenburg after her husband's death in 1971. She died October 6, 1987.

his name since he lives in town now) who owed 300 dollars without interest. He gave Henry 300 dollars. Henry gave him 20 dollars back. That was maybe the biggest sum collected from one person, but any sum helped.

The bank had the first mortgage on anything we owned and the Traders Finance had the second mortgage. So I started writing to the Traders Finance. They had a mortgage for 6,000 dollars. They had repossessed a lot of used cars. They sold them for whatever they could get and the shortfall was charged against the garage account. So I wrote to them. They wrote back saying we had a good half section of land with good buildings. I wrote them describing that the house was an old log house with a rotting floor and it was being sold for back taxes. I don't remember if we made them an offer or if they set a price. I am not even too sure what we settled for but I think it was 2,000 dollars.

After we had paid or settled with the Traders Finance we had to redeem the land. They had it for tax sale for 350 dollars. Nobody had much money then so it wasn't sold yet. We had another quarter section of land bought and made the last payment on it. It was in my name so they could not put a mortgage against it. There were oil rights on it which we leased to an Oil Company for 80 dollars per year for ten years. We rented the land. There were better crops on that land and when grain prices went up we got money to help pay for the taxes on the other land and pay the Bank. When we got the bank debt down to 1,200 dollars Henry borrowed money from Hugo Yeske and paid off the bank. Then we got all the notes and statements from the bank and found that for ten years the bank had been collecting the crops from the half section of land but it hadn't received even as much as we had paid for rent in town and we had cheap rent. There were buildings on the farm, a poor house but good barn, sheds, good well, portable granaries and hay and green feed. The rent the Bank collected for this half section was not as much as we got from the other quarter section. I couldn't understand it and to this day I don't. But later there were better crops and better prices. We paid off Mr. Yeske and other outstanding debts. I felt free again. I would have boarders, Florence Popp, when she went to school in Langenburg, and Luella Kendel when she worked in town. Henry would often have a helper who would board at our place.

I was saving for a fur coat. When I thought I had enough saved there were good fur sales advertised in the Winnipeg papers so I decided to go to Winnipeg and buy a fur coat. I had taken the ads along. But either they didn't have my size or they were sold out. I did a lot of shopping. I went to Rudolfs, a furrier. He had a beautiful muskrat coat for 365 dollars. I liked it, but I had had a long-haired coat when we got married and knew that the hair would break. I wanted Persian Lamb. The Bay had nothing under 600 dollars, but they were having a March sale with coats for 495 dollars. I couldn't go back in March so they said I could place my order. They took my measurements. They had skins so I could pick what I liked.

Henry had told me before I left, "You won't buy". So I decided to order. I gave them a cheque for 495 dollars a few days after. One evening, after I had returned to Langenburg, one of the bank boys came over. I had overdrawn my bank account by five dollars. So I had to put some money in my account. I felt so disturbed about spending that much money for a coat when we had been so hard up for so long. I nearly worried myself sick over it. The coat didn't come for a few weeks and when it came I was almost embarrassed to wear it, but it was a very good coat, the warmest I've ever had. With a few repairs and alterations, after twenty five years it still was a good coat and no longer was I sorry that I had bought it.[22]

While Ella was in training there were times I wasn't feeling so well - going through a change of life. One day I went to Yorkton to see Dr. Portnoff. At the time we didn't have a doctor in Langenburg. Dr. Portnoff examined me and told me I was pregnant. He was pretty sure but I was to come back in six weeks - then he would be sure. I was 48 years old. I told him we were getting a doctor in Langenburg and I could go to him. Well Dr. Portnoff was very interested. He asked if our doctor would get in touch with him. Well I was not elated. In fact, I felt sick to my stomach. I went to eat, ordered soup, but couldn't eat, so I went

---

[22] Mary Popp's fur coat is now owned by her granddaughter Beverly Kesslering.

out and walked. I looked in store windows at baby clothes. I saw a woman who had a sweater on. It was buttoned, but her coat wouldn't close, only the belt. My coat was fitted. I thought that was what I would look like. Then I met Kay Popp.[23] She asked me what the doctor had told me. I told her. She laughed and said, "Imagine Uncle Henry pushing a carriage."

Then I went to brother Rudy's place. My sister-in-law Tug didn't think it was so funny at my age. I had gone up on the train. When I got home Henry met me at the station. He asked me what the doctor had said. When I told him, he said, "I don't believe it. He is crazy."

That night we went out to a party a Welkes. Next night there was a vanity fair at the hall. I went. I wanted to tell someone and couldn't. Mrs. Thomas, one of the teachers was fixed up telling fortunes. She told me my fortune. Then she asked if I had a special question to ask. I did, but would not ask her.

I had started writing a letter to Ella before I had gone to Yorkton. I was going to mail it from there, but I didn't, so I kept on adding to it, explaining what the doctor had said. I wrote some every day until on Wednesday when I found I wasn't pregnant. So I finished the letter and sent it. Dick lived in Winnipeg then. Ella got excited until she got to the end of the letter. She took it over to Dick's. They read it. By Saturday I was called to the phone at Mrs. Romboughs. The kids had phoned to tease me. We had not told anybody in town but then it got out. We were teased a lot about that.

In 1944 when Ella was home for holidays we were still collecting debts. We heard that Martin Schepp[24] was having an auction sale. He had refused to pay on his notes, so Henry and Rudy took a judgment or lien against his property. The day of the sale we went there. Henry was still on crutches. He had to have someone to serve the paper on Schepp. John Betz was also there to collect and he offered to serve the paper. He gave the papers to

---

[23] Katherine Popp, born March 3, 1911, daughter of Jacob and Elisabeth (Schoepp) Popp, married Anthony Senger on October 12, 1973.

[24] Martin Schepp and his wife Katharina (Fatteicher) farmed in the Zorra District. They had three children: George, Ewald and Marie.

Martin Schepp and after a while the two Schepp sons picked a fight with him and started beating him. Mr. Betz was a stout man. They threw him down. He couldn't breathe and they were kicking him in the face and side. Henry wanted to go and help him but I held him. I was afraid they would break his leg again. To this day I don't understand how people looked on and let that happen. Then the son's uncle, Henry Fatteicher, came and got the boys away. Mr. Betz got up. He staggered, his nose and eyes were full of blood. Somebody got him into a car and took him away. So our collections were not always easy. But then not all people were like that. A lot of people were hard up, but honest.

Ella graduated in 1945. We went to Winnipeg for her graduation. We picked up Irene at Moosomin and went a day earlier to do some shopping. The next day the war ended. The city went wild. You couldn't get uptown. The streets were packed - people, cars, everybody shouting, singing, throwing streamers, papers. The day after was the graduation. Ella and Irene came home with us. Dick was in Australia then.

After Ella graduated she did some private nursing in Langenburg then in Yorkton. While home she met Ernie Parkinson,[25] and in 1946 they decided to get married. She was still working in Yorkton and Ernie, after his discharge from the Navy, got a job at Flin Flon in the mine. They set the date for June 16, 1946. Ella was earning some money so she picked her wedding dress at Yorkton. Everything was still rationed - meat, butter, sugar. Liquor was rationed, so we decided on just a family wedding. And I was not well. About three weeks before the wedding I had hemorrhaged and was to take it easy. So we had a house wedding. Our house was small so we just had family and a few friends, which was hard, as everybody had been so good to us.

They had a shower for Ella and offered their cars and help. It felt mean not to ask them to the wedding, but we asked them to

---

[25] Ernest H. Parkinson was born March 11, 1922 in the Clumber District near Bredenbury. He joined the Navy in 1942 and served until 1945. Ernie worked at the Langenburg Hardware Store from 1950 to 1956. In 1956 Ernie bought the dray business from A. Hemauer. He was Town Secretary from 1960 until he was employed by Canada Post in 1962. He retired from the post office in 1987.

drop in later. It was a lovely day. Arnold and Meta came from Winnipeg. Dick and Irene came from Mossbank. They had no car so my brother George had to bring them. My sister Helen and Bill Hauser were on a trip and wrote that they would come for the wedding on their way back. We really wanted them to come since their place was Ella's second home while she was in training. They were so very good to her. Ernie's family was closer and outside of Elda and Orvill Gamble[26] we didn't know his family until the wedding.

It was a nice wedding and everything went well. I had Mrs. Reles get the food ready to serve. Arnold and Meta and Dick and Irene came and helped organize things. Ella and Ernie just left for a few days then came back and moved to Flin Flon. In 1944 you could only get to Flin Flon by train.

Again I marveled at how my mother did it. In 1914 she had three big weddings in one year with hot meals and all.

---

[26] Elda Gamble was Ernie Parkinson's sister. Orvill Gamble was a pharmacist. He built the drugstore in Langenburg and the residence at 216 Carl Avenue East.

TIME FOR OURSELVES

After the war, Dick did not feel he wanted to continue his studies at the Seminary in St. Louis. They rented a suite at Mrs. Rombough's house. Their first son, Brian, was born October 24, 1945. Then, in 1946 Dick got a job with Social Welfare in Mossbank. Later he got a job in Melfort, where Barbara was born on August 27, 1947. I went up with Irene's parents on August 29th, 1947.

When Heptons[1] moved away, Dick bought his business and they moved back to Langenburg in the winter on a very stormy day. The roads were blocked and with two small children they had lots of trouble. In 1950, they bought lots and built a house in Langenburg.

---

[1] William Hepton (1892 - 1982) and his wife Florence (Turner) were born in England. They moved to Langenburg from Regina in 1921. Mr. Hepton was a lawyer in Langenburg from 1921 until the 1940's.

In 1947, a year after Ella and Ernie were married, they came home for holidays for about a week. They had just gone back to Flin Flon when Mrs. Rombough asked me, "How would you like to go to Flin Flon for July 1st?" Henry thought we should go. We started out about four o'clock in the afternoon. It was a hot day. The men were drinking beer. We thought they made twenty miles per bottle. Jakie did all the driving. We had supper at Swan River. I thought the country was beautiful. We were going as far as Birch River that night, where Mrs. Rombough's brother lived. It was dark when we got there. They had had a heavy rain so the road to their place was under water. The car was pushing water ahead, then it stopped. We had to get out in the muck. The men walked to town, about three quarters of a mile, while Mrs. Rombough and I crawled through a fence and started through the bush to the house which was dark. Her brother wasn't home and the family was in bed. We stayed only until the car was pulled out. Then we went to the hotel, had some lunch, got rooms and went to bed.

Next morning, July 1, we started out early. We thought we would get to The Pas and see when we could get a train to Flin Flon. When we got closer to The Pas we drove along the railroad track and saw a train going on the track. When we got to town, we drove right up to the station. The men got out and asked where the train was going. They said to Flin Flon. It was just leaving. They asked them to hold it. We grabbed our bags and ran for the train. We got on in time, got seats, then sat and laughed at how lucky we were to catch the train. I couldn't stop looking at those huge spruce hills. The track was so crooked that sometimes you thought you saw another train, but it would either be the front end or the back end of the train we were on. It was a long train and went very slowly.

When we got to Flin Flon I remembered I hadn't taken Ella's address along. I knew they lived on Hillcrest, but couldn't remember if it was 61 or 62. We had no idea where it was. So the men asked a Chinese laundry man. He said he would take us. It was up and down hill all the time. When we got there, we had to see if we were at the right house. We knocked - no answer. So we opened the door and went in. The dog growled but let us in. I looked to see if I recognized any of Ella's things. The first thing I saw were some pictures I'd made for Ella. So we were at the right house. We were hungry so we went back uptown to eat at the cafe.

Mrs. Rombough and I looked around a bit then we walked back to the house on the raised, wooden sidewalks. When we got to the end therc were no steps down and so we had to go back and find steps. We didn't know we were walking on the water mains. Flin Flon was all rock so their water pipes were boxed in above ground and packed with sawdust. Later when we told Ella and Ernie about their funny sidewalks, they laughed.

The men had taken a taxi and went to a picnic where they thought they would find Ernie and Ella. When they got there the first people they saw were Ella and Ernie. Ella saw her dad coming. They sure had a surprise. The next day it was still very hot but we went sightseeing and walking. There weren't many cars in Flin Flon then since there were no roads. That night we took the train out again. The next day we went as far as Birch River. Mrs. Rombough had some business there. We had spent another night there, then went a different way home, through Togo and Calder. Calder had a sports day so we went to the sports day and returned home that night. It was an unplanned trip, but we sure had a lot of fun.

July 8th, 1947, was Langenburg's sports day. I helped in the booth. Those years we had to take a lot from home - tub, canners, knives, dippers, ladles and pies. We came home late with a tub full of dirty dishes. I could hear the phone ringing. It was Arnold phoning from Winnipeg. My sister Helen was critically ill; we were to come at once. I had about three quarters of an hour to catch the train. I was dirty from frying hamburgers and working at the sports ground. I tried to get ready but I was so confused. I put a blouse on inside out until somebody told me. I had to leave everything as it was and I just made the train. When I got to Winnipeg, Helen was in the hospital, paralyzed. She could move one arm a bit and talk some. She was so surprised. Why had I come to Winnipeg so unexpected? I couldn't tell her there was no hope for her, though the doctors tried with a certain type of blood transfusion, all to no avail. She couldn't swallow. She died July 14th, 1947. It was very hard to see her go. Her daughter, Elaine, was eight years old and her son, Brian, five years old. I missed her a lot. (It was later established that she died of polio.)

Sister Katie then lived in Winnipeg. Her life had been hard. After she married Pete Rathgeber in 1914 they lived on a farm then bought a house and garage in Inglis. They had six children.[2] But business was poor, especially for those who had no experience in business (as we too found out). People bought on credit and couldn't pay. Pete left and Katie moved to Winnipeg with the children where she got a job. The children grew up and all got work. Katie got a job cleaning at Riedles Brewery where she worked until she got sick and died.[3]

I went to Flin Flon again when Ricki was born on November 2, 1948. She took her time arriving so I spent a few weeks there. When Ella was in the hospital Ernie would work or sleep days so I walked. It was a long way to the hospital and the road was stony so I would get on the water mains. It was easier walking and I knew which steps to get off or on. I did a lot of walking and tried different ways. I'd go by the United Church. There was a long, winding stairway but then I would have to climb the hill to the house, but found it all interesting. It was a good way to lose weight.

I went to Flin Flon again that year after Christmas. Ella had written that she had a sore breast. They thought it could be cancer. I took the train to Yorkton. At Bredenbury Ernie's folks got on. Ernie was surprised when he met us in Flin Flon. When I had received Ella's letter I talked to Dr. McManus[4] and he advised we take her to Regina. He did not think they were equipped in Flin Flon to do surgery of that kind. By the time we got there they were quite sure it was not cancer. That was my last trip to Flin Flon.

---

[2] George, 1915 (who later adopted the English version of "Rathgeber" - Advice); Helma, 1918; Frieda, 1920; Lillian, 1922; Alice, 1925; and Rudolf, 1927.

[3] Katie died September 29, 1953 at 61 years of age.

[4] Dr. McManus was a doctor in Langenburg in the 1940s. He was known as an excellent doctor and had served in the Canadian army. In 1946 he built the house at 216 Road Avenue East. The Town of Langenburg designated it a heritage property in 1994.when it was purchased and used by Don Layh as a law office. Don and Jan Layh had two children: Adam and Avery.

Ella and Ernie liked Flin Flon at first; it was a young people's town. Before Ricki was born, Ella worked at the hospital. But both being on shift work sometimes they would meet, one going to work and one coming home. They also found the smelter smoke disagreeable. They didn't think they wanted to stay there so they sold their house and furniture and came back. Tony Reichmuth[5] had bought a store in Binscarth and was waiting for Ernie to work for him. They tried it but didn't like it.

Then in 1950 Mrs. Rombough asked me if I wanted to go to Port Arthur with them to visit Arnold and Meta. Again Henry said, "Go." Mrs. Rombough, Jakie Baumung, Gustie and Eitel Zorn were going through Port Arthur, then on to Oshawa to pick up a new car. Oh yes, I wanted to go along.

We left July 24th. We went through Winnipeg and got to Port Arthur at 5:00 a.m. We had breakfast and then went to Wilson Motors where Arnold worked. He took us home and phoned Meta at work. They both took the day off and drove us around. We went to a mixed beer parlor, the first we had ever been in. We made arrangements to eat at the Flamingo Club, a new place that had just been opened. It was such a snazzy place. Jakie and Eitel wore big white felt hats. People thought they were Americans. Bill Thurber[6] was telling stories. I had ordered the smallest steak and it was big. The men ordered chicken in a basket. Jakie put catsup on his then couldn't eat it. So Bill put a serviette over it. First they tried to buy the basket but the waitress said they couldn't sell it. So Bill opened his pants, put the basket in and zipped it up and walked out. They knew the basket was gone but couldn't see how it got out.

That night Mrs. Rombough asked if I wanted to go along for the rest of their trip. Well, I sure wanted to. I got so excited I

---

[5] Anthony (Tony) Reichmuth (1899 - 1967) came to Canada from the United States with his parents in 1901. The Reichmuth family operated a General Store in Marchwell for several years. In 1927 Tony married Louise Yont. Tony and Louise moved to Binscarth in 1950 after selling the Marchwell store to Johann Schepp and Ernest Hande. Tony operated a hardware store in Binscarth until his death in 1967.

[6] Bill Thurber had been the high school principal in Langenburg from 1930 - 1938.

couldn't sleep the rest of the night. I was still packed. I didn't have too much money along but they said they could help me. Next morning they came to pick me up and we went back to Thurbers for lunch. (They had gone back to Flamingo Club to return the basket.)

We left Port Arthur and drove through forests along lakes and crossed the International border at Pigeon River. All I had to show was my Legion Auxiliary card but it was enough. It was my first time in the States. We went through Duluth. We got on the wrong highway but that just meant driving around in Duluth and I could see more. It all was so very interesting to me - the different trees, lakes, and ships and barges loading ore. Mrs. Rombough would explain it all to me. At Sault Ste. Marie we crossed back to Canada on the ferry. An American band played on the ferry. On the Canadian side we ran into a very big parade. It was a civic holiday there. We stayed in cabins or hotels and we would leave real early, then have breakfast at taverns later. We by-passed Ottawa on the day of MacKenzie King's funeral. At Sudbury the country was so different. It was iron range mining. We went to Cornwall and stayed in the Lloyd George Hotel right by the lake. It was all so beautiful, too nice to go to sleep.

Saturday morning we went to Oshawa. Eitel picked up the new car. We went to Toronto and looked up Rudy Baumungs[7] and William Schicks[8] and other cousins and my niece. We saw Casa Loma.[9] I hadn't even heard of it so it was very interesting, this real castle. We had guides who explained it all.

---

[7] Rudolf Baumung was Mary Popp's cousin, the son of Johann Friedrich and Elisabeth (Haberstock) Baumung.

[8] Minnie (nee Bessler) was Mary Popp's cousin, born in Landestreu, Austria on April 6, 1903. Minnie was the daughter of Christian Bessler and Elenora Lowenberger. Minnie came to Canada in 1922, joining her siblings Elisabeth (Nerbas), Fred and John. She married William Schick. They had one daughter, Wilma. Minnie continues to reside in Toronto.

[9] Casa Loma is a "medieval" castle built by Sir Henry Mill Pellatt between 1911 to 1914 on a 25 acre estate in Toronto. The castle was designed with several technological features uncommon for that time - wiring for electric power, a central vacuum system and its own telephone exchange. Because of financial problems, Sir Henry occupied the castle for only nine years. The City of Toronto took over the castle for unpaid taxes in 1924. In 1937, the Kiwanis

From Toronto we went to Blenheim, stopped at Millie and Wilbur Rooke's.[10] It was beautiful country there. The fruit trees were loaded - applies, cherries, peaches and grape arbors, all of which I'd never seen. At Grimsby we looked up Bob Beckers.[11] We went to Niagara Falls and rode in the *Maid of The Mist*. From there we went through tobacco-growing country, fields of it, and saw many drying sheds. We arrived in Windsor late that night. Next day we looked up Paul and Emma Mensch[12] and did more sightseeing and partying. That night we went to Detroit through the tunnel. We went to a bar and had martinis, my first. In that bar I saw my first television. It was very snowy and all they did was advertise razor blades. Then we all went to a burlesque show, my first too. It was smutty and I didn't like it. I would rather have walked through the streets and looked at the skyscrapers.

We continued our return trip. With two cars it was hard to stay together in the traffic. We returned to Canada at Pigeon River and arrived in Fort William at 2 o'clock. Patsy Thurber and Jeanette,[13] our granddaughter, came home with us. We reached Kenora by evening. We couldn't find rooms so we slept in the cars.

It was a most interesting trip as we stopped at any place that seemed interesting and took pictures. Gustie was getting anxious to get home. She had left their baby Billy[14] at home. We stopped in Winnipeg at Henry Kauk's,[15] had lunch, and brought

---

Clubs of Toronto acquired the castle and opened it for public tours. Several television shows and movies have been filmed at the castle, including portions of recent movies like *Cocktail* with Tom Cruise and *Goosebumps*.

[10] Millie Aasen, daughter of John Aasen and Mary Kendel (Mary Popp's cousin) married Wilbur Rooke. They moved to Ontario.

[11] Robert Becker was the son of Carl and Anna (Wohlers) Becker of Langenburg. Robert served in the RCAF in Eastern Canada where he met his wife Janet Smith. They had two daughters, Shirley and Barbara.

[12] Paul Mensch, born in 1910, was the son of William Mensch and Katherine (Haas) Mensch. Paul married Emma Rudoski in 1933. They retired in Windsor, Ontario.

[13] Jeanette Popp, Arnold and Meta's daughter, was born May 13, 1934.

[14] William Zorn was born November 10, 1948.

[15] Henry Kauk was married to Anne Aasen, the daughter of Mary (Kendel) Aasen.

Loretta Aasen[16] who was there, home. We were gone one day less than two weeks and every day of that time was something new to see. I had borrowed money and still came home C.O.D.

[16] Loretta Aasen was Norman and Mae Aasen's daughter.

A NEW HOUSE

In 1951 Mrs. Burkhardt wanted to move into her house so we decided we would build a house.[1] We had already bought the lots. But I was not feeling well. I had poor teeth and would get bad toothaches. So I went to Yorkton to see Dr. Large to have a tooth pulled. He said if he pulled that front tooth, I couldn't wear my partial plate. He said he would pull the remaining seven teeth and make a complete upper plate right away. I told him I hadn't been well and was afraid to have them all pulled. He said there was nothing to be afraid of, he had pulled a lot of teeth. So I decided to let him pull them. I phoned Henry and told him that I would not come home that night. I had the teeth pulled Saturday morning. Dr. Large had the plate ready and put it in. My face felt stiff. He said, "Smile." I couldn't.

[1] The new house was built at 209 Wells Avenue East. Mary remained in this house until 1993 when, at the age of 96, she moved to the Langenburg Care Home. She sold her house to Gord and Fawn Wickham.

I came home with Albert Werschlers.[2] I spit blood into a bag all the way home. That night it bled worse. At 6:00 a.m. Henry got Ella. She didn't know what to do. Dr. McManus was at the hospital across the street[3] so she went over to tell him to come over. He said he had no time. He told her to take cotton-batten and pack my mouth after taking the plate out. She did that. After a while it stopped bleeding. I put the plate back in which was torture. Then my face started swelling. By Monday morning it was very swollen, so I phoned Dr. Large. He said to put on intermittent heat, fifteen minutes hot, ten minutes cold. I did that all day. The swelling went down, but my face went green and blue.

On Tuesday night we had our last bridge party at Mrs. Romboughs. I phoned her to tell her I could not come, but she wanted me to come - Henry could bring me. I wore dark glasses and went. I didn't feel poorly, but everybody tried not to look at my face. When lunch came I was hungry and could eat turkey with my new teeth, but I spoiled it for the rest of them. When they looked at my face they weren't hungry. Anyway I thought I would be fine after that. But I wasn't. I guess I had lost too much blood. My face stayed discoloured. It looked decomposed. I wore dark glasses if I went out, but I was not feeling well.

Six weeks later I started getting dizzy spells. I went to see Dr. McManus. He told me to go to the hospital right away. I began liver shots and pills, but it didn't seem to help. My whole body seemed cold, chilled. I went home for a few days while they moved from the hall to the new hospital,[4] and went back in for another four weeks until I really got scared. I left the hospital and Ella and I went to Yorkton to see Dr. Large from the hospital. He X-rayed and said he could see a loose bone and he would not touch

---

[2] Albert Werschler, son of Rudolf and Carolina (Busch) Werschler, married Helen Mack, daughter of George and Katherine (Burkhart) Mack and farmed northeast of Langenburg. They had three boys, Harold, Donald and Raymond.

[3] In December, 1946 the Langenburg Community Hall was converted to St. Francis Hospital. The stage of the hall was converted to the case room. The Felician Sisters of Grandview set up and administered the Hospital.

[4] In April, 1951, at an approximate cost of $250,000 Langenburg Union Hospital was officially opened with 31 beds. On September 30, 1993 the Hospital was closed.

me again for a million dollars. So I went back to the hospital. My face would still swell and was discoloured. Dr. Large said to go to a specialist. It could be cancer. I felt I had to get out of the hospital. I couldn't stay there any longer. I guess my nerves were shot. I couldn't eat. So I came home. The first thing I did was go into the garden and get some winter onions to eat. I wasn't hungry. The smell of food made me feel sick to my stomach.

By then the carpenters had started working on our house. The way I felt, I didn't think I would need a house, but we had to get out of the house we were in. My face was so sore. One day Henry took me to Russell to see Dr. Graham. He X-rayed my face and said my left jaw bone was broken. He thought the plate didn't fit and suggested I see a specialist in Winnipeg. But he was going on holidays so I just tried to get used to it.

I tried to work so hard on our house, to putty nail holes and sand. I had a garden, but I was freezing all the time. I wore a heavy jumbo sweater all summer. And I'd fall all the time. I fell a few steps down in the cellar on some jars of dill pickles. I'm sure I cracked a bone. It was very sore and green and black for months, but I was afraid I'd have to go to the hospital if I went to see the doctor. Also I was afraid of him, he had given me an overdose of thyroid before. I was on three grams which Dr. Hunter told me was dynamite, so I just struggled along. I don't think I took any medicine.

Then on our anniversary Fred and Mary Mitschke came over. We had some beer. Mary and I shared one bottle, then another. When I made sandwiches, I felt hungry. So we decided maybe I should try stout. Henry brought a case home. I had a bottle in the fridge and drank a glass full before meals. It was too cold, but it seemed to make me hungry. I felt a little stronger and worked hard to get our house finished. It was getting cold and Mrs. Burkhardt cried that she had no more coal and she wanted to move. It was such a wet summer and fall that the plaster did not want to dry in our house. Even the paint and varnish were very slow drying. But we did get moved in our new house early in November 1951. I thought I'd be so warm. We had an oil furnace, but I didn't understand how to work it and the house was so damp.

The windows and walls were frosted up thick. It was cold and damp for just the first few months.

After a while I could get the heat up and I could eat. I ordered some wheat germ oil. My hair had fallen out badly but it started growing in. I tried all the home cures I could think of and began to feel better. My face would still swell and get discoloured. The first chance I got when I felt stronger I went to Dr. Houston. He had been our doctor while we lived in Calder and I had great faith in him. So he asked me a lot of questions and took blood tests. He told me I had infection of the bones in my head and that it would take some time to clear up. I'd just have to be patient. Just talking to him helped me. He gave me some medicine. I also saw Dr. Large and he again told me to go and see a specialist. He gave me the name of one in Winnipeg. He also said my upper plate would not fit until I had my lower teeth out and a lower plate made. Dr. Graham had also told me to go and see the same specialist.

By February I felt strong enough to go to Winnipeg. My niece was getting married so we went to the wedding and I went to see the specialist, Dr. Freeman. He looked at my plate and said it did not fit. The roof of my mouth was raw from the plate. He wrote a note to Dr. Graham and told him if I would have a plate made of Luxeem it would solve my trouble. So I went back to Dr. Large and told him. He said the specialist was crazy. He didn't believe me so I showed him the note the specialist had written to Dr. Graham. Then he got mad because I had gone to another dentist. He said if I wanted a plate of that material and wanted to pay 75 or 85 dollars, all right, but it would not help. I told him I had already paid more for the plate I had and it made my mouth so sore. So he told me to take it out while I was working around the house and just wear it to eat or when I went out. Well I went back to Dr. Graham and he took an impression and built a set. I had to go to Russell about three times. When he had a good fit he sent it to Winnipeg to have a plate made. Then my mouth healed and my face didn't swell. He just charged me 45 dollars for it. I thought it was all just too much. I wasn't well, not quite over a change of life, then I started with new teeth, then a new house - too much at once.

One day in the summer of 1952, Henry came home and said we should go to the Calgary Stampede. Phillip and Minnie Daum[5] and Lou and Annie Brenner[6] were going and wanted someone to go with them. Henry wouldn't have to drive. I was surprised as he never wanted to go away. That year there was so much to do at home. We had no walks and the yard needed a lot of work, but if we didn't go away he would get no holiday. So we decided to go along.

We took two days going to Calgary. Brenner's car was new so we didn't drive too fast. In Calgary we stayed with Henry's sister Rosie Chittick in her small house. We enjoyed staying at Rosie's. She did not come to the Stampede with us. She thought it would be too hard for her. We went with Phillip and Minnie Daum and their friends. We did have fun. Then we went to Banff where we went on a tour. It was cool. Henry was so cold he stayed in the bus. The next morning we went to Lake Louise. It was lovely driving but it was drizzling. The bears were walking on the road. One was limping so we stopped. He came and stood up on the car. I opened the window and fed him cinnamon buns while Lou took his picture. A row of cars had lined up behind us so we went on. Later we came to a sign that said "$500.00 Fine for Feeding Bears." We didn't have 500 dollars so we kidded that I'd have to go to jail.

Lake Louise was disappointing. There was such a heavy drizzle you could hardly see the lake. We walked around. It was muddy and they were spreading fertilizer on the lawns which smelled like dead horses. Then we tried to find a place to eat. We were told to go to Chateau Lake Louise. When we got there everything was such high style and we wore such low style clothes and muddy shoes. They had heavy carpeting on the floor with uniformed waiters. They brought us juice and chipped ice. I ordered porridge. It was brought in a pot, set in hot water and served in a dish at the table. The coffee, cream and sugar were

---

[5] Phillip and Minnie (Schaan) Daum lived in Churchbridge where Phillip was the grain buyer for the Consolidated Elevator.

[6] Louis and Annie (Bessel) Brenner farmed in the Churchbridge area until 1953. Louis then purchased the Wotherspoon and Westman Garage and renamed it Churchbridge Motors.

brought on a big silver tray and set before me to pour, but Henry reached across the table and poured his own. It wasn't too expensive, but we didn't get too much to eat. We ended up with finger bowls. Well we had so much fun of it all. That experience was the highlight of our trip. They did have the cleanest bathrooms that we had come across on our trip. I don't even know if we left a tip. We weren't used to tips. We missed the beauty of Lake Louise because it was such a dreary day but the drive was lovely. We went back to Calgary that night and next morning started for home. We were glad we had gone, as that was the last time Henry saw his sister Rosie.

Early Saturday we started home. We had dinner at Hannah then stopped at Netherhill at Ferd Popp's. They had just moved there and hadn't finished unpacking yet. We had lunch and went on to Saskatoon where we stayed the night with Henry's sister and brother-in-law, Caroline and Art McRae. Next day Brenners picked us up and we drove home. The garden was lovely when we got home. We were just gone a week but there was a lot to do when we got home.

Ella and Ernie lived in a suite. They weren't too happy there so they bought a house. Ernie was working at Best's Store.[7] Beverly was born December 13th, 1952 in the Langenburg hospital. Before then all patients were taken to Russell. Ella nursed at the Langenburg hospital quite a bit when she could.

I babysat sometimes when people went away, like when Venns went to a bank convention to Toronto or when Threadkells went to Winnipeg or when Bergers went to Hawaii. I was saving money for a deep freeze. Henry didn't believe in a deep freezer, but to me it meant a lot to freeze vegetables from the garden and have them when I wanted. So I saved enough and bought one. Then Henry thought it was a good idea.

There was a lot of work on our new house. We made walks and steps, had the yard filled in and grass seeded. I wanted trees so I planted two apple trees and two cherry trees. In about three years they were covered with blossoms and fruit. The Heyer No 12 was

---

[7] Cliff and Maxine Best moved to Langenburg in 1946 when they bought the Hardware Store. They left Langenburg in 1975.

just loaded. It was lovely. I also planted two White Mountain Ash and spruce trees. I loved trees. I also planted raspberries and strawberries - the kind of garden I liked with everything in it. Yes it was a lot of work but the kind of work that was interesting and such good healthy exercise for me.

In 1952 Ella, Ernie and their girls asked us if we wanted to go with them to Port Arthur to visit Arnold and Meta. We had intended to leave a couple days earlier but Henry was worried about grain mites in the bins. So we left the next morning. When we got to Portage, I found I didn't have my wallet. What had happened? The night before Martha Kohnen had come for a stamp. I got my wallet and instead of putting it back in my purse I put it beside my purse. But I wasn't even sure of that. I had also gone over to Ella's for a while the night before and left our doors unlocked so I wasn't sure. Henry teased me. He said I didn't want to spend my money that's why I left my wallet at home.

When we got to Port Arthur I asked Arnold to cash a cheque for me so I had money. Henry just carried his money in his jacket pocket. They had gone down to a cafe. Ernie went in and Henry sat in the car with Ricki and Bev. A bum came along and asked Henry for a quarter. Henry gave him one. Later two men walked past the car. One bent down and picked something up and said, "Now I'll buy the coffee." Henry felt his pocket. His money was gone! He dashed into the cafe and asked the men if they had picked up his money. They had picked up some money but asked Henry how he knew it was his money. They asked him how much it was. He had about 70 dollars and he knew what bills he had. So they gave him his money. He bought coffee for them and talked to them. It happened the man who picked up the money was Arnold's lawyer. Then I teased Henry back - I left my money at home, but he lost his.

Arnold and Meta ran a cafe then. They were very busy but they took time off to show us around. They went with us through the grain terminals and their new arena which had a canteen in a club room with lovely furniture and drapes. We had a very nice time. We talked Henry into coming home the American way. He was not enjoying the holiday too much. He was too worried about the mites in the grain bins. We spent a night in Bemidji and shopped at Grand Forks, North Dakota. We were glad to get home. I found my wallet okay.

When our house was built there were many nice pieces of leftover boards. The builders would throw them on a pile to burn. If I'd come in time before they would light it, I'd pick out the good pieces of board and put them in the basement. Henry wanted to know why I was saving all those pieces of board. I'm sure they burned a lot of nice pieces when I wasn't around.

One winter when I was feeling better I went down the basement and looked at my pieces of boards and decided I'd make a little bench. I had no tools other than a poor hand saw that cut crooked (though good hand saws cut crooked for me too). I had a hammer and new nails so I tried to find a good piece of straight board and build something around it. I wanted a sewing bench. I built one with a lid on it like one I'd seen before. Henry put hinges on the lid. Then I wanted a stand to keep the silver chest on so I built one and called it my tea wagon. Henry put castors on it. Then I made a bedside table, a front hall bench with a lid on it, a magazine rack and two or three tables.

I had all that stuff in the basement covered with a big sheet of paper as I had them all nicely sanded and I was raising a lot of dust. When I had most of them made the women wanted to see them. So when bridge was at my place I took them down the basement and unveiled my work. They were surprised as I had done pretty well, especially since I had no tools.

For my birthday that year Henry bought me a plane, a screw driver and a marking pencil. The pencil didn't help much. I still cut crooked. I had become so engrossed in my building I'd get up early and go down and work until late at night. Oh yes, I had made a smoking table for Henry for his birthday and when we tooled copper pictures, I made the frames. I made a lawn chair but I didn't have enough lumber. I had to use pieces. The chair was comfortable but didn't last long. I just wanted to make things. I have no idea what I would want to make or how. I just had an urge to make things. Then suddenly the urge was gone.

The same happened with copper tooling. I saw a profile picture of the Queen in MacLean's magazine so I traced and tooled it. Faces were hard to tool but it went pretty well. The hair went well. She wore a three-strand necklace and earrings - they looked nice. It looked so nice Ella asked "Are you going to send it to her?" Well I hadn't even thought of that. Then I started thinking, “Why not?” So I started wrapping it - but how do you address a parcel to thc Queen of England? I didn't tell anybody. When I got to the post office I nearly didn't have the nerve to mail it. I told Mr. Thompson.[8] Maybe he thought I was crazy that I had tooled a picture of the Queen and was sending it to her. It took a few weeks. Then I got this official letter from the Governor General in Ottawa. I was afraid to open it. It was a letter from the Queen thanking me for the copper tooled picture. I didn't tell anybody for a long time.

I also tooled Ella and Ernie’s wedding picture. The first one I poked a hole through Ernie's nose so I tried another one. I got Ella's dress pretty nicely. I found faces very hard to do, but I tried.

---

[8] Norman Thompson (October 23, 1893 - March 1, 1984) was postmaster in Langenburg from 1926 until 1961. He married Katherine Walz. They had two daughters, Grace and Gloria.

HENRY'S RETIREMENT

In 1956 Henry turned 65 years old and retired from the Saskatchewan Wheat Pool. The new Pool agent was Ralph Alberts. One day Henry and I decided late in the afternoon to go picking saskatoons. I made some sandwiches. It didn't matter what time we came home. We found lovely berries so we stayed out until after 9 p.m. As soon as we drove into the yard Ralph Alberts drove in. They were having a party for Henry and had looked all over for us. Dick and Ella didn't know where we were - we had just picked up and left. I quickly got dressed. Ralph didn't say it was a wiener roast and I had put a fancy dress on. They took us out to Alfred and Betty Walzs.[1] They had waited and waited for us.

---

[1] Alfred Walz, born 1910, was the son of Joseph and Anna (Buchberger). He married Betty DePape in 1934. They had four children: Leroy, Earl, Gordon and Inez.

The local Pool committee presented Henry with a gold watch which he hadn't received from the Pool since he had just bought grain for 24 years and six months when he was 65 years old. They just gave gold watches after 25 years of service. They had another party for Henry at Marchwell and at a meeting at Yorkton. The agents gave him a pen and pencil set.

After Henry retired from the Pool, his pension wasn't big enough to live on. He thought he would ship cattle for the Pool. He took one car load of cattle to Winnipeg. While he was there he became very sick. He thought he was going to die; he was still sick when he got home. Dr. Zbeetnoff gave him an electrocardiograph but nothing showed and Henry got better. But he didn't want to ship cattle any more.

He was asked to take a job slinging beer at the beer parlor and to caretake at the bank. Then an oil agent asked if he would take charge of a service station. That sounded like a good deal but Henry would be responsible for giving credit. I was scared of that since it had taken us so many years to clear the debts of "Lowenberger & Popp". I was even afraid to play Monopoly - it was too true to life.

Then Mr. Hiere from the Western Producer came from Regina looking for someone to sell subscriptions. He talked Henry into it. Henry didn't do too badly but he had to drive a lot and he sold at regular subscription prices while a sheet writer on a bicycle was ahead of him selling for different papers as well as the Western Producer at a cheaper rate. So Henry quit.

Then Henry started talking about getting a job at an oil rig to run a steam boiler. He still had his boiler certificate from when he ran the steam engine for threshing. He spoke to Roy Brown from Spy Hill who had worked on a rig the year before. So one Sunday in the early fall of 1956, we went to Spy Hill, picked up Browns and went to an oil rig around Frobisher, Saskatchewan. Henry talked to the boss who thought he would have a job for Henry after freeze up. But he never phoned. Roy Brown had already gone so Henry decided he would go by himself. I got his clothes ready and he left on October 31st. When he got there the company already had enough men. He heard that the Regent

Company needed a boiler man so he went to see them and they gave him a job.

Henry was not a letter writer but I went to the Post Office every day. Nothing. I couldn't write to him since I didn't know his address. He finally wrote about the trouble he had on the road getting there and getting a boarding place. He liked the work and liked the gang. Before Christmas they moved north of Kamsack. On Christmas he worked double shift and gave someone else a chance to go home. Between Christmas and New Years they moved down to Elphinstone, Manitoba so he came home for a couple of days. While he was home we had a little Christmas and birthday party for him and he left again. We had an early spring in 1957. Since they were drilling in a lake they had to quit early.

That fall Henry waited for a call to return to the oil rigs but they didn't phone until December 14th. It was a different company that needed a man at Alameda, Saskatchewan. So again I got him ready and he left. He didn't like his boss or the gang. He couldn't find a boarding place so he stayed at the hotel. It was very cold. He had a turkey for Christmas from Can American, the company he worked for. At Christmas he was so homesick he said he cried like a baby, and thought, "What am I doing here?" He quit and came home in January 1958. He liked the work but it wasn't easy being away from home. Next year he got a couple of phone calls. One was not far from Russell. It was close to home but it was shift work and sometimes very cold weather. The pay was good and the kind of work he liked but thought it wasn't worth it.

Then, in the summer of 1958, he got a job building roads with the Municipality. Sometimes it would be very hot, but he would go out early and come home earlier. He was proud to be able to do it and he liked it although sometimes he would get aggravated at the men. They would sometimes play tricks on him which he didn't always think were funny and in the evening he would come home and scold about them. I told him to quit, but he wouldn't. But his back and leg got sore. So he just worked part time. He continued to work until 1966.

TRAVEL AND COMMUNITY

When we moved to Langenburg in 1938, we quickly got to know people. I joined the bridge club so I got to know those women. After a year or two Henry was elected president of the church board[1] which he held for 12 or 13 years. They organized a Board of Trade in which Henry was active as an executive or committee member. The community then started working for a hospital. He was on that Board[2] and helped organize meetings in MacNutt, Churchbridge, Beresina and Langenburg. Government men were out to speak. In preparation of a plebiscite Henry went to see a lot of people in the MacNutt and Landestreu area. Henry knew the people and I went along. The plebiscite carried and everybody was happy.

---

[1] Christ Lutheran Church

[2] The original Board was formed in March 1949. The Langenburg Union Hospital was opened in 1951. Dick Popp became administrator of the new hospital.

Then when the rink[3] was built, Henry was on the committee. A group went to other towns to look at rinks and inquire about costs. The rink was built with a lot of free labour. Henry kept a record of his time. I think his time book is still around. After it was built they had a monster car bingo. So he went out selling bingo books. One day I went with him to Calder, Wroxton, Togo, Roblin, Inglis and Shellmouth. Henry sold the winning ticket to the druggist at Esterhazy.

The women had formed a community club, later known as the Red Cross Society. We sewed pajamas and baby clothes and did a lot of knitting after the war. On February 11, 1946, the Ladies Auxiliary to the Canadian Legion was organized. I was on the first committee. On October 18, 1946 we had a hobo dance which went over well. It was the last dance in the hall because it was being converted into a hospital until a new hospital was built. The Legion men were building the Legion hall and the Ladies Auxilliary raised money to help and to furnish it. We had one meeting and one social a month. After the Legion hall was built, we often had whist drives. On November 11th, 1948 the mortgage was burned. But there was still a lot to be done so the Legion put on sports days. The first one, on a Sunday, was a great success. We were sold out of everything.

When the hospital was started, we organized the Hospital Auxilliary. Again we worked hard raising money to buy an autoclave. We had teas, bazaars, bake sales, and a booth on sports day. We served for the bonspiels and had plays. We also helped with canning food at the hospital. We made sheets, pillow cases, gowns and baby clothes. We also did the mending at the hospital for a number of years. Then we paid Mrs. Reles to do the mending until the Board made other arrangements. For many years we would have a tag day[4] every fall. We bought a lot of needed things for the hospital and for patients' comfort.

---

[3] The rink was built in 1957 - 58 with four sheets of ice.

[4] On tag day canvassers would give people a tag (a piece of paper with a design on it promoting their particular cause) in exchange for a donation. Donors wore their tags all day to show they had supported the cause and to avoid being asked for further donations.

In 1949 Christ Lutheran Church started building a church. So we started a Ladies Aid and sponsored fowl suppers, bazaars, teas, bake sales and mission festivals. Sometimes we cleaned, painted and sewed. Sometimes it was interesting work; sometimes not so interesting, and often not appreciated. But I guess we all tried the best we knew how.

During the summer of 1957 Eitel and Freda Schendel[5] asked us to go along to Port Arthur. We left on Sunday, August 4th and went as far as Winnipeg. We stayed the night with my brother Jake. Schendels stayed at Howard Kendels. We left early Monday morning and got to Port Arthur at 7:00 p.m. Arnold and Meta still owned the cafe so we had supper there.

We didn't know that Schendels had planned to return through the United States. We left Port Arthur on Thursday morning and stopped at Duluth then went on to Grand Rapids where we spent the night and went sightseeing next morning. We went to Bemidji and saw Paul Bunyan and the blue ox. We travelled, shopped and stayed at various places: Grand Forks, Devil's Lake and Minot. Sunday morning we crossed the border at North Portal.

We returned through the Beinfait coal mining area and had dinner at Oxbow - turkey special at one dollar each. Henry and I just had $1.93 between us so had to borrow seven cents from Eitel to pay for our dinner. We were already coming home C.O.D. We stopped at Estevan to see the new power plant and a brick plant. At Frobisher we saw a lot of oil wells. Then we noticed a Regent Oil Drilling rig so we drove up to it. It was a rig Henry had worked for the winter before, running a steam boiler. We got home at 6:00 p.m. Sunday. It had been such a nice trip.

In October of 1957 Lou Brenner came to see if we were ready to go to California as we had planned five years ago. Henry said he couldn't go. He thought he would get a call to an oil rig and he didn't want to go on a three week trip. He said it was too far. I didn't know what to do. I wanted Henry to come along, but he wouldn't come. I hadn't seen brother Adolph since he moved to

---

[5] Eitel Schendel married Freda Metz, Mary Popp's niece. Eitel was the Pool agent in MacNutt and Yorkton.

California in 1930. That was 27 years ago. I had to decide in a hurry, because they were leaving in a week. I worked very hard to get all my work done - stuff out of the garden, windows washed, storm windows on. It was a good time to go but I didn't like to go alone.

Everybody told me to go, I might never get a chance for the rest of my life. I hadn't seen Al for so many years and had never met Mary,[6] his wife. I wrote him a letter that I was planning to come. He phoned back. Then I got excited. I told him we intended leaving on Tuesday. I started getting ready. Al forgot to tell me to bring warm clothes. I went summery. Lou Brenner came on Monday to say they would leave at 6:30 the next morning, October 8, 1957. They were taking food along so we could save a lot of time by making our own meals. So I made pies, took eggs, bacon, summer sausage, cabbage rolls, cookies, Christmas cake, jam, tea, coffee, a frying pan and some dishes. Mrs. Brenner had chicken roasted and a lot of food to last us until we got there. It was a cold morning when we started. Brenners had a new Dodge car but we still took blankets.

We crossed the border into Montana at Regway and travelled through Plentywood, Scoby, Wolf Point and Glasgow. We stayed in a motel in Harlem, having travelled 592 miles that day.

The next day we went through Great Falls and travelled along the Missouri River and through Mount Helena, a lovely place surrounded by beautiful mountains, through Boulder, Butte and Great Falls. We crossed very high mountains and arrived in McCannon, Idaho that night where we got a motel for $5.50.

On Thursday morning we crossed the Utah state line and reached Salt Lake City by 11:00 a.m. I sure wanted to look around. It was such a beautiful city and I had read about the Mormon Temple. At 6:00 p.m. we crossed the state line and arrived in Las Vegas, Nevada about 8:00 p.m. on October 10th. We

---

[6] Adolph and his first wife, Anne Drawson (1905 - 1939), divorced. They had one daughter, Patricia. He then married and divorced Lillian Adeline Kirk. His last marriage was to Mary ? to whom he was married at the time of Mary Popp's visit. Adolph changed his name from Lowenberger to Lowe.

got a fairly nice motel with a hot plate at six dollars. It was nice and warm that night. We had supper, fixed lunch for the next day and wrote letters although we didn't find a place to mail them until we got to Long Beach, California the next day. We left Las Vegas on Friday at 7:00 a.m. It was lovely out but too dark to see much of Las Vegas except all the taverns lit up. There were many casinos. We got into California at 8:00 a.m., and travelled miles and miles through desert. We ran into heavy rain about noon so we had to eat our lunch in the car.

We drove through Riverside at 1:00 p.m. It was beautiful. The streets were lined with palm trees. We saw orange and lemon orchards. We went through Anaheim and arrived at Long Beach at 2:30 p.m. The Bennetts (Lou's sister) lived at Garden Grove, Magnolia Avenue. When we got there, nobody was home. We had travelled about 2,200 miles from Langenburg. A kind neighbour went with me to a pay phone several blocks away to phone my brother Al. I reached my brother's house. They weren't home, so I left a message. Then we sat in the car from 2:30 until 6:30 p.m. After 6:00 I went again alone to the pay phone. I stumbled over a trailer shaft and hurt my foot. I got Mary on the phone. I told her where I was and asked her if they could come get me. Well, she thought they could have come and got me from Langenburg. They lived 50 miles away. At that moment I wished I had stayed home.

I had counted houses when I left Bennetts and thought I'd know Brenner's car when I came back. But the car was gone and I missed the house at first, but found it. The Bennetts were home. They thought I had got lost. They didn't have street lights yet since it was a new development.

Al and Mary also had trouble finding the house. They too looked for a Saskatchewan-plated Dodge car. They had a flash light to look at house numbers. When they came in we were strangers. I didn't recognize Al, nor he me. But it had to be him. He thought I'd be as skinny as I was when he had last seen me. Mary was glad that other people were plump. We had some lunch and started for Al and Mary's house. Next morning I went for a walk to see the tall palm trees which lined the streets, the oleander trees in bloom and the hibiscus trees, some low, some tall with single and double blossoms. Al said they bloomed year round.

There were beautiful roses and creeping ivy geraniums climbing all over, on buildings, over roofs, along the banks of the freeway, blooming in all colours. There was so much to see but my eyes needed a rest. All the looking and map-reading had made them sore.

On Sunday morning, October 13th, Al and Mary had planned to take me sightseeing but it rained all day. Mary had tickets for the cinema where they showed *The Seven Wonders of the World*. It was a wonderful show. They showed new things that had never been shown from all over the world such as flying over a volcano, filming down into the smoldering crater, the River Jordan, the Red Sea, Mount Sinai, the Himalayan Mountains, Niagara Falls. It was all filmed from a airplane with the narrator commenting from the plane. They also showed films taken from different countries and a very good comedy. It was one of the newest screens then. It seemed as if you really saw the things happening. When a train came towards you, you ducked. It seemed to come right at you.

Al and Mary planned to take me to a fancy place for dinner where a lot of movie people ate, but my eyes felt so sore and it was raining so hard I asked if we could just go home, have lunch and watch T.V., which we didn't have at home. They were showing the Queen opening Parliament in Canada and we could rest.

On Monday, October 14, we went sightseeing. Along the ocean drive we saw big boats stopped at the Glass Wayfarers Chapel near Portuguese Bend. The chapel was built of glass and chimes played hymns all the time. The grounds were beautiful. We went to the Long Beach Amusement Park which is miles of fair, ferris wheels, rides, games, merry-go-rounds and booths of all descriptions. We stopped and had pig burgers for lunch. Al took me to a big station where he had worked and introduced me to friends and acquaintances.

Then we went to Elvira St. where they had stalls for different wares you could buy. You could also watch them making them - blowing glass and basket weaving. I could have spent hours there looking if my eyes hadn't been so tired. My body was getting tired too. We went to Chinatown. They made me play the mouth organ and a man played the flute until people started gathering around us. We bought some flutes and went home.

On Tuesday morning Al and Mary had to attend to some of their housing units. I went along and looked at the different trees, especially the banana trees with their blossoms and little bananas. In the afternoon we drove to West Covena, to one of their houses which had a walnut tree in the yard. I shook some off but they were wormy. The tree hadn't been sprayed. Then we went to Mary's daughter's house. While they were fixing it up it had been vandalized three times, windows smashed, roof chopped, paint poured around inside - a terrible mess. Then we went to Dortha's, Mary's other daughter and had a nice visit there.

Wednesday morning Mary was sick. We had worn her out. Al went to work and I did a lot of walking around to see things. In the afternoon Al took me to Ferndell, a beautiful zoo.

Thursday morning we left early for Anaheim. I wanted to see my niece Pat.[7] After some inquiring, we got there but there was nobody home. The neighbor thought she had gone to Los Angeles.

Then we went to Dr. Acheson's place.[8] The housekeeper said that Ricki had gone shopping. The housekeeper phoned the doctor. I talked to him. He told me to stay, they would come home. They came, picked us up and took us to the Palms for lunch. It was a dine and dance place, very classy. The palm trees seemed to be growing right through the floor. The food was delicious, and they piled up my plate. They had so many kinds of food that I did not know what they were. I was hungry. Dr. Acheson was very busy so he visited while we ate. I enjoyed that visit very much.

When Al and I got back Mary was feeling better and she had got tickets for a show - *The Drunkard Playing the Wayward Way*. It was so different, like out of the past. Helen, Mary's daughter, and her husband came. They served refreshments all the time and at intermission they brought sandwiches and coffee. After the show they announced that they had a visitor from Canada, Mrs. Mary Popp. My mouth dropped open and I looked at Mary. Well,

---

[7] Pat was the daughter of Adolph and Anne Lowenberger. She was born July 29, 1932 in Los Angeles, California. She married Donald Krebs in 1954. They had three children: Donald, Eric and Susan.

[8] Yvonne Ryckebosch (Ricki) was in nurse's training with Ella Popp. Yvonne married Dr. Charles Acheson.

I had to stand up and the performers sang *I Got a Lovely Bunch of Coconuts*. They welcomed a lot of other people like that. It was a big party.

The entire visit was like a dream, to see so much. Everything was so different. But Los Angeles was too big and scared me. It wasn't homey.

We had got in touch with the Brenners. We left Friday morning at 7:00 a.m. for Reno, Nevada to stay at Mary Willis' motel. We got a motel right across from her place.

Saturday morning, October 19th, we drove out to Virginia City and Ghost Town. It started raining and when we got there it was snowing very heavily so we didn't get out of the car. We contented ourselves seeing what we could from the car. It was a deserted town with a huge old school, houses, museum, church, famous cornstalk saloon, big cemetery and gold mines. Some buildings were braced so they wouldn't fall over. It was snowing real hard with thunder and lightening, real ghostly.

When we got back Mary had a big turkey dinner prepared. We were so hungry. It was delicious. After dinner we went to the famous Harold Club that we had seen advertised everywhere along the way. There were seven floors of gambling and all kinds of games of chance, with a bar on each floor. Everybody played like they were possessed. The Brenners and I just looked. You could find money on the floor. If people dropped money they didn't bother to stop and pick it up. We gambled it. Then I got a dollar's worth of nickels and played a nickel machine. I won a little and played it back. Then I won the jackpot of $7.50 - all in nickels. They brought a paper bag and put it in. I cashed some in for silver dollars. I had two to bring home. And this went on all day and all night and was busier on the weekends. We saw a couple playing a 50-cent machine. They won a jackpot of 250 dollars. But people seemed crazy. Then we went home. I lay on the bed with tea bags on my eyes.

It was October 20, 1967, our 43rd wedding anniversary, and I was in Reno and homesick. On Monday morning we had breakfast at Mary's. I thanked her for having been so very kind to me - she treated me like family. We left at 6:00 a.m. It was very cold. The car was covered with ice. The radio said 30° F. It was hard to see highway signs. We went through Salt Lake City again, but took a different direction as we were going home a different way. We travelled 600 miles that day.

Next morning we started out at 4:30 a.m. When we crossed from Utah into Wyoming it started raining. The mountains weren't that high but they were beautiful, like castles and all colours. We went through Laramie and from there it was a lot of farm land. We stayed at Paxton, Nebraska that night where we found a motel with a stove, cupboards and two rooms for $4.50.

On Wednesday we started out at 5:00 a.m. and went through North Platte, Nebraska where we saw fields of corn and sugar beets. We crossed into Iowa, then Minnesota. We arrived at Jeffers, Minnesota and stayed at Gus Heidemans, (Brenner's brother-in-law), who owned a store there.

On Friday, October 25th, 1957 we crossed the international border at Emerson where we declared our purchases. From there on we saw some of the nicest farm lands we had seen in all the miles we had travelled. We arrived in Winnipeg at 5:00 p.m. Brenner's took me to Jake and Fantie's. They stayed at their son Leonard's place. I did some visiting while I was in Winnipeg on Saturday and on Sunday went to church with Jake and Fantie.

Monday morning we started for home. We got home at 1:30 p.m. It had been a wonderful holiday. I was gone nearly three weeks. It was sure good to get back home.

FIFTIETH WEDDING ANNIVERSARY

We celebrated our 50th Wedding Anniversary in 1964. Ella had gotten in touch with Arnold and Meta. They wrote that they could come if it was on the Thanksgiving Weekend - October 11th. We did no inviting around Langenburg, other than put an invitation in the local paper: "Everybody Welcome to a Come and Go Tea: No Gifts."

I tried to buy a dress which seemed impossible. I just couldn't get anything to fit so I bought material and sewed myself a dress. I so wanted Henry to get a new suit but he didn't want to.

We invited Reverend and Mrs. Wiegner (he had confirmed me and married us). He came from Winnipeg. Henry was working on the road so he was busy and thought we were making too much fuss. It was hard to know just how much food to prepare as it was open house and on Sunday. I still have the lists of all we used. Everybody brought cakes. Gustie Zorn made the wedding cake. By the time I decorated it I was getting nervous.

The granddaughters cut out big numbers and letters "50th Anniversary". I sprayed them gold and put glitter on them. A number of women made sandwiches, some decorated the hall. We took all our fancy cups and saucers to the hall and others brought theirs. Arnold, Meta, Jeanette, Bill[1] and the boys came on Friday. Brother Jake and Fantie came from Winnipeg. Jake was still feeling fine and he had bought a new suit, hat, shoes and overcoat. He was all dressed up and so cheerful. And Henry hadn't even bought a new suit.

Ferd Popps came on Saturday from Netherhill, Alberta. Ella had a big supper at their place the night before for us all. There was just so much excitement. There had been a long rainy cold spell. But that day turned out lovely, almost as nice as the day we were married. We took pictures outside before we went to the hall.

None of our attendants could come. Sister Katie was dead. Frank Wagner at Salmon Arm was in a wheel chair with an amputated leg and Minnie couldn't bring him and couldn't leave him. They had planned their golden wedding for the same day. At the hall they had a long table where we sat with the cake and flowers on.

Reverend Wiegner gave a sermon. Lillian Keays[2] sang "*Jesu Geh Voran*", the song sung at our wedding. The hall was very crowded. After 6 o'clock a lot of people came to the house. We did not want gifts but received some anyway.

---

[1] Arnold and Meta's daughter, Jeanette, married Bill Langlia. They had three sons: William, Douglas and David.

[2] Lillian Keays was the wife of the station agent, Elmer Keys.

OUR LAST VISIT WITH ARNOLD

After our 50th Anniversary I got sick with the flu and was in the hospital for a while. There was a hum in my head and I was dizzy. Dr. Neilmeyer said my arteries were drying up. Then Arnold and Meta wrote saying I needed a rest and we should come to Port Arthur for Christmas. We decided to go. All the time I wasn't feeling well. That night I woke up and started vomiting, couldn't stop. Henry called Ella. I thought it was the end. They called the doctor. When he arrived he gave me a needle. He asked me to sit up and it started all over again. So I had to go to the hospital. He thought it was my gall bladder. He was going to give me tests, but after a couple of days I felt better.

I had to miss Albert and Bertha Yeske's golden wedding anniversary. I had been to Fred and Mary Mitschke's anniversary before that but I felt bad about missing Yeske's anniversary. After a few days I came home. I still had the hum on the left side of my head but we started planning our trip again. By then we had decided to get somebody to drive us to Moosomin to the train so we wouldn't have to change trains. I hadn't been on a train for a long time. The train had come from Vancouver. It was dirty but I still enjoyed it. Arnold and Meta were at the station in Port Arthur to meet us on December 23, 1964.

That morning their son-in-law's dad (Mr. Langila) had died. The funeral was next morning, a sad happening just before Christmas. We went to the funeral.

We had a nice Christmas. Arnold and Meta had a lot of people in and took us out a lot. By then I was feeling better and I wanted to eat all the time. Wherever we went they had such lovely food. And I ate. I was afraid Arnold and Mete would be ashamed of me. Even the humming in my head got better. Henry enjoyed it all very much. On Christmas Eve Arnold took him to the rink to meet some of the curlers and they came home in the evening. We were late getting to church. During a conversation Arnold said he might die before any of us. He did go to a doctor while we were there and was asked to come again if the doctor told him anything bad. He didn't tell us anything.

A few people dropped in after we had been to church. Nobody seemed too merry. Bill's father had been buried earlier that day so Bill, Jeanette and the boys were often in tears. On Christmas morning, Meta took us to a different church. Arnold took Henry to the rink and when they came home some men came along who all played instruments. A small orchestra played carols. It was lovely. But they were all sad. One of the group had died two weeks before. They played a piece for him. They were all Arnold's friends. They said they had come every year on Christmas day to play. They seemed so nice.

Boxing Day was a beautiful day. Arnold took us for a ride to show us Port Arthur and Fort William. The cities were decorated beautifully. We were invited to the singer, Bobby Curtola's parent's home.[1] Mr. Curtola and Arnold had both worked for Wilson's Motors for many years and were good friends.

---

[1] Bobby Curtola as born in 1944 in Thunder Bay, Ontario. He was one of Canada's early teen idols. He started his career with his high school band, Bobby and the Bobcats. *Hand and Hand with You* was his first hit in 1960. His best known hit was *Fortune Teller* in 1962, a huge hit in Canada and the United States.

When we got there Bobby had left early that morning for the West to appear at Brandon that week. His younger brother, I think his name was Billie, had got engaged that day. There were so many people there. They were showing us their new big beautiful house which somebody said Bobby had built for them. While we were there the Wilsons came. Mr. Curtola was still working for them. Arnold had quit a few years before and had gone into a cafe business for a while. Then he went into an electronics business with a partner. I got talking to Mrs. Wilson. They had lived in Regina before and were friends of the Saville Taylors (Henry's niece) in Regina.

Then the Fishers came. Douglas Fisher was the newly-elected Federal N.D.P. Member of Parliament. Henry wanted to talk politics with him. Mrs. Fisher was telling us how she went along to the sessions. At that time the flag debate was on and it dragged on and on. It was getting close to Christmas and the Members wanted to go home. Finally Mike Pearson got mad and he gave them all a real talking to. Mrs. Fisher said Mr. Pearson always seemed so calm but he flared up and got that bill passed. Then the Members could go home.

Again there the food interested me so. Mrs. Curtola had stayed up all night cooking and getting Bobby ready to leave. It was a lovely spread, buffet style. There was turkey and trimmings, all kinds of salads and ravioli - which I hadn't seen before. It was the "eatingest" Christmas I ever had. We were there a week, a very interesting one.

Arnold and Meta took us to the train. The night before we left, Ed Rowens[2] came to Arnold and Meta's house. We had a good visit, reminiscing about when we all lived at MacNutt. He remembered some very funny things that happened there. They left when we had to leave for the train. It left at 11:00 p.m. We said good-bye to Arnold, not thinking we would never see him again.

Our trip was like a second honeymoon, after our 50th wedding anniversary. We couldn't have had a lovelier trip. We both enjoyed it, though there was some sadness connected with it which I will not mention.

---

[2] The Rowens farmed at MacNutt.

I wasn't feeling well when we got home but the buzzing in my head slowly got better. I got busy with the baby clinic, bridge club, Ladies Aid, Hospital Aid, Ladies Legion Auxiliary and all our birthdays within a week - Ella's on January 15, Henry's on January 16, mine on January 18, and Dick's on January 20. So there would at least be one party somewhere during the week. That year the party was at Dick's. Henry's brother-in-law, Ferdinand Becker,[3] died on January 16, 1965 at 90 years old. He had been in the Anderson Lodge in Yorkton. We went to the funeral in Zorra and saw all the family. Some we hadn't seen in years.

At the end of October 1965, we got a letter from Meta. Arnold had been in the hospital with a coronary and was in an oxygen tent. I did not know how serious that was but Ella said it was very serious. I should maybe have phoned. I got a card and wrote him a letter. I still had it lying on the table when the phone call came. It seemed he had been better and was allowed out of bed the day before, but he died suddenly in bed while he was shaving. That was such a terrible shock. I phoned Ella and Dick. They got Henry home from the road. I had just started hanging out clothes and kept on washing. I could cry as loud as I wanted to. Ella and Gustie came over. We talked about going down to Port Arthur. Dick wasn't well. He had to go see doctor in Yorkton.

Dick, Irene, Ella and we left early next morning. Dick didn't tell us he was having dizzy spells and thought he would have to go back home. But he got better and we went on. He had to do all the driving. The last 20 miles was in very thick fog so we got to Port Arthur late. Meta was just going to bed. She didn't think we would get there that night. Her sisters Evelyn and Gloria were with her. People were so good.

Next day we went to the church parlor to see Arnold. He looked so alive and so young, but he was dead. The funeral was on Thursday. There was a bitter cold wind. I had taken my fur coat along and stood to protect Henry and the others from the cold. It was a Legion graveside service. Then some friends served lunch at the house. So many people came to the house. I saw a lot of

---

[3] Ferdinand Becker married Henry's sister, Katherine Popp (December 20, 1876 - December 23, 1918) on November 26, 1896.

people whose houses we had been at during Christmas holidays. I had intended to get their addresses and send them Christmas cards but after seeing them again and talking to them, I wasn't in the mood to send gay cards.

The next day we left for home. The girls had made sandwiches and packed some food for us. We started out quite early. We had gone about 20 miles when Dick started getting dizzy. There was a lot of traffic - big trucks - so Ella sat next to Dick to get the wheel and step on the brake in case he blacked out. We were driving very slowly. We stopped at Kenora for dinner. From there I phoned Winnipeg to brother Jake to tell him that we were coming there for the night as we didn't think Dick could drive all the way home. We got to Winnipeg and stayed with Jake and Fantie. Dick, Irene and Ella went to Howard Kendels. There Dick got very sick and they called a doctor to the house. He gave Dick some medicine and made arrangements for Dick to go for X-rays and tests next morning. By the time he got the results we were late getting started from Winnipeg. Dick wasn't to drive but he drove out of the city. Then Ella drove to Minnedosa. She had phoned home for Ernie to meet us there and bring another driver along. We had a late supper at Russell and came home. It was such a very hard trip for us all.

Dick had been to Yorkton doctors and was waiting for a bed to have a gall bladder operation. After his surgery he felt better for a while but those spells came back. He had other tests. It was getting very cold then and Henry didn't go back to work. He took Arnold's death very hard.

We got so many sympathy cards. So I got busy writing letters, then Christmas cards and getting ready for the holidays. Being busy was such good medicine. We had the family in as the Christmas before we had spent at Arnold's. We were so glad we had gone.

LIFE AS A SENIOR

1965 was a busy one for Langenburg and Saskatchewan. It was our Diamond Anniversary of becoming a province. There were functions everywhere; everybody wore old-fashioned clothes.

Langenburg's committee worked very hard. They had got a load of slabs from a sawmill and boarded up the front of stores and buildings. We had a dinner and show for all the old timers the night before. A lot of the older people found old clothes from the past. I made myself a dress and wore my mother's knitted wedding bonnet.

It had been dry for a long time. We needed rain very badly. The night before the celebration we had a heavy rain, but the next day, August 17th, was a nice day. Everybody was happy about the rain.

The day started with an outdoor pancake breakfast and street dancing. The parade started at 1:00 p.m. Floats of all descriptions were so very good. We, the Hospital Aid, made a big float with a flower garden on. Mrs. Schoepp and I were the oldest so we had rocking chairs on the float. We sat there, rolling bandages. We also had an umbrella without any cloth on, just the ribs. It was nice sitting on the float but we missed seeing some of the floats. There were several bands even a Scottish Bag Pipe Band. It was such a good parade. People were in the mood and everybody made up something to enter. In the afternoon the Senior Citizens Units were opened with guest speakers. There was an antique show in the new Municipal Auditorium. An asphalt floor was put in the arena for dancing. They had hired *The Six Fat Dutchmen* orchestra. The curling rink was fixed up for a beer garden; they even had bunny girls. We had prepared so much food, gallons of chili con carni and pounds of hamburger.

We had another parade with floats and bands for Centennial Year on July 24, 1967. But it didn't go over as well as the 60th Anniversary, though there were very good floats. They went out to the sports grounds and were going to end up with a picnic. I guess they had a lot of people out there, but a lot didn't go out. The floats came back to town and it started raining pretty hard.

One of the highlights of 1966 was my first pension cheque on February 24, 1966. I didn't mind getting older for it. Life seemed busy. Our Ladies Aid served for a lot of weddings, banquets and anniversaries.

That summer was very busy. When we moved into our house in 1951 I wanted fruit trees. I had always dreamed of apple trees. I ordered a Heyer No. 12 apple tree, a Dalge crab, two cherry trees and two white mountain ash. After a few years the trees were beautiful in the spring, all white with blossoms, then loaded with fruit in the summer. The No. 12 apple tree was so loaded I'd put posts in and tie a rope on to keep the branches from breaking. I would stand and admire that tree. Later it got fire blight. In the spring hundreds of cedar waxwings would come. They were lovely birds. But in a few hours, they would have all the petals eaten off the trees. The trees would still bear fruit but I think those birds brought fire blight. The Heyer No. 12 apple tree slowly died. I had to chop it down but by then I had planted a North Battleford apple, a pear tree, raspberries, strawberries, more apple trees, spruce and cedar trees, which all kept me very busy.

Henry still worked some, but wasn't feeling well. In June his stomach got sore. Dr. Neilmeyer took him to the hospital for X-rays and tests. He said Henry had a hiatus hernia and put him on a diet with no coarse foods. He also said Henry should have no beer and should quit smoking. He liked going to the pub where he met his friends so he started drinking wine, but sometimes he would mix beer and wine. That was no good. He decided to quit smoking, and on October 2, 1966, he just quit. But he snuffed which was maybe worse since when he snuffed he spit all the time.

In April 1967, the Legion Auxiliary had a tea for all the Senior Citizens. We wore our centennial gowns. Then our Ladies Aid also had a tea for the Senior Citizens and we put on a skit - the *Schwabische Frauen Verein,*[1] which the senior people enjoyed. But I didn't because Henry had a lot of stomach trouble and we had taken him to the hospital the day before.

Henry developed bladder trouble while in the hospital and Dr. Neilmeyer said he would send him to Regina. I phoned Dick and Ella. They came over and decided to take Henry to Yorkton. They gave him tests and X-rays. Henry became very confused while he was in the hospital in Langenburg and worse in Yorkton. He could not remember to do what the doctors or nurses told him to do. I wasn't feeling well so we made an appointment to see Dr. Gable on May 8th. When I came in to see Dr. Gable he told me to sit down. He then told me Henry had prostate cancer. That was a terrible shock. The doctor gave me tranquilizers to take, four a day, and said not to tell Henry about the cancer. He said they would send him to Regina to the cancer clinic. They might operate, but they had pills which would control it pretty well. Henry could maybe live a few years. Meanwhile they were giving him blood transfusions in Yorkton and were trying to settle his stomach. All this time he was not smoking. He had stopped October 2nd and this was May. But one day Irene went to see him and gave him a cigarette and that did it. He was taking cigarettes from patients and asking everybody for cigarettes. So I went and bought him cigarettes and matches. It was dangerous for him to smoke in bed.

---

[1] *Schwabische Frauen Verein* means Schwabisch Ladies' Club. The skit was a meeting conducted in the German dialect spoken by many of the German women in the congregation.

At the same time Phillip,[2] his brother, was in the hospital. He was burning grass and his clothes caught fire and he was very badly burned and suffered a lot.

I stayed with Pauline Zorn. She had breast cancer and had had an operation about ten years before. By then she was full of cancer. She would go to Regina for check-ups. She said a lot of doctors would come when she was being examined. She said they used her as a guinea pig. Her cancer was a rare case but she could talk about it as if she were talking about someone else. She told me she had the hymns and pallbearers picked for her funeral and had everything arranged. She was a wonderful person with such a sense of humor. We would both cry and she would say something funny and we would start laughing.

We got Henry home from Yorkton May 20, 1968. We took him back in a week to see the doctor. He made an appointment for June 5th at Regina, with Dr. Barootes. We still were not to tell Henry he had cancer.

Meanwhile Ella had surgery in Regina on May 31st. She was still there when we took Henry in. They put him through the cancer clinic for a day and a half. When the doctor called me in he said Henry had to have surgery. He was very weak by then. Henry was a very difficult patient as he was so confused and didn't do what he was supposed to. They did not seem to realize that he couldn't remember and therefore he was sadly neglected. I had asked for a special nurse, but they said he didn't need one. He was in a nice ward but without a bathroom or toilet. He was so weak and mixed up. He was throwing up his food which didn't seem to be reported to the doctor. Henry did not know who his doctor was. He thought the orderlies were doctors.

The beginning of July, Ernie and Ella came to Regina to get Ricki home. I showed Ella how her dad was neglected. There was dried-on b.m. on his legs and feet and blood on the sheets. Ella started crying but since she was a registered nurse she got water and washed off her dad and got sheets and changed his bed. I was afraid to do anything like that. I had just tried to rub Henry's leg once when he had a cramp. The orderly came and asked whether I

[2] Philip Popp died October 24, 1974.

should be doing that - “You’d better ask the nurse.” But after I saw Ella, I washed him and also changed his bed when necessary. Then one day I came in and he wasn't there so I went to the desk. They told me he was moved to Self Care. He was in a semi-private ward, such a lovely clean room with a toilet in it. A big orderly put him in the bath tub and gave him a bath. He got such good care there but he still couldn't eat and would still vomit sometimes so they gave him more tests. He received about 26 blood transfusions while he was in the hospital at Regina. He developed an itch and was confused.

He was discharged on July 17, 1968. When we got him home, he weighed 134 pounds. He was sick and weak and so mixed up. He would get up during the night then could not find his way back to the bedroom. And he was so very itchy. After he was home a week I thought he needed blood. So they tested and took him to the hospital in Langenburg and gave him two pints. He started eating. I gave him juice and a cup of raisins each day. He was gaining weight but his itch was getting worse. Dr. Basset was in Langenburg then. He tried different pills. Nothing seemed to help. People told me different things to do, like calamine lotion, witch hazel and other cures. Nothing would help. He scratched so badly he got pusy scabs. He would sit up in bed all the time and scratch. I couldn't sleep so I tried to sleep on the chesterfield, but he would get up and walk around, looking for me and switching on the lights. I couldn't go upstairs, I was afraid he would wander out. I became very tired.

Henry was to go back to see Dr. Good. Dick was going to Regina for a convention so we went in the day before and stayed at the Kings Hotel. It was terrible night. Henry didn’t sleep and was scratching all the time. I had locked the door and he wanted out. We didn’t get any sleep.

The doctor said his condition was fine. He gave him a lot of tests for his itch but couldn’t find anything. He tried to get an appointment with a skin specialist for that day but we couldn’t stay over. Dick was coming home and to spend another night and come home on the bus - I couldn’t take it.

We came home and started with saltpeter baths. Dr. Bassett also gave me some cortisone pills. Henry’s itch got better and he wasn't as confused. We tried to take him out as much as possible as he was getting stronger. If he was out he didn't scratch as much. I guess nerves had a lot to do with it. On November 13, 1967 we went to Adolph and Margaret Kendel's 50th Anniversary and he seemed to enjoy that.

That Christmas we had the family in for dinner. All the cousins and friends dropped in. Henry enjoyed it but when he didn't he could sit in his chair in all the noise and go soundly asleep.

January 1, 1968 was Dick and Irene's 25th Anniversary. By then Henry could go uptown and to the pub. He wanted to ask some men over for his birthday. When he told me I said we should ask some women too. So I phoned them and we had a luncheon at 5 o'clock. That was on January 16th, Henry's 77th birthday.

Since 1967 had been a very difficult year in many ways, I hoped for a brighter 1968. I planned what I could do. The inside of our house needed painting. I started on the kitchen cupboards but I seemed so stiff so I phoned Gordon Park.[3] I did all the inside work, the cupboards, the windows, doors and woodwork. Gordon did the ceiling and walls and all the downstairs. I did the floors and painted the basement walls and floor and the back porch. I won a gallon of paint at the lumber yard so I painted the car shed. I worked very hard but it seemed the harder I worked the better I felt. It gave me such a good feeling to do things.

In April 1968, Trudeau become Prime Minister. We went to Lou and Clara Miller's[4] 44th Anniversary in March and Joe and Minnie Popp's[5] 40th on March 16th. We went to Carl Welke's funeral on June 19th.[6] On July 24th the Ladies' Aid served for LaVonne Miller's[7] wedding.

---

[3] Gordon Park began his painting business in 1964 and, as of 1998, continues to operate his business.

[4] Louis Miller married Clara Richter on March 5, 1924.

[5] Joseph Popp married Wilhelmina Andres on March 16, 1928.

[6] Carl Fredrick Welke came from a family of eleven boys and one girl. He was the councillor and Reeve of the R.M. of Langenburg for many years. He never married.

[7] LaVonne Miller, born January 16, 1946, the daughter of Robert and Alma (Mitschke) Miller, married Roy Graham of Binscarth, Manitoba.

Our granddaughter, Ricki Parkinson[8] got married on August 17, 1968. Gustie Zorn made the wedding cake. I was going to ice it. I had it in a crock in the basement. It seemed too moist so I put it on wax paper on the table to ripen. One day I went to look at the cake. I smelled turpentine. I had been cleaning the tables downstairs and had upset a tin of turpentine. I thought the tin was empty but it had a little turpentine in. It ran under the cake. I was sick. I brought it up to put a first coat of icing on. I cut a little off and tasted it. It tasted awful of turpentine so I phone Ella to come over. We decided we couldn't serve any of that cake. I thought we could bake another one if Gustie would do it. I phoned her and she came over. It was evening and the stores were closed; so we phoned Mrs. Van Joff[9] who went to the store. Gustie got enough stuff for half a recipe and baked it early next morning. She got two layers out of it. So we iced and decorated the turpentine cake - real fancy. Ricki helped. We iced and decorated the new cake too. We didn't cut the big turpentine cake. I asked them not to tell anybody about my accident. I just felt too bad to talk to anybody just then. Later I could tell people but not just then.

We had to dismantle the cake because we needed the pillars and stand for Barb's cake. I thought I didn't smell turpentine so much anymore so I put the cake in the freezer. After a while you couldn't taste turpentine at all. The smell came out.

Our granddaughter, Barb's wedding was August 30, 1968. The Ladies Aid served supper for the family in the church basement followed by a reception in the hall. There was no dancing as her husband, Daryl Lentz, was a minister's son who did not approve of dancing.

Between these two weddings we had Reverend Borchardt's Anniversary in the arena.[10] I made corsages for the family. It was a very big do.

---

[8] Ricki Parkinson married Carlyle Murray of Marchwell, Saskatchewan, son of James and Mary (Mattheis) Murray. Later they divorced.

[9] Peter and Agnes Van Joff ran the IGA grocery store in Langenburg.

[10] Reverend Borchardt came to Christ Lutheran Church in August, 1928. He retired in 1970 after serving 48 years in the ministry. He died June 27, 1985. All three of his sons became Lutheran ministers.

The summer of 1968 had been a busy season for me. Then on September 17, I had washed clothes and made some pies. I was boiling potatoes, intending to make *Berhae*, and was frying liver and mushrooms for dinner. I had my old clothes on, all paint-spotted, and old shoes, as right after dinner I was going in the garden to clean the raspberries. Dinner was just about ready when I decided to take a pail down the basement. When I was on the last step, I don't know what happened - I fell. I guess I was knocked out for a minute as I was lying on my back, my leg twisted. I tried to move but it hurt. I tried to roll around but could not. By then my leg was very sore. I started calling. I knew Henry wouldn't hear me. He usually had his hearing aid switched off. I called and yelled until I couldn't anymore. I was getting chills as I just had a thin sleeveless blouse on. The basement floor was cold. I didn't know what to do. Luckily we hadn't eaten yet. So at 12:15 Henry wondered why there was no dinner and he came to the kitchen. He could hear me call. He came down. When he saw me he didn't know what to do. I told him to phone Ella. Ella came and it didn't take long for Dick and Dr. Choi to come. They got the stretcher and Wally Becker with his station wagon and some men from the pub to help carry me up.

They took me to the hospital and X-rayed my hip. It was fractured and I had to go to Regina. Ella came with me. The plane ride was a little bumpy. I was operated on late that night. My hip was badly splintered so they couldn't pin it. I got a plastic hip which the doctor said was like a new hip and that I would be walking in a few weeks. In a week they took me down to learn to walk on crutches. I was in for six weeks. My leg felt fine but I had some bladder trouble.

After I got home I wanted a bath. For the six weeks I was gone I never had a bath. So I sat on the side of the tub and got in with my clothes on then took my clothes off and ran the water. This worked fine. When I was home for nearly four weeks I did it again. I turned the hot water tap on then couldn't open the cold water tap. I panicked and yelled but Henry didn't hear me. I had to lean forward to turn the hot tap off and my leg kinked. I thought I had rebroken it. I got the cold tap running and got some more water in the tub. I sat in the tub crying out loud. I thought I would have to go to Regina again. When I got out of the tub my leg was terribly sore.

I was shut in the rest of the winter. I didn't mind; I made a big nylon quilt and a couple of little ones. Ella did our washing and once a week she would come over and clean the house and do our shopping. We had Christmas dinner at their house.

Dick and Ella came for Henry's birthday in January, 1969. The next day the girls came for a surprise - only somebody had told me. But I acted surprised. I was sitting making quilt blocks. They brought a punch bowl with cups and fixed a punch and brought us so much food and candy. I was so pleased about it all. It was my 72nd birthday.

Henry was feeling well enough to go for the mail, to shovel the path and help me in the house. He could get things from the basement. They had made me climb stairs on crutches a lot in Regina but I was afraid at home. I found I could get downstairs on my seat, take the crutches down and get a bag to get things out of the freezer. Then Henry could bring it up.

They told me in Regina that I'd be able to walk in a couple of months with my new hip and it was going on five months and my leg was still sore. I was supposed to go to Regina in November, 1968 to see Dr. Kim but Dr. Choi said it wasn't necessary. I wrote Dr. Kim. He wrote back and told me to come in on March 26th.

I also made an appointment for Henry at the cancer clinic. His report was pretty good but Dr. Kim was very disappointed in my progress. He said I'd have to stay in for six weeks of therapy. Well I just couldn't. When we got home I remembered I had heard about therapy at Yorkton Hospital. So I got in touch with Dr. Choi who had moved to Yorkton. I went up and stayed with my brother, George.[11] He took me to the hospital every day and stayed with me all afternoon.

I had to do many kinds of therapy. Mr. Stewart was in charge. He put me back on crutches. I stayed in Yorkton for a week and came home on Friday. I had to walk on my knees which

---

[11] George Lowenberger (May 23, 1902 - August 23, 1987) married Adelheid Mack, daughter of Valentine Mack and Katherine Nerbas on October 16, 1922.

hurt my leg terribly. The exercises were very difficult but I worked hard. Sometimes tears or sweat would run but I felt the therapy helped. After a few weeks he started me with one crutch, then canes. I started therapy in Yorkton on April 7, 1969. By May 5 he told me not to use crutches all the time and he put me on canes. I would go out in the garden, leave the crutches, get on my knees and work. Mr. Stewart said that was good.

When I went to Yorkton in April I phoned Pauline Zorn. She was too ill to talk that day. Then a couple of days later George took me over. She was so very sick and thin, dying of cancer. She died April 26, 1969. She had suffered so much. I felt so bad as she was a very dear friend. Rudy seemed fine. He had been working but was home to look after her for the last few months. Then he worked buying grain in Regina. He died December 28, 1969 - found dead in his motel room. So two of our very dear friends, younger than us, were gone. It was so sad.

Another person I had come to rely on so very much was our granddaughter, Ricki. She was training at the General Hospital and would come to see her granddad a lot. When I was in she would come in every day. I'd know what shift she was on and would wait for her - the bright spot of my day.

In 1969 Dick got a job in Edmonton, Alberta. They had a sale on June 28th. It was very hard to see them move away when we were getting older and Henry wasn't well. We felt we needed them here. But Dick was not happy in his job. There was so much trouble[12] that it was best for them to move and we understood that.

For our 55th Anniversary in 1969 I didn't want to have anything as it would take a lot of planning and work. I thought I couldn't do it again but Ella said it was just a "must". The only way we could have it in the house was a come and go tea. We planned it for Sunday afternoon, October 19th. Ella did the inviting, a come and go tea, from 2:00 to 5:00 p.m.. We served wine, sandwiches, dainties, coffee and tea. Reverend Borchardt had a little service for

---

[12] Langenburg's Hospital Board was often at odds with one of the town doctors, Dr. Zbeetnoff, who began his medical practice in Langenburg in 1953 and is still practicing in 1998.

us. Then people came and went. It was nice but I would have preferred it if people could have come and stayed.

My brother from Yorkton came late and others stayed so we served supper and later played silly games, like full show when somebody would ask where would we go for our honeymoon. I sneaked into the bedroom and put on a long gown and hat to go away. Ella had noticed. When I came out they couldn't find the rice so they threw corn flakes at us. Henry was feeling well enough and enjoyed it all. They took some silly pictures. It was all so very funny, in fact I thought too silly for our age, but I enjoyed it very much as that was a time that wasn't too happy for us. We had a lovely day and some fun. But it seemed our fun days were growing fewer and sad days oftener.

Pauline and Rudy Zorn had died. Mary Mitschke died September 3, 1969. Henry McCullough[13] died November 15th. Fred Kendel died December 11th. Mrs. Burkhart[14] died December 14th. Laura Geith,[15] my cousin, had just been visiting us a week before. She died suddenly. All those people, all good friends, had come to visit Henry while he was sick. It was so sad to see friends go. Yes there were some weddings and anniversaries but there was always somebody who wouldn't be there any more. Somebody else was gone.

In January 1970 our granddaughter Beverly Parkinson married Roy Ferguson. In February there was a bad earthquake in Los Angeles so I phoned brother Al to see how they were. They had felt it but were not in the area where it was bad. That was something else. You could phone all the way to Los Angeles and hear them as if they were in Langenburg.

---

[13] Henry McCullough had been the bank manager in Langenburg. Henry and his wife Babs (Barbara) were close friends of Henry and Mary Popp.

[14] Mrs. Burkhart was the fifth wife of Johann Burkhart, one of the four original settlers who came to Langenburg with Mary Popp's parents. See footnote 16, page 5. Mr. Burkhart and Philip Bieber made arrangements to bring two woman from Germany to become their wives. Clara's maiden name was also Burkhart.

[15] Laura Geith was a daughter of Rudolph and Dora Baumung. She was Mary Popp's cousin.

On February 17, 1970 Daryl and Barbara Lentz had a baby boy, Darren, another great-grandson for us.

Then in April 1970 Mary Aasen died suddenly. She wasn't well and always worried that she would have to go to a nursing home. When she came from Austria our home was her home. She was our family. I felt sad when she was gone. I missed her a lot.

Then came the time we couldn't drive our car any more. We sold it. After having a car for many years we felt lost without it.

In June I received a Certificate of Merit for being in charge of the Child Health Clinic, sponsored by the Hospital Auxiliary. I volunteered to be in charge to take the appointments, get helpers and put up posters every month and to see that we had a place to have the Clinic.

In August 1970, Paula, Dick's daughter, and Daryl Orth were married. On the day of the wedding after we came back from the family dinner a phone call came from Regina. Roy phoned. Their baby had come stillborn. Beverly had not been well. She was in the hospital. Ella had just come back from Regina the day before. That was a shock to everyone. It put a damper on the wedding. Ella and Ernie left for Regina. Barb Lentz was kneeling on the floor changing little Darren who was six months old when the phone call came. She was kneeling and crying.

In 1971 we went to the MacNutt Homecoming for Old Timers at Adolph and Margaret Kendels. Ferd Popp brought his sister Elsie Donahue from Sacramento. She had been adopted by Reverend Predoehl and taken to the United States after her mother died of tuberculosis. We hadn't seen Elsie for many years.

In September I asked Ella and Ernie if they would take us to Winnipeg for a weekend. I wanted to see my brother Jake. Henry stood the trip pretty well but he thought we were going the wrong way and he got very disturbed about it. We had two very poor nights in Winnipeg. I knew that we couldn't go anywhere again overnight as his nights were not good, even at home.

We did go to Gustie and Eitel Zorn's 30th Anniversary in June, to Phillip and Laura Popp's 60th Anniversary, to Mr. and Mrs. Rudy's 50th Anniversary and to a few funerals.

On October 5 we took Henry to the Cancer Clinic in Regina. Dr. Preston told us they had to keep him in for cobalt treatments. I came home with Ella and Ernie and went in next weekend with Pastor Morgret.[16] Henry was so very confused. When we got him home he wouldn't even know who I was. He would get out of bed then he wouldn't come back to bed because he didn't know who was in bed. I'd have to get up and get him back in bed. During the day he was better though he'd have good and bad days.

On December 11 we went to Jack and Gertie Lundgren's 40th Anniversary. Henry was fine for a while but when evening came he wanted to go home. We came home. Then he worried, "Where were the horses we had come home with?" "Where had we put them?"

On New Years Day 1972, Dick's son, Brian, got married to Louise Krefting. We couldn't go to Edmonton. I planned a wedding party for them when they came through on their way East on Sunday, January 9th.

Ernie and Ella took us to George and Della Lowenberger's 50th Anniversary. Henry was all right but on the way home he got disturbed that we were going the wrong way. He was very glad when he saw the Langenburg water tower and more glad when he saw our house. But then he often thought this was not our house - that we had another house.

We could go out for a while. We went to the Henry Lowenberger's funeral. He had been in the hospital with Henry. Then Albert Yeske, our next door neighbour, died. Henry missed him a lot.

Henry would get nose bleeds and bladder infections. He had to go to the hospital more often. Some nights I would get little sleep. I was afraid to take sleeping pills as I felt I had to wake up when Henry got out of bed. He might smoke or plug in the tea kettle.

On November 15, 1972 Paula and Daryl had a baby boy, Warren. Dick and Irene did not come home for Christmas that

---

[16] Pastor Morgret was the Lutheran Minister of Christ Lutheran Church from 1970 to 1972.

year. They had all their family at Edmonton. Daryl Lentz wasn't very well. We had the Parkinson family over for Christmas.

On February 1, 1973 we got a colour T.V. but we didn't watch much as my eyes bothered me all winter. What changes since I was born! When the first phones came out what a wonder that was. All through our lives there have been such wonderful changes, like people landing on the moon. Some of the changes are maybe not for the best - they make life more hectic.

Henry was in the hospital several times during the year. Physically he did not too badly but mentally not well. He had his 82nd birthday in the hospital on January 16, 1973. We both had good appetites so I spent a lot of time cooking and baking.

On February 14, 1973 Lizzie Hande (Henry's sister) died in Esterhazy. On February 15th, Dick phoned saying Daryl Lentz had passed away. Both funerals were on Saturday. We went to Lizzie's funeral in Marchwell.

On March 1, 1973 Ella phoned that Lori Scherloski said there was an opening for Henry at the Esterhazy Special Care Home. That was such a shock to me. I didn't know how long I could look after him, especially since I had been suffering with terribly sore eyes all winter.

On March 27, 1973 Dr. Newton[17] got an appointment for me in with Dr. McCrossen in Yorkton. He examined my eyes and said it was nothing to worry about. It was little ulcers that kept growing all the time. He gave me two bottles of drops to use every hour. I explained that I was writing my memoirs and he asked if I would mention his name in my memoirs.

Conditions seemed a little easier with us. Henry slept better at night and wasn't in too much pain so I got more rest. I started house cleaning. I did the upstairs, washed the kitchen cupboards, ceilings, walls and bathroom.

In June I stepped on a step stool to water the tomato plants on the basement window. The stool broke and I fell. I hurt my ankle, skinned my elbow and all the other sores hurt all over again. I thought, "I'm jinxed." I tried to be so careful. I was so tense and clumsy. I started exercising again and became more active outside.

---

[17] Dr. Newton was a doctor in Langenburg.

The summer of 1973 was one of the hardest, most trying summers of my life. Dr. Newton came on June 8 and said to bring Henry to the hospital to do some tests and regulate his medication. He didn't seem too ill. I could look after him pretty well. He seemed hungry all the time. That day his cousin, Minnie Wagner came from Salmon Arm to spend the weekend. She had been one of our bridesmaids. Her husband Frank was also Henry's cousin and had been our best man. They were married three weeks after us.

Minnie visited Henry in the hospital but he didn't know her. That was not surprising as often in the last six months he didn't always know who I was, or Ella or Dick. Henry was discharged June 24th and I got him home in the afternoon. He got a nose bleed at 10 o'clock when I was getting him ready for bed. We didn't sleep much that night. Next morning he got another bad nose bleed so I phoned the doctor. Ella took him back to the hospital.

On July 5th Gustie took her mother and me to the hospital. When Henry talked we couldn't understand him. Next day, they phoned that he was discharged. Elna Baumung took me to get him. He couldn't talk or walk. He was so sick. I couldn't understand why they sent him home in that condition - don't think I ever will. Dr. Newton had left. Dr. Fanner took over but he'd gone on holidays and Dr. Bahee from England took over. He discharged Henry. I just couldn't handle him. I had to phone Dr. Ramadan during the night and get the ambulance to take him back to the hospital.

When I got there the next day they told me he couldn't swallow. He must have had some kind of stroke. I went every afternoon and give him water with a spoon. On July 17th the hospital phoned and asked me to come - Henry was not responding. Gustie took me to the hospital. Henry was dying. Pastor Konrad came out and stayed with me. Gustie, too, stayed. He died very easily, just kept breathing slower until he didn't breathe anymore. The nurses were so very good - Joan Mund[18] and Phyllis Dixon[19]

---

[18] Joan (Mattice) Mund moved from Portreeve, Saskatchewan to work at the Langenburg Hospital as a registered nurse. She married Earl Mund, son of

were on. Gustie brought me home and all the cousins and neighbours came over.

It was Pastor Konrad's first funeral at Christ Lutheran Church. Braendle & Bruce were undertakers. There were very helpful. It all seemed like a dream.

My brother Rudy and Tug were on holidays. We didn't contact them. Brother George was in the Yorkton hospital, very ill. I phoned Adolph. He couldn't come. But Jake who was ill and Fantie came with their son Bob and his wife Mavis.

Henry's only living brother, Phillip, two years older than he, was in hospital in Yorkton. His sister, Mary, 88 years old, couldn't come. His youngest sister, Lena, had just returned from holidays and couldn't come either.

Acting pall bearers were Ewald Popp, Leslie Popp, Joe Becker, Henry Hande, Edgar Popp, all nephews of Henry, and Bob Lowenberger, my nephew. Honourary pall bearers were Jake Baumung, Eitel Zorn, Adolph Kendel, Lou Miller, Jim Murray and Henry Rudoski. The organist was Margaret Mitschke. The choir sang *Lass Mich Gehen.*

There was so much thinking to do. My mind got very tired and I was so hungry. There was something missing - it was the release from the constant day and night worry which had been with me for so long and then wasn't there.

Henry had been sick in body and mind for so long. He prayed for the Lord to let him die and it was a blessing when he died. I knew it, but it was hard to see your life partner leave you. I did not want to cry. If I cried I felt I was feeling sorry for myself and I did not want to do that. Even after some months, it still seemed unreal. I was in the house alone, in the bed alone and ate alone. I could always talk to him, even if he didn't always know what I was talking about.

Christian and Barbara Mund. Earl and Joan had three daughters: Shauna, Lareen and Denyse.

[19] Phyllis and her husband, Clarence, the Saskatchewan Wheat Pool agent, moved to Marchwell from Fertile, Saskatchewan in 1965. Phyllis began work at the Hospital in 1972 as a nurse's aide after the death of her husband. Clarence and Phyllis had four children: Murray, Kay, Darla and Cameron.

I put off writing about this as I was afraid I would get emotional. I did. But it would have been 59 years in October that we were married. We had troubles and tribulations in those 59 years, but we also had a lot to thank the Lord for.

WITHOUT HENRY

After Henry died so many others followed him: Harold Grube,[1] a good friend of Henry's, Albert Werschler, Katie Nerbas (my cousin) and Lou Bahsler. I went to their funerals and felt for those people and their loss.

On my birthday, January 18, 1974, Minnie Popp and Helen Popp[2] came early in the afternoon. Later, they had planned a surprise birthday supper. Ella came with roast chicken, Gustie Zorn with a salad and a lovely birthday cake and Thelma Hartung[3] with a casserole. I was so happy I could have cried. Aunt Lizzie came and Jake and Elna came as well. I also had several phone calls.

---

[1] Harold Grube (1911 - 1973) was born in Minnesota. In 1936 he married Lily Remus. They had three daughters: Gwen, Carol and Fay.

[2] Helen (Ohlinger) was born May 29, 1913. She married Ewald Popp in 1938. They had no children.

[3] Thelma was the daughter of Mary Popp's cousin - Mary (Kendel) and John Aasen. Thelma was born May 16, 1913 and died August 24, 1996. She married Leo Hartung, son of Alfred and Lydia (Froelke) Hartung in 1950. They had one son, John.

On January 24, 1974, I heard on the radio that the government had approved a 35-bed, special care home with one, two and three level care to be built in Langenburg for 525,000 dollars. This meant so much for the area as so many older people were not well enough to stay in their homes. There were such long waiting lists in all the hospitals and special care homes.

1974 was a hard year for me, hard on my nerves. My eyes bothered me terribly and I got serious infections. The doctor gave me antibiotics from which I got such a bad reaction that I had to have surgery. And while in the hospital, I got the flu. Then the nurses went on strike so I came home too soon and became ill. I would lie in bed or on the chesterfield with my head covered, very depressed. I had very dark thoughts.

In early July, Ernie and Ella went East on holidays. I went along as far as Winnipeg to see my brother Jake who was ill. I stayed with Jake and Fantie for a couple of days and came home by bus on Sunday morning. Jake had had cancer of the mouth for over six years. First the doctor said it was borderline. Then they operated on a growth and gave him 30 cobalt treatments which were hard on him and dried up his saliva glands. He could just speak about three words and had to wet his mouth from a spray bottle. His food had to be put through a blender and washed down.

I had so many ill friends and so many had died: Henry's brother, Phillip Popp; my cousin - Lizzie Busch, and Henry's niece and a good friend of mine - Minnie Moore. I missed her. We wrote often and were very close. I felt I was being left behind.

In August we had a memorial service and pot luck dinner in the Hoffenthal Church in memory of our dead buried there.

In 1974, the New Horizons Senior Citizens Club was formed. At first we met in the Municipal Auditorium, and later in the Catholic Church Auditorium. We would bring a lunch and play bingo, cards and shuffle board. We bought a piano and had sing songs. Sometimes we would get outside entertainment. We had a lovely Christmas dinner party with turkey, cabbage rolls, salad and all the trimmings, oranges and chocolates.

On September 8, 1974, unidentified flying objects were seen on Edwin Fuhr's farm, a few miles north of town.[4] He was swathing grain when he saw a large shining object hovering over a dry hay slough. He started walking towards it to see what it was. When he was within 15 feet, the object started spinning and shot straight up with a sweep of wind which temporarily flattened the uncut crop. He backed up to his swather and while he was watching, frozen with shock, four additional objects shot straight up in the air. Only rings were left where the objects had been. The rings were about 10 feet in diameter with an impression the size of a saucer in the centre. For about two feet on the outside of the ring the grass was curled clockwise. This was on Sunday, 10:00 a.m. On Monday or Tuesday, another circle was added. People heard about it and came from miles around to see it. They said over a 1,000 people came in the next few weeks.

The Special Care Home had been approved but troubles detained the starting of it. Then inflation made the price of materials rise and they had to go back for more money. So by early 1975, it still had not been started, although the water mains were laid in the location.

Also during the year, most of the unpaved streets in town were paved. After a late fall, spring and summer, people had to go through knee deep mud to get in and out of their houses.[5]

When Brian Popp, my grandson, and his wife Louise left for Germany, they invited me to visit them. I started dreaming about a trip but knew I could not go alone. I talked to Ella about it. When she said she would come with me, my dream started taking shape. Dick was going for six weeks. Then Ernie decided he would go so we started planning. I made a smaller garden and kept very busy.

I had one very big worry -- my brother Jake in Winnipeg was dying of cancer. I had gone to see him in May 1975. He was very ill and we knew he wouldn't live much longer. I expected a phone call any day. Often, I was afraid to answer the phone.

---

[4] Edwin Fuhr was born April 28, 1938 to Gustav and Helen (Schuttler) Fuhr. He married Karen Yeske, daughter of Leo and Hedwig (Off) Yeske, in 1967.

[5] Mary Popp makes a comment at this point in her memoirs stating "Notice that I did not write anything in 1975 which was a very full year for me. I am now 79 years old."

On July 2nd we drove to Winnipeg. We checked our luggage at the airport. I phoned Fantie and told her we were going to the hospital to see Jake. I was happy about that as it was the last time I saw him and he knew us all and could talk to us.

We went back to the airport and boarded the plane. I felt as if I had shed all my troubles and left them behind. I loved the plane ride and the service on the flight. Then we were in Germany, a very different country. Brian met us at Frankfurt. It was so nice to see a face we knew in that mob of strangers. The drive to Lahr where Brian was stationed was lovely, but we had to fight to stay awake as we had lost a night's sleep.

Our trip was so very interesting, with so much to see. With Brian and Louise's help, we made arrangements to go to many places. The first place we went was to Vienna, Austria. I would have liked to have gone to the part of Austria where my parents were born, but I was told it was in the Russian zone and had been completely destroyed. But we went through a lot of Austria on the train. Our parents had told us a lot about their homeland, but since they had left there in 1888, there would have been great changes.[6]

Our next trip was to Lunen and Kamen to visit my cousins, whom I had never met. I had written to some of them. Others I didn't know existed. Again, it was nearly a day's train ride. When we got there, who would we look for? One cousin was there with four of her nephews and nieces. Ernie was the first off the train. She asked "Langenburg?" He said "Yes, Langenburg." They could not speak a word of English; Ernie, not a word of German. Ella and Dick's German was poor and mine not that good. It was an odd situation but it went fine. They smothered us with kindness and overfed us. We spent four fun-filled days there. The time was too short and I did not get to see all of my cousins and relatives there, but we got to know the ones I had written to.

From there we took a five-hour Rhine cruise from Koblenz to Mainz. From Mannheim we took a bus tour through Heidelberg

---

[6] Austria, after World War I was greatly reduced in size from the time that Mary Popp's parents left. Vienna, Austria, is several hundred kilometres from Landestreu where Mary Popp's parents were born. In 1975, when Mary Popp was in Europe, the village where her parents were born was in the Ukraine.

and other towns to Langenburg, Germany, which was a must on our trip since Langenburg, Canada was named after it. After we told the *Burgermeister* (Mayor) who we were and where we were from, we were very kindly received. He took us for coffee at the Castle Rose Garden, showed us the town and took us to his house for refreshments. He showed us his very large garden then took us back to our 750 year old hotel, the *Gast Hof Zur Post*. We got up early next morning and toured the *Schloss* (castle) Langenburg von Hohenloh.

Ella and Ernie went to the post office to meet the postmaster. Since there was no train into Langenburg and there was no bus until next evening, they made arrangements to take us by car, about 45 kilometres to Schwabische Hall to get a train to go back to Baden to Brian and Louise's home to get ready to go home. Brian took us to Frankfurt.

When we landed in Winnipeg we took a taxi to Jake's place. When we got there, Fantie told us that Jake had died July 18th and the funeral had been July 22nd.

It was so good to come home on July 24th, 1975, very tired. It was a wonderful trip, something I had not expected in my lifetime, especially at my age. I enjoyed the trip so very much. I should have made arrangements to stay six weeks. There had been a heat spell the three weeks we were gone. The garden needed me. The flowers and weeds had gone to seed. The raspberries had started ripening. The lawn had dried up and there was an armload of mail and bills to pay.

On August 8, 1975, I went to Regina to my granddaughter's wedding. Ricki and Tom Jackson got married August 9, a small, very nice wedding.

On August 21st, I went by bus to Edmonton to my grandson's wedding, Brant Popp and Joan Zuk. The wedding was August 22nd, a big, very nice wedding.

On December 26, Dick, Brant and Joan came to Langenburg so I roasted a turkey and had the family and friends in for dinner. For my birthday in 1976, family, cousins and nephews came and brought the whole meal with birthday cake and all. It made me so happy and I was so thankful that they were so thoughtful and kind to me. Yes, there were times when I was lonely and blue, but after a party like that I would scold myself for being blue.

I also went to many meetings. I had the Hospital Auxiliary meeting at my home on January 22, 1976. I had been a member since 1946. The most welcome happening that year was the Special Care Home was started and they expected it to be finished within a year. I did hope that I would never have to go in, but it felt good to know it would be there in case I would need it. So many people were waiting for it.

On Easter Sunday, 1976, I put a ham on to cook and fell asleep. I cooked the ham to pieces. I was mad and thought I would carry the garbage can out. I stepped on a little patch of ice and fell down and broke my wrist. I was so mad at myself that it didn't hurt. I could have asked Ernie to take the garbage out. I didn't have to carry it out on Easter Sunday. I didn't have to step on that little patch of ice, but I guess it was to be. I got myself up and phoned Ella and Ernie. They took me to the hospital and X-rayed my hand. Both bones on my left wrist were broken.

I was in the hospital for a couple of days and had to learn to do things with one hand, my teeth, knees or feet. Sometimes it was funny. I used my teeth for so much, to hold things or open things. A neighbour brought me a small fish and, for the first time, I felt hungry. So I tried to cut it up. It slipped back and forth. I wouldn't hold a raw fish with my teeth so I put paper towel on it and lifted my sore arm on top of it and got it cut. I couldn't tie my shoes since I couldn't get my teeth down there. I didn't wear a brassiere because I couldn't close it. Then, too, with the help of my teeth, I learned I could close it.

A short while later, I was going along to the Hospital Auxiliary meeting and while getting into the car, somebody closed the door and caught the fingers of my right hand in the door. They were flattened, the middle finger split open. I had my hand X-rayed and had a cast put on. Then I had neither hand. But I was lucky no bones in my fingers were broken. The two middle finger nails came off my right hand. I had the cast on my left hand for over 10 weeks. When the cast came off, I asked the doctor not to cut it since I wanted to make a flower vase of it. But when I saw my hand I forgot about making the vase. My hand was all scabby, crooked and looked awful. But it came back and I could carry and dig in the garden by fall.

One day, after I had come home from the hospital and I got a letter from Helma White,[7] my niece from Vancouver, with an invitation to come visit her. I wanted to go and Ella said, "You have to go." I decided to go by bus so I wrote Helma. My raspberries were just starting to ripen. I hoed through the garden and told them to just leave it. I didn't care. I had never been to B.C. and always wanted to go. I wanted to enjoy it, and I did. I was gone for four weeks. It gave my arm and fingers a chance to heal.

I visited Victoria, Chiliwack, Nanaimo, Burnaby and Surrey. I stayed mostly with my niece. I also visited my sister-in-law, Caroline McRae. I was interested in seeing people I hadn't seen for a long time, like my nephew, Buddy Barker,[8] who had stayed at our place when he was about 12 years old and went to school with our boys. He was a rascal, but was good to me. He always helped me with the supper dishes. I had not seen him for 48 years. I phoned him and he came to see me. He looked like his Dad had at the time he stayed at our place. Buddy remembered so much about our horses, the farm and the threshing gang. He told me he had learned to milk at our place.

I had always wanted to go to Vancouver. The trip was lovely. But I liked my home, Langenburg, a small town. When you went downtown, you could say hello to everybody.

I got very busy in the garden and yard. My arm got stronger and I found I could dig in the garden, wash windows and put up the storm windows myself.

One of my cousins, Lisa Kandel,[9] with whom I stayed for four days in Germany, died the summer of 1976. She had been so good to me. I was so glad I got to know her. So I wrote sympathy and Christmas cards to Germany. It seemed I was forever writing letters. If I got lonesome I would write a letter to somebody.

---

[7] Helma White was the daughter of Julius and Elisabeth (Lowenberger) Metz.

[8] Buddy (Arthur) Barker was the son of Alan and Mary (Popp) Barker.

[9] Lisa Kandel (Baumung), born October 11, 1902, was the daughter of Johann Friedrich Baumung and Elisabeth Haberstock. Her husband, Rudolph, lived to be 103 years of age, dying in 1995.

1976 was a year of dissatisfaction with governments worldwide. In Canada, the change of government in Quebec with René Levesque caused such a stir. It seemed that countries all over the world were interested. In the United States, Jimmy Carter became President and people seemed to expect big changes.

I was on the entertainment committee for our senior citizens club. We were trying to come up with a program which wasn't easy as some of us didn't hear, see or walk too well. I thought we should have a kitchen band. Some hadn't seen a kitchen band so I invited them to my place. Another woman and I played mouth organs. We had wash tub drums, washboards, pot lids and whatever I could find in my drawers. We had a majorette who used an old curtain rod. The practice was fun and seemed to be enjoyed.

During the summer our kitchen band played at a picnic at the campground. Then we were asked to go to Melville for a senior citizens' rally. We added more members and more instruments like kazoos, tea kettles, coffee pots and dustpans. We were asked to perform at the Care Home in Langenburg, then an anniversary, a picnic, a parade at Marchwell and the thresherman's reunion in Yorkton. We were asked to come on *Profile*, a program on Yorkton T.V. We got a little nervous and thought we should have a piano. Our performance went over well as everybody who saw it said it was good. Months after, every so often, somebody would say, "Oh, we saw your kitchen band on T.V."

Eventually, we had 17 members, including a conductor, majorette and banner bearer. We did small parts of old fashioned dances like the seven step, three step, finger polka and French minuet. It was fun, but not all fun. Sixteen old women have 16 different ideas how things should be done. I did a lot of phoning. My partner and I even practiced playing the mouth organ over the phone. It was all very silly, especially at my age, but I did enjoy it. Later, different senior citizens groups set up kitchen bands.

In 1977 I decided I would get a typewriter. I ordered a cheaper new one and learned how to type. It wasn't easy at my age. I always hit the wrong keys and the space bar when I wasn't supposed to. I started with German letters which proved too much. I had to think what to write, to translate, to spell and find the keys all at once. My first try was a disaster, but I was quite taken with it. I always liked to try things.

To start 1978, Jake Baumung, my cousin, neighbour and friend, died suddenly. It was a great shock to us all. My brother Al's wife, Mary, also died as well as many other relatives and friends. I missed them all.

That summer I bought myself a small lawnmower to cut my own lawn. I got scolded for it but felt that walking was good for me. And the doctor said, "Do it." My garden and yard, trees, raspberries, apples and vegetables all kept me very busy.

There were also happy occasions - Joe and Minnie Popp's 50th anniversary and brother Rudy's 50th anniversary. It was at these gatherings that we could meet old friends to reminisce about times gone by. But they were getting fewer all the time.

In 1978 our kitchen band had 15 performances. Most important to us was being asked to Regina to demonstrate how to start a kitchen band. We received 100 dollars for expenses and supper. We were asked to go to the Wascana Hospital to entertain the patients. We were also winners at the Bredenbury talent show and went to Lemberg for the regional play-offs where we got a tremendous applause and honourable mention.

During 1978, Dick got divorced and remarried on November 11 in Edmonton. Ella and Ernie, Gustie and Eitel and I went to the wedding. He married Mary Jacob,[10] a widow. She had three daughters.

During the summer of 1978, my brother Al came from California. He left Canada in 1928 and came back once 30 years later, in 1958 when my brother George drove Al and me out to the old Lowenberger home place. The house, then, was very much the same. They still used the wood stove and the cistern pump and most of the old buildings were still there.

When we returned to the old home place in 1978, we saw tremendous changes since we had been there 20 years before. The big bush that almost surrounded the old house was gone, but a new shelter belt had been planted. All of the old buildings were gone,

---

[10] Mary Chancellor was born July 6, 1919 in England. She was previously married to Roy Jacob and had three daugthers: Ellen, Arlene and Joan.

but the granaries, one at each end with the buggy shed between, remained. The new house was not in the same place as the old one, so the well didn't seem to be in the right place. I remembered when Johnson, the well driller, dug the well. We didn't like the water at first, but that didn't matter because we didn't have to haul all that water, barrels and barrels full, and carry it in. In 1978 they even had a cow waterer out there.[11] I just wanted to walk around and look, try to imagine where things had been. The slough we used to bathe in and skate and slide on in winter had dried up. It all brought back such fond childhood memories.

On Monday morning, February 26, 1979, we had a total eclipse of the sun. I watched it on television. In Langenburg it was very cloudy and no sign of the sun. It slowly grew darker. At about 11:15 a.m. it was very dark. It was so interesting as they said it was a once in a lifetime event. The next eclipse is to be in 2024, but not in this area. Men are getting too clever, exploring too much of God's creation, like landing on the moon and foretelling events. But if it wasn't to be, the Lord would stop it. And it is all interesting.

In the spring of 1979, we got word that our cousins, Willie and Kathy Harth and Adolf and Hilda Kendel[12] were coming from Germany. They arrived on May 14th. Hilda Kendel was my cousin and her husband, Adolf Kendel, was my second cousin. They stayed three days. We had so many dinners, parties and get-togethers while they were here. John and Mary Baumung[13] also

---

[11] This land is now owned by Daryl Kendell.

[12] See genealogical chart of Mary Popp's cousins. These couples, as young adults, left Landestreu, Austria in 1940 and lived in German-annexed Poland during World War II. They escaped the Russian advance in 1945 and settled in Schneverdingen, West Germany.

[13] John Baumung (1906 - 1995) was Mary Popp's cousin, brother to Hilda Kendel. John and Mary left Schneverdingen, Germany in 1948 and settled in Langenburg with their three daughters: Charlotte, Martha and Gertrude. They left Langenburg in the early 1950s and moved to Melville and eventually to Vancouver. John's wife, Mary, was born in Landestreu in 1910. Her mother was Luise Mack (1890 - 1979). Luise had fallen in love with a young German Catholic. Luise's father, Friedrich Mack (1851 - ?) forbade the relationship. When Mary was born, the young man returned and again asked to marry Luise. Mr. Mack disallowed the marriage. Mary was adopted by Luise's sister,

came from Vancouver. On May 24, we had a pot luck dinner at the senior citizen's hall for all the cousins and relatives - what a noisy, but nice party. The German cousins enjoyed it. It would never happen again.

On August 28, 1979, I went to Thunder Bay by bus to my great-grandson's wedding. It was a beautiful wedding. I was sort of an honoured guest. The day after the wedding, we went to Arnold's grave. I had not been there since his funeral, nearly 14 years before. I took pictures of the grave.

1980 was the 75th anniversary of the Province. Before then, it was known at the North West Territories. My older sisters, my brothers and I were all born when it was still called the North West Territories. Saskatchewan didn't become a province until 1905.

My 83rd birthday came and went. I didn't feel any different but felt my time was running out.

In March a Heritage Dinner for senior citizens was held with a lovely beef dinner for some 400 people. The Honourable T.C. Douglas, former Premier of Saskatchewan, was guest speaker. At 75 years of age, he was as old as Saskatchewan, although not born in the province.

On February 9, 1980, Elsie Donahue died. She was Jack and Lizzie Popp's daughter who had been adopted by Pastor Predoehl soon after she was born. Elsie moved to the United States and was raised by the Predoehls. She died at 63 years of age from lung cancer. Her wish was to buried with her mother and sisters at Landestreu. So her brothers, Ferd and Joe, and her sister, Kay, had her body brought from Sacramento to Landestreu.

A young teacher brought me a book to read about Austria.[14] At first I thought I wouldn't be interested since the print

---

Elisabeth who had married August Haas. She was rasied with her cousin Hetti Haas who married Friedrich Lowenberger. Luise came to Canada in 1912 and worked for a short time for the Busch family at Shellmouth. Luise married Carl Daum (1897 - 1968) in 1913. They had seven children: Julia (Gurski/Bieber), Louise (Schepp), Friedrich, Elisabeth (Becker), Elsie (Layh/Mack); Edwin, Evelyn (Jabs).

[14] The young teacher who brought the book was Don Layh. The book was *Zeitweiser der Galiziendeutschen, 1976.* This book was given to Don Layh

was small and there was a lot of reading. But then I started reading about places like Landestreu where my parents were born. There were even pictures of the village showing where their homes had been. A lot of it was written in the *Schwabisch* language, a dialect they spoke there. I had so much fun reading it, even though it was difficult, as we had never learned to read the dialect. I told others about it, but I guess it was boring to them. I read until my eyes got too tired. There were also very sad parts about the wars when people had to flee and come back and rebuild. After the World War II their village was destroyed.

On October 5th, 1979, Dick had a heart attack and was in the hospital for weeks. I dreaded to hear the phone ring since when Arnold died, we had just heard on the Friday that he was ill and on Monday the phone call came that he was dead. Dick slowly recovered and began to feel better.

One blustery day in March 1980 I went to the rink to watch my great-grandson, Warren Orth, seven years old, play hockey with the Snowflakes in a tournament - little specks falling down on that big sheet of ice. Warren was the smallest. They lost their game but were second in the tournament and were presented with silver medals.

I didn't go to the rink often but there had been a time when we spent so much time there. We used to sell pie at five cents, soup ten cents, sandwiches fifteen cents. In 1980 pie was forty cents, coffee forty cents, and hamburgers seventy-five cents. They were also using paper cups and plates so there was no dishwashing.

In May I got a surprise - a parcel from Langenburg, Germany, from Fritz Gronbach, the former mayor of the town. He sent a box of *Wievele,* tiny cookies, and three of the town's newspapers, *Langenburger Amtsblatt.* The year before, after Langenburg's 75th anniversary, I sent him some of our newspaper clippings and wrote him a little history of our town. They printed it in their newspaper in three installments, one in May and two in June. They sent me the three issues. Fritz Gronbach had translated

---

during a visit to Germany in 1975 when he visited Karl and Maria Layh who lived in Munich. Karl Layh was born in Ugartsthal, a village neighbouring Landestreu.

it, not so well, but there are some things that don't sound the same when translated.

May 20, 1980, was the Quebec Referendum. The "No" vote got 60 percent, meaning that Quebec would not separate, but stay in Canada, which is what most Canadians had hoped for.

During May, after days of hot winds, many forest fires were raging out of control. People were being evacuated and families had to leave their homes and possessions, not knowing whether they would be there when they came back. Then Mt. St. Helens erupted. So many people were missing and there was so much damage. In Langenburg it was hazy with strong hot winds. And we complain - we shouldn't.

Our kitchen band was asked to perform a couple of numbers for the "Celebrate Saskatchewan" August long weekend. We also entered a float which involved a lot of extra planning and work and even some worry. A pancake street breakfast was held in the morning. We had to get home and get dressed and get on the float as it started lining up at 11:00 a.m.. It was all great fun. That was the last time our kitchen band played that I was in. At that time, there were the following members - Alida Schepp,[15] Annie Goehring,[16] Beatrice Hogberg,[17] Betty Kriewaldt,[18] Eva Leis, Julia Schmidt, Lillie Grube, Lizzie Poier, Lisel Nolan,[19] Margaret Bily, Mary Zorn, Tillie Goetz,[20] Dora Haberstock and myself.

---

[15] Alida Schepp, daughter of Peter and Emma Schepp, married John Schepp, son of Jacob and Caroline (Geres) Schepp. They had two children: Marvin and Elaine.

[16] Annie Fingas was the daughter of Elisabeth Kendel, Mary Popp's cousin who married William Fingas. Annie married Joseph Goehring in 1932. They had three sons: Harvey, Orland and Brian.

[17] Beatrice Wenzoski was born June 20, 1912. She married Alex Hogberg in 1934. They had four children: Clifford, Donna, Edsel and Faye.

[18] Betty Zentner married Herbert Kriewaldt, son of Ferdinand and Beatha (Lowenberger) in 1934. They had one daughter, Mardell.

[19] Elisabeth Fuhr, born 1909, married Gerald Nolan in 1934. They had two children: James and Patricia.

[20] Mathilda Kammermayer was born January 25, 1908, the ninth child of Otto and Maria (Kain) Kammermayer. She married Joseph Goetz in 1928. They had a family of nine.

By then, we had lost Millie Hartung[21] who died of cancer that spring. Clara Miller had quit and Helen Fieseler[22] had fallen. Betty Kriewaldt had a stroke; Julia Schmidt died of a throat ailment and Margaret Bily died of a heart attack.[23]

On September 3, 1980 I was in the garden picking corn with Hulda Weinheimer.[24] She said she was cold in the house so she put on a sweater and came out to work. Rudolf had gone to the farm. We talked and planned our garden for next year. She decided she wouldn't plant so much next year. I told her to remind me not to plant so much corn. We worked while we talked. When I had picked and husked my corn, I came in. She was still working. Next morning, I was told she had just died. I missed her so very much. In the summer our gardens were side by side. The funeral was September 6th. I kept on working in the garden, but Hulda wasn't there digging vegetables or trimming trees.

September 23, was a cold day. The forecast was for rain and snow so I got dressed and went to clean the garden. Earlier, when I had picked apples, I broke a big branch which was still hanging from the tree. The ladder was there so I thought I would cut off the branch. The ground was soft from the rain and the ladder fell over and down I went. It wasn't high. I landed on my seat and didn't feel hurt. But when I tried to get up, I saw that my right ankle was twisted. My left leg was under me. I pulled it out and knew that it was broke above the knee. Then I started calling for help. I was among the shrubs and couldn't move. Nobody could see me. Since it was a nasty day, nobody was outside. It was about 3:30 p.m. and although cars were going by, they could not hear me call. And, oh, the thoughts I had - I was sure my leg would have to be taken off. I prayed I wouldn't have to suffer too

---

[21] Amelia Fuhr married Robert Hartung in 1926. She died March 21, 1980. They had two children: Margaret and Ruben.

[22] Helen Metz, the daughter of John and Matilda (Werschler), was born December 29, 1914. She married William Fieseler in 1936. They had two daughters: Bonnie and Kathleen.

[23] In 1983, Mary Popp noted that the kitchen band had started again with new members. Bob Miller was the conductor and Ella Miller played the piano

[24] Hulda (Yeske) Weinheimer was born January 24, 1916. She and Rudolf (1909 - 1991) raised ten children.

much pain. What would happen to me? When would I be found? The forecast was for snow. The hymn, *Wer Weiss Wie Nahe Mir Mein Ende*[25] went through my mind while I sat there. I wondered, would it be my end with my legs so badly broken? I almost wished it would be, but God had not meant it to be yet.

I saw Mrs. Geres come out of her house. She couldn't hear me. I was getting very tired but couldn't lie down or I wouldn't see anybody walk by. Then Matteis' puppy barked and kept on barking. They came out to scold him and heard me calling. They phoned for the doctor and the ambulance. It took a while until they came. By then my leg was starting to hurt badly. They took me to Yorkton. I had just walked out of the house perhaps an hour ago and little did I know that I wouldn't get back in for six months.

I was in traction for two and a half months with my ankle in a cast. During that time I had so many problems. My bladder wouldn't work so they used a catheter. I got infection and had to have needles. I developed bed sores and they used a heat lamp on them. I was burned and raw and the sores didn't want to heal. My stomach wouldn't work from all the medication. I was on my back for two and a half months with thoughts I didn't want to share or talk about. A lot of people were telling me that at my age I shouldn't get on a ladder, which didn't help any since when you are alone, you have to do things for yourself.

Three months after I came to the hospital, I could stand on my right foot and swivel to sit in a chair. Two nurses were going to give me a whirlpool bath, but my legs wouldn't bend enough. Then something snapped. I nearly fell in the pool. Next morning, they X-rayed and the doctor told me my ankle had come apart and that I needed surgery the next day.

On December 24, 1980, I had surgery. I don't think the doctor knew what had happened. I cried and when some of the nurses came and said how sorry they were, it just made me feel more sorry for myself. Anyway, it had been building up and I felt

---

[25] *Wer Weiss, Wie Nahe Mir Mein Ende!*
Hin Geht die Zeit, her kommt der tod.
Ach, wie geschwinde und behende kann kommen meine Todesnot!
Mein Gott, ich bitt' durch Christi Blut
Mach's nur mit meinem Ende Gut!

better after the cry. So my Christmas wasn't so nice even though I got many gifts, flowers, cards, letters and prayers.

After the surgery, I got a heavy cast on my leg. After a few days I was learning to walk with a cast using a walker. I was transferred by ambulance to the Langenburg hospital on January 15, 1981 with a heavy cast on my right ankle. I had my 84th birthday in the hospital.

On March 21, after being in the hospital for six months less two days, it felt oh so good to be home. I just moved around the house with a walker to look at everything. Ernie and Ella had the house all clean.

Then Ella became sick. Her ailment seemed so serious and doctors and specialists don't seem to know what caused it or how to treat it. She had been in the Regina General Hospital and the Plains Hospital for tests and examinations.

It was so good to get outside in the spring. Ernie came and put in some garden. I couldn't bend down at first, but later I was able to so I planted more vegetables. I managed to look after the garden, pick strawberries, raspberries and apples. The tree where I had fallen the previous fall was so loaded. I wanted to pick all the apples myself and give them away. I picked about twenty pails. It was a lovely summer and fall and I was out as much as I could without getting too tired, walking with crutches or the cane. I even made a cane with a little board at the bottom that wouldn't sink into the soil, just to be outside. The doctor said that was good for my leg so I couldn't be scolded about it.

On September 14, 1981, I was greatly surprised when Anette Kandel from Bremen, Germany arrived in Langenburg. I had met her six years ago when we were in Germany. I had stayed at her grandparents, Rudolf and Lisa Kandel, in Schneverdingen. Lisa (Baumung) was my cousin. Anette had come to her grandmother's every day. She wanted to learn English and to know all about Canada. She stayed overnight with her grandmother so we slept in the same room and talked a lot. I asked her to come to Canada some time. So six years later, she decided to come.

She had flown to Los Angeles and hitchhiked to Langenburg in about three weeks. She had not let me know that she was coming. She had grown a lot and could speak broken

English. She was hungry and dirty so I fixed us up a big supper. Then I asked her questions about her travels. The night before she had slept in a corn field in Minnesota. She had a map with her route all marked out. She left Langenburg in early October by bus for Vancouver. We were all worried about her, but she got there. I received a letter from her in Oregon. She was heading for Mexico.

In February, 1982, my neighbour, Theresa Geres[26] as well as my neighbour across the street, Herb Hildebrandt,[27] died. Death seemed to surround me.

On April 17, 1982, there was an historic, once in a lifetime occasion. The Queen brought to Canada and signed the Canadian Constitution - the repatriation of the Constitution - giving Canada full independence. It was a three-day celebration with the Queen and Prince Philip riding in the 97 year old horse-drawn Landau. And to think I could just sit at home by my T.V. and see and hear it all with a mass choir singing *Praise God From Whom All Blessings Flow* - history in the making.

In 1982 Shellmouth had its 100th anniversary. My brother, Al, came from Los Angeles for a couple of weeks. My brother Jake's widow, Fantie, her son Bob and his daughter, also came. So I had a chance to go with them for just one day.

I could still do most of the garden work myself. I cut the lawn then wondered if I could dig. I asked the doctor and he said it would strengthen my muscles, but to be careful not to fall. So I tried near the house where I could hang on and finally I could dig in the garden, even though it was risky. I found that there was so much to do, things that had been left undone. I could walk downtown to do my business. I had letters to write and had so much I wanted to read, eyes permitting.

Then I got involved in family history: Popp, Lowenberger and Baumungs. I was trying to update all my records. D'Arcy Hande[28] sent me a Popp family history dating back to the 1700s.

---

[26] Theresa (Bardua) Geres was born December 16, 1899. She married Jacob Geres in 1926. He was born in Landestreu, Austria on July 6, 1883. They had two sons: Walter and Reinhold

[27] Herbert Hildebrandt (February 8, 1918 - February 20, 1982) was the son of Carl Hildebrandt and Annie Severin. He married Alwina Remus in 1941. They had two sons: Glen and Roy.

In the fall of 1982, Isabel Welke[29] phoned me and asked if I would go along to Yorkton to the Lutheran Layman's League to put on the *Schwabische Ladies' Aid Meeting* - a program we had first done in 1965 at the Landestreu church. I recalled how at Landestreu they had such a nice religious program in the church and there we were with such a silly thing. I remembered getting all hot and cold and nervous.

When Isabel Welke asked if I would get a group together to go to Yorkton, I had to think. It was a challenge. I said, "Yes." So Isabel got a few ladies to her house and we talked it over. When we got to Yorkton, the same thing happened. I went through the same emotions I had gone through 17 years earlier in Landestreu. That's what I told the audience - how nervous I was. That saved me. A lot of people told us how they enjoyed it so I was glad I had gone. I got home late but couldn't go to sleep.

The winter of 1982/83 was very mild. Everyone told me how well I was doing. I was thankful for what I could do for myself. I loved hearing from my friends but sometimes their letters were sad. Everyone was getting older and having different ailments or were left alone. Yes, it was hard to grow old alone and to depend so much on others. I felt I was a burden. For how long? But that is what life is all about. I didn't want to be young again as I would have had to go over it all again and make the same mistakes.

---

[28] D'Arcy Hande, born 1951, was the son of Ernest and Isabel (Bennett) Hande.

[29] Isabel (Langford) Welke (1926 - 1994) was born in Castelavery, Manitoba and raised on a farm near Shellmouth. In 1952 she married Frank Welke (1915 - 1991), son of William and Ida (Yeske), a widower with four children. Frank and Isabel Welke had four children, Corinne, Allan, Gayle and Joy.

LOSING ELLA

After Easter I had another big worry. At Easter when Dick was home he got sick in the morning - one of his spells. He went white then red and got so dizzy we had to get him on the chesterfield. I had not seen him like that before. It scared me. I couldn't go to church. Then when Dick returned to Edmonton, Mary phoned that he was in the hospital. He had a rectal polyp removed. It was not malignant.

Then Ella began feeling ill and getting worse. It was such a worry. They worried about me and that also worried me. Ella went to Regina in May for appointments for stress tests and to see what they could do for her. She was in the hospital for a week. They sent her home with different pills so she felt better and went back to work.

In May, the weather was getting warmer and I felt stronger so I went outside. The grass was getting long so I started to cut the lawn. Ernie had fixed the mower but it made a lot of noise and didn't seem to work. One of the knives didn't turn so I went to turn it with my hand. The knife turned quickly and caught the third finger on my right hand. It was cut and bled badly. I couldn't see how bad it was until I came in and held it under the tap. It was bad, but I was so glad that it had not taken my fingers. I was ashamed to tell anyone what a foolish thing I had done. Ella took me to the hospital and I had stitches. But there was so much to do and I needed my right hand. I was thankful I had my fingers. It would heal.

I decided to put the typewriter away as I had a lot of neglected work to do - fingers permitting - like digging dandelions. On June 14th, lightning struck my house, hitting the T.V., the phone and the electric clock on the fridge. I was eating dinner when I heard a terrible crash. I heard something fall and I could smell smoke. The lightning had knocked the channel master box onto the middle of the floor. The mat that was under it was partially burnt.

In August I went to Regina to my granddaughter Beverley's wedding to Steve Kesslering. I stayed with granddaughter Ricki and Tom Jackson and enjoyed it very much.

I also went to Luella and Wilburt Andres'[1] 40th wedding anniversary at MacNutt with Ella, Ernie, Gustie and Eitel Zorn and Helen Popp. Those were occasions I really enjoyed, seeing relatives and friends. It made old age seem not so old when you could meet with friends. But then there were also times when you heard that another of your family had passed on or had become disabled.

In the spring of 1984 I had another accident - I broke a bone in my right foot when I stumbled in the back porch and fell. I had to call Dr. Bhatt and go to the hospital for X-rays. I stayed in for 13 days. I had been feeling well and catching up with my work and then that had to happen.

Then I had another not-so-nice experience when a slick salesman came and insisted that my house had to be insulated. He stayed nearly all afternoon until I gave him a cheque for $383.33. He said I wouldn't have to do anything - there would be no mess.

---

[1] Wilburt was the son of Fred Andres. Luella was the daughter of Adolph Margaret (Becker) Kendel.

But his workmen left a terrible mess. I thought I wouldn't be able to clean it. But I had to and I felt so sorry for myself. I had to crawl into different spaces but while I was at it, I found a lot of things to throw away. I started going through letters, cards, re-reading and burning. I burned some papers I still needed. I hoped there were copies in the basement that I hadn't yet burned. Then I found the Shellmouth book which I had read and re-read. I always found it so interesting, especially the beginning of Shellmouth.

On May 14th, I watched the swearing in of the new Governor General, Madame Jeanne Sauve. She arrived in a limousine wearing a full sleeved coat over a floor length dress. She was the 23rd Governor General of Canada. All the dignitaries gave speeches. She changed into a fur coat to inspect the Guard. She received a 21 gun salute with jets flying overhead. She was the first woman to become Govenor General in Canada and she was born in Saskatchewan.

In 1984 the Progressive Conservatives elected a new leader, Brian Mulroney. Pierre Trudeau resigned making numerous appointments before he did. At the Liberal convention, John Turner was elected as leader and Prime Minister for the shortest time in history. Then followed the election campaign for weeks and the Progressive Conservatives going into power with the biggest landslide ever. Brian Mulroney was sworn in as the new Prime Minister and he appointed a 40 member cabinet.

Then followed the Pope's 12 day tour of Canada. (It was too long.) He was on every T.V. station with his popemobile. Too much fuss was made and there was a five million dollar bill to pay.

On September 24, the Queen landed in New Brunswick. Brian and Mila Mulroney were there to welcome her. It was all very interesting to be able to see this on T.V., but it also took time and I neglected my work.

Langenburg continued to grow during 1984. Ten more low rental units and some homes were built during the last year. The drug store was enlarged. But our hospital continued to suffer.

On Hallowe'en evening, we were struck by a bad blizzard and cold weather so no one called for treats. Luckily I had bought candies I liked. I put them in the freezer before I could eat them all.

On March 17, 1985, our senior citizens had a social and presentation of ten-year pins. The president, Bob Miller, had done a lot of work. Bob had planned it so that everyone was to sit down and then the honoured guests were to pick up their food first. But soon there were about 20 people at the food table filling their plates. Senior citizens just won't listen or maybe they don't hear. It was just hard to work with over 100 of us. And then they write letters about their gripes and take them around for everybody to sign. When we are old we think we have the right to do as we please. Maybe it should be like that because it is very hard to get old or be old. We have to live one day at a time. Sometimes seniors are lonely. Golden age maybe is not so golden.

I noticed I didn't write anything in 1986. No wonder - it was not a good year for me. I got the flu then I fell in the back landing and got my little finger on my left hand caught in the railing. It was all torn up so Dr. McDonald came and took me to the hospital and sewed it up. I was to go to Regina to Dr. Kim to have it taken off but I didn't go. So I had a very sore little finger. It was in a splint for a long time so I couldn't put it in water and had to do everything with one hand. After seven weeks, the other finger was swollen badly and I had to go to the hospital to have my ring cut off. I had it enlarged to get it back on.

January of this year was my 90th birthday. How did I feel? I really don't know. On my birthday we went to church in the morning and then to the Legion for a catered family dinner and picture taking. Then at 2:30 p.m. there was an open house at the hall. A lot of people came.

The snow went early so by May I was outside trying to catch up with what was left undone in fall. Although I put the typewriter away in May, I found I was talking to myself so decided that if I typed I wouldn't need to talk to myself.

In November, I was given a new awkward gadget for my wrist - an emergency alert. If I pressed the buttons it rang Ella's phone. It's really wonderful what they can invent to take care of old people. I also had to have my phones changed to push button.

Christmas 1987 came and went and so did my 91st birthday. I didn't really feel any different, only stiffer and afraid of falling. I tried to be so careful and tried to exercise more. I continued to do all my own work - that is supposed to be my exercise but I'm so slow. I was always behind, like doing my fall house work cleaning after Christmas.

I wrote a lot of early Christmas letters in 1987 so I got a lot of letters and even some phone calls from family and friends. I read my memoirs over and had been told to have them published. But it's just about my life and who would be interested?

Good Friday was on April 1st. That was a very hard month, though it started out good. Easter Sunday was Joe and Minnie Popp's 60th anniversary. It was very enjoyable as their family was home and we were asked to stay for a lovely turkey dinner. On April 4th, my nephew, Bob Lowenberger phoned that his mother, Fantie, was very sick. On April 7th, 1988 she died.

But during all that time, I was crying. Ella was very sick and had to go to Melville for X-rays. Then she was called to Regina. Ricki phoned to say it was cancer on her lungs. That shock was just too much. I cried for ten days. I couldn't control myself. Then they phoned that she would have surgery - there was hope. She had surgery on April 29th, 1988, when they removed one lung. She was doing all right but had to learn to breathe on one lung.

During the summer, I was always so busy, but slow and tired. I didn't do things as I planned them - something always came up that I had to do before the thing I had set out to do. There was so much that I wanted to do. I made dill pickles and then tried to make a little order in the basement. I mopped up the floor and then got to the typewriter.

On November 22nd, Ella went to Regina for a cancer appointment and to see a specialist. She was crying when she phoned before they left. So I cried and cried. I tried to keep busy washing dresses, blouses, pants and sweaters. Ella's report from Regina was heart breaking - cancer on the brain. They were giving her some pills which seemed to perk her up. I was so tired in my head but life went on.

Ella went to Regina again in December for treatment. She had lost all her hair. She told me to buy a new dress for Christmas.

I bought one at Yuen's Store.[2] We went to church on December 24th and to communion then left for Regina in the afternoon for Christmas. I didn't feel too good about going but the girls thought it was best since Ella wasn't well. We had a lovely supper and evening at Bev and Steve's and came back to Ricki and Tom's where I stayed.

When I went into the house I lost my balance on the patio and fell backwards. I hurt my head badly and also pulled some muscles in my side. When we came home from Regina, Ernie drove me to the hospital. They kept me in for a week and I got the flu. Then they took me to the Care Home for two weeks of respite care. There I was unhappy as I was sick and during that time Ella became very ill and I couldn't go to her.

Ella was getting sicker all the time until I could see there was no hope. Why Lord did I have to live so long to have to see my children die? If only I could have taken Ella's place. Ella was taken to the hospital on January 5, 1990 while I was in respite care at the Care Home. On January 9 Dick and Mary came from Edmonton. We went to the hospital. Pastor Mohr[3] came to give us a family communion.

On February 18, Ernie got Ella home from the hospital. When I got there after church Ernie was sitting in a chair and said Ella insisted she was not going back to the hospital. She had a good dinner but by 5:00 o'clock she was getting very tired and was ready to go back. I think that was about the last of her walking. She just kept getting weaker all the time and was eventually put on oxygen.

On March 19, 1990, Ella died at 10:32 a.m. She had not taken food or drink for the previous two days. She did not respond and died in a coma. Although we had phoned Ricki and Dick and Mary, they did not make it in time. She went quicker than we thought. Bev and Steve were with her when she died. I just

---

[2] Sonny and Debbie Yuen and their four children came from Hong Kong in 1969. In 1976 they opened Yuen's S & D Enterprises Ltd., a clothing and footwear business.

[3] Reverend Dale Mohr was the pastor at the Christ Lutheran Church from 1985 to 1995.

couldn't make myself believe that she was gone, forever, and I was still here.

The funeral was on March 22, 1990, a cold, blustery day. I couldn't believe it had happened and I am still crying - but life has to go on.

On Sunday, July 22nd, Ernie took me to church and then to Joe and Lydia Buchberger's[4] 10th anniversary. There was a big crowd with lovely food and a lovely party. Harry Zorn brought me home but, as always, I felt so very alone.

On Monday I tried to do everything - pull weeds and pick beans. Ernie took me to the musical ride at the sports grounds. There were thousands of people. By the time the musical ride started it was getting dark and cold but the ride was great - what you could see of it as people would get up in front of us. But the horses were beautiful and it was worth the long sit and wait.

In September I was so busy doing this and that. One day I dug, washed, dried and carried the potatoes down to the basement. I tried to clean the garden but would get so tired. Then the plums were ripe and falling. I picked some and sat on the back porch. I had so much of everything but no one to give it to.

I was so tired in mind and body just trying to make some order in my house and not moving things too much or I wouldn't remember where they were. I just had too much stuff around. I didn't know what to do with it. Oh how I wished Ella were there to help me.

Minnie Popp died on Saturday, February 23, 1991. Then Gustie Zorn phoned that her sister, Lydia,[5] had died on February 23, as well.

Then Laura Popp, Philip's wife, died at 99 years of age. The funeral was on March 16, 1991. Frank and Laverna Kentel[6] took me along.

---

[4] Joseph Buchberger (June 24, 1913 - September 1, 1994) was the youngest son of Mike and Julia (Aman) Buchberger. After his first wife, Hedwig Mitschke, died in 1974, he married Lydia Matheis (Nerbas) in 1980.

[5] Lydia Baumung married Jacob Andres of MacNutt. They had three children: Kenneth, Patricia and Gerald.

The spring of 1991 left me feeling so alone. I still missed Ella a lot but kept very busy, probably because I was so slow. I could work faster but I couldn't think faster. I went through things trying to throw them away but got sidetracked all the time. I had too much stuff around and didn't know what to do with it and didn't have anyone to talk it over with. Oh how I missed Ella.

I did such stupid things. I bought onion sets and then couldn't find them. I thought I had not bought any. Then I got a loaf of bread out of the freezer and found my onion sets in a shopping bag under the loaf of bread, frozen hard. Then while cleaning in the shed I found a box with some good garment bags in it. How did they get there? I don't know, but I wondered.

In September, Dick and Mary came from Edmonton and Meta and Jeanette came from Thunder Bay. Dick and Mary stayed at Ernie's and Meta and Jeanette stayed three days with me. We all enjoyed it.

October 20th, 1991, was a terrible, terrible stormy Sunday. Elna Baumung was going to take me to church but I phoned to say I would not go. It was our wedding day, 77 years ago, which was such a beautiful day.

I hadn't added to my memoirs for a long time. By March 1992 I hadn't done any typing for so long that it was hard to find the letters. I just hadn't felt like saying anything on paper though I had written a couple of letters. But my mind didn't want to help me. I felt confused.

March 19th, 1992, was two years since Ella died. I still missed her very much but I could think of her without my eyes filling with tears, but not always. It became harder to see her in my mind. Why did she have to go before me? Only the good Lord knows the answer to that. We pray "Thy Will be Done" so I have to accept it though it is very hard at times.

---

[6] Frank Kentel was the son of Andreas and Christina Kentel. He married Loverna Popp, the oldest daughter of Joseph and Minnie Popp. They had three children: Darcy, Jane and Eldon.

MY FINAL HOME

It is Tuesday, May 14, 1996.[1] The weather is dark and cold. I just don't seem to get anything done. Somebody had brought some little puppies in today so I stayed and watched them and that is why I didn't get anything done. I forget how to type and I would like to keep it up, if I can. Only I am getting more forgetful every day.

[1] Mary Popp moved to the Langenburg Centennial Special Care Home in March, 1993. It seems she did no writing between the time of her arrival in 1993 until 1996. The sheet of paper upon which this portion of her memoirs was recorded was found in her typewriter in February, 1998.

I am always trying to make order and it always gets worse. But what can I expect of me? I am nearly 100 years old and my mind doesn't do what I would like it to.

This is Sunday and I am confused, like I wasn't here at all. I wish I could snap out of it. Today Jeanette and Bill Langilia came to see me and will be coming back tomorrow for a longer visit. They are on their way to the Yukon to visit Doug at Faro. Jeanette came on May 24th to visit with me and we talked about family and even all the trouble the Queen has had with her children. On May 25th Jeanette and Bill are heading to Edmonton and will visit with Dick and Mary for the day.

I guess this will be my last typing as I don't think my mind will improve any. So I will put the typewriter away and see, but I don't think there is any hope. But I am thankful for what I could do. I am now 99 years old and know I must give up, put the typewriter in the case and let whatever will be, be. For now, I am a very tired Mary Popp.[2]

---

[2] Donald Layh interviewed Mrs. Popp in February, 1998 with the intention of asking questions of her to complete her memoirs. She indicated that she had thought about getting out her typewriter which had been put away for a couple of years. Upon hearing Mrs. Popp express an interest in using her typewriter, Carol Schaab at the Care Home helped Mrs. Popp get her typewriter out of storage. After moving the typewriter into the light of the window, Mrs. Popp began typing. The faded ribbon in her old manual typewriter was worn out. She could not see the print. She typed one phrase, "When they told me there was room in the Care Home I had....." then rubbed her eyes and told Carol Schaab that she couldn't see the print. Then with characteristic humour she typed, "Shucks, I don't see so good -- The heck with Don." Those were Mrs. Popp's last typed words at the age of 101 years.

EPILOGUE

Mrs. Popp left her home at 209 Wells Avenue East and took residence at the Langenburg Centennial Special Care Home on March 24, 1993.

Mrs. Popp assumed an active role in the daily activities of the Care Home. Staff at the Care Home described how she would take residents under her care, visiting those who were unwell or reading the activity bulletin board for those whose eyesight was failing. In 1995, at the age of 98, I asked Mrs. Popp if she would attend at the Langenburg High School to assist me in presenting a guest lecture to the grade nine students about local history. She enjoyed the opportunity to explain to the students some of the interests she held as a young person.

In January, 1997 Mrs. Popp turned 100 years old. The Care Home hosted a Hawaiian theme party for her and presented her with a harmonica manufactured by a company that was commemorating its 100th anniversary by producing a limited edition harmonica. Mrs. Popp played a few lively tunes and cut and served her birthday cake. In response to Mayor Dave Schappert's request that he only wanted a small piece of birthday cake, Mrs. Popp, without further word, cut and placed upon his plate a minuscule tidbit of cake. Not until she had served everyone else with cake, did she quietly place upon Mr. Schappert's plate a modest slice of cake. As always, Mrs. Popp had a sense of occasion.

To commemorate Mrs. Popp's 100th birthday a number of people in the community made donations to a special committee which chose an original piece of Jan Layh's artwork to purchase and donate to the Care Home to remain there as a special tribute to Mrs. Popp. Today it prominently hangs in the Care Home.

After I had decided to edit and publish Mrs. Popp's memoirs I visited her in March, 1998 to update her reflections over the previous few years. Although she said that she often felt confused, her ability to engage in conversation about a variety of topics, both past and recent, was remarkable.

Mrs. Popp recalled that in 1993 when she learned that there was room for her in the Care Home, she realized that she couldn't stay alone any longer. She was prepared to leave her house on Wells Avenue, her home for over 40 years. She recalled that she wasn't sad to leave her house. She kidded that the house had some "mistakes" in it anyway. She hadn't liked the design of the roof line which had never "looked good, inside or out."

Mrs. Popp explained that she thoroughly enjoyed living at the Care Home. She was pleased with the care that she received - meals were prepared for her, the staff looked after her in every way and she had nothing to worry about. She admitted that she could even be confused and it didn't really matter because someone was always there to look after her. The Care Home was her home.

When asked what was the best time of her life she recounted her childhood on her parents' farm growing up with her brothers and sisters. She reflected on her close relationship with her sister, Katie and their story-telling while they did outside chores. She recounted the times Katie pretended to be "Jakob" and she pretended to be "Konrad". Jakob and Konrad lived in the "Old Country" and were characters in many stories that Mary and Katie invented to pass time.

When asked what was the hardest time of her life, Mrs. Popp laughingly said, "Having babies." In reply to the question whether she would do anything significantly different if she could lead her life over she laughed and said, "No, I would probably make the same mistakes all over again."

Mrs. Popp spoke about her children dying. At Dick's funeral in the summer of 1997, Mrs. Popp, then 100 years old, walked down the flight of stairs at Christ Lutheran Church to attend the lunch reception. She walked back upstairs by herself as well. Mrs. Popp felt that Dick's death was a relief since he was not well and his mind had become "poor". When asked how a mother felt to see her children die before her, she replied, "They had to go. That is life."

Mrs. Popp said she was not afraid of death, saying "In fact, sometimes I think I would welcome it." She explained that there was no secret to living 101 years, "It just happens." When asked if she took pride in being 101 years old she quickly offered that it wasn't easy being that old - "It's not easy to be 101 years old. Everyone looks at you and says 'Oh, she is 101 years old'."

When I explained to Mrs. Popp that her memoirs would be published she expressed her hopes that she would be well enough to read them.

On the morning of Friday, March 20, 1998 Mrs. Popp was not feeling well. After she had her morning bath and had her hair done, she apparently suffered a minor stroke or heart attack. By noon the nursing staff at the Care Home had become quite alarmed by Mrs. Popp's quick deterioration. I quickly went to the Care Home and found Mrs. Popp with the staff who had just given her oxygen. I was uncertain if she was aware that I was there since she seemed to be drifting in and out of consciousness. After remaining with her a few minutes I quietly spoke to her, telling her that the nurses were concerned about her. I wished her well and told her that she had won my admiration and respect during the years I had known her. I told her that we would enjoy her memoirs for many years. She slowly opened her eyes and whispered "Thank-you." That was the last time I saw Mrs. Popp.

By Friday afternoon, however, she had rallied and when Pastor Koenig came to visit her she was able to converse in a whispered voice. After reading a psalm to her, Pastor Koenig asked if he could sing a hymn to her. When she paused, her granddaughter, Paula Orth, suggested *In the Garden.* When Pastor Koenig admitted that he did not know all the words to this hymn, Mrs. Popp, began to softly sing the words in perfect pitch:

I come to the garden alone,
While the dew is still on the roses;
And the voice I hear, falling on my ear,
The Son of God discloses.
And He walks with me, and He talks with me,
And He tells me I am His own;
And the joy we share as we tarry there
None other has ever known.

Pastor Koenig joined her in singing. When they finished she said, "And now you know it."

On Saturday, Mrs. Popp's family had gathered around her. She faded in and out of sleep. Everyone expected the end to come soon.

On Sunday morning she seemed miraculously improved. She sat up and had porridge for breakfast and seemed surprised that she had been in bed for over two days. Her family was relieved that she had rallied and had apparently overcome whatever had struck her. Her granddaughters, Ricki Jackson and Bev Kesslering, left the Care Home in the early afternoon and were making arrangements to return to Regina when the Care Home called and advised them that Mrs. Popp had died.

Her family later agreed that Mrs. Popp would have considered dying a personal matter, not to be watched by others. She had spoken to her family and, reassuring them that she was "okay", she proceeded with characteristic dignity to the last task of her 101 years, 72 days. Mrs. Popp died peacefully on Sunday afternoon, March 22, 1998. She was buried beside her husband, Henry, in Christ Lutheran Church cemetery on Wednesday, March 25, 1998.

BIBLIOGRAPHY

Barry, Bill, People, Place: Saskatchewan and Its Names, Canadian Plains Research Centre, University of Regina

Bauereiss, Betty, Then and Now: Dropmore, Castleavery, Grainsby, Rochedale, 1995, UNISCO Press, Box 5027, Station "E", Edmonton, Alberta

Evangelisch Lutherische Gemeinde Hoffenthal (1892 - 1992), Printed by Jasper Printing Group Ltd., Edmonton, Alberta

Konrad Gross (Kurator von Katharinendorf seit 1933, geb. 27.12.1897), *Alexanderdorf und Katharinendorf von 1863 - 1940*, Die evangelischen Gemeinden in der Bukowina, Schriftenreihe des Hilfskomitees fur die evangelischen Umsiedler aus der Bukowina

Hande, D'Arcy, *Genealogical Notes: Descendants of Jacob Popp and His Wife Katherine Hartung of the Austrian Empire*

Hunt, Ian and Helen, Flower Valley School District, No. 1098, May 31, 1987

Joubert, Michelle, Die Glockengiesser von der Bukowina und Galizien: The Geib Family, Michelle Joubert, Box 32212, Juneau, Alaska, 99803

Meyer, Henry George, Meyer family Tree, Henry Meyer, 54 Krauss Street, Regina, Sask, S4T 6G3, Focus Publishing Inc., 1170 Eigthth Avenue, Regina, Sask., S4R 1C9

One Hundred Years in the Fellowship of the Holy Spirit, edited by Irene Adams, St Paul's Evangelical Lutheran Church, Langenburg, Sask, 1889-1989

Our Heritage - Family and Friends, Langenburg, Saskatchewan, 1997, Custom Printers, Yorkton, Sask.

Sawkey, John Andrew, Those Were the Days: The History of MacNutt, Calder, Dropmore and the Surrounding District: "Pioneer to Present", Friesen Printers, Altona, Manitoba, ROG OBO

Schaan, Rudy Landestreu: A Village No More (unpublished)

Shellmouth Our Century, Shellmouth Historical Club, 1982

Tell Me About the Good Old Days: Marchwell & Districts History, Marchwell Histroy Book Club, Box 98, Marchwell, Sask, SOA 2AO, Friesen Printers, Altona, Manitoba, ROG OBO

The First Hundred Years Around Churchbridge 1880 - 1980, 1980, Evergreen Club, Friesen Printers, Altona, Manitoba, ROG OBO

Walk Back Through Time: A History of Langenburg & District, A Celebrate Saskatchewan Project, 1980, Modern Press, Saskatoon, Sask.

Zeitweiser der Galiziendeutschen 1976, Herausgegeben vom Hilfskomitee der Galiziendeutschen, Konto Nr. 20470-702, Postgiroamt Stuttgart, Landesgirokass, Stuttgart, Germany

Zeitweiser der Galiziendeutschen 1988, Herausgegeben vom Hilfskomitee der Galiziendeutschen, Konto Nr. 20470-702, Postgiroamt Stuttgart, Landesgirokass, Stuttgart, Germany

NAMES OF PERSONS APPEARING TO TEXT AND FOOTNOTES

(Women's names are entered by their maiden name. Birth dates have been given in some instances to avoid confusion.)

Please send **A Century in the West: Life of a Pioneer Woman – Mary Popp's Story** to:

NAME: ______________________________

ADDRESS: ______________________________

____

PROVINCE/STATE: ______________________________

POSTAL/ZIP CODE: ______________________________

____ Number of Copies

Payment: $20.00 (CDN) $13.95 (US) per copy

(All prices include GST and shippingand handling costs)

☐ Cheque or money Order

☐ VISA Account #_____________ Expiry Date: ____________

Please send cheque or money order payable to Twin Valley Consulting Ltd., Box 250, Langenburg, Sask., S0A 2A0, Canada

---

Please send **A Century in the West: Life of a Pioneer Woman – Mary Popp's Story** to:

NAME: ______________________________

ADDRESS: ______________________________

____

PROVINCE/STATE: ______________________________

POSTAL/ZIP CODE: ______________________________

____ Number of Copies

Payment: $20.00 (CDN) $13.95 (US) per copy

(All prices include GST and shippingand handling costs)

☐ Cheque or money Order

☐ VISA Account #_____________ Expiry Date: ____________

Please send cheque or money order payable to Twin Valley Consulting Ltd., Box 250, Langenburg, Sask., S0A 2A0, Canada